Westerns and the
Trail of Tradition

Westerns and the Trail of Tradition

A Year-by-Year History, 1929–1962

by BARRIE HANFLING

McFarland & Company, Inc., Publishers
Jefferson, North Carolina, and London

Publisher's note: Barrie Hanfling died on May 31, 2001, after seeing and correcting the page proofs of this book. His wife Judith, his sister Dawn Perch and her husband David, and Mr. Hanfling's brother Brian (compiler of the index) were of great help in the final months.

Frontispiece: Roy Rogers, King of the Cowboys, on Trigger.

Library of Congress Cataloguing-in-Publication Data

Hanfling, Barrie, 1944–2001.
    Westerns and the trail of tradition: a year-by-year history,
1929–1962 / by Barrie Hanfling.
        p.   cm.
    Includes bibliographical references (p.) and index.   ∞
    ISBN 0-7864-1125-2 (illustrated case binding : 50# alkaline paper)
    1. Western films — History and criticism.   I. Title.
PN1995.9.W4 H355   2001
791.43'5278 — dc21   2001032638

British Library Cataloguing data are available

Manufactured in the United States of America

On the cover: A scene from *The Man from Laramie* (1955), with Jimmy
Stewart's back to the camera.

McFarland & Company, Inc., Publishers
  Box 611, Jefferson, North Carolina 28640
    www.mcfarlandpub.com

This book is dedicated to
Judith and Patrick —
"for all of the years."

Acknowledgments

To all those who helped in the construction and publication of this book I extend heartfelt thanks. Some of this goes to the authors of various books and articles as listed in the bibliography. Special thanks go to family and friends who encouraged me; to Colin Momber and Boyd Magers, whose advice was invaluable; to many readers of my monthly magazine who have, without knowing it, urged me on by their stated enjoyment in my writing. Thanks also to Mike Richards and Bob Moreton, who provided material, and to Eddie Brandt's Saturday Matinee organization in Hollywood, who helped with the stills.

My sister Dawn Peach, and her husband David, who typed and proofread the manuscript, have been invaluable, and my brother Brian indexed for me.

In the final analysis all errors, misjudgments and sins of omission are mine alone.

Contents

Preface

The history of western movies stretches back nearly a hundred years, if 1903 is accepted as the birth year with *The Great Train Robbery*. Over these years the western film has fluctuated in popularity and today probably stands at its lowest point. Contrary to the view of many critics, however, the western is not dead. It lingers on in the hands of creators and artists who are, however, quite different from the practitioners of the mid–20th century, men and women to whom the old West is long gone. The western film as it exists today does not appeal to oldtimers like myself who remember it in its heyday.

Times have changed. When the makers of the old-style westerns (of the 1930s, 1940s and 1950s) were born, the transformation of America's western lands from "wild West" to tame civilization had barely been completed. To them the wild West was the immediate past, and they had a certain feel for it. As these men passed away, so passed that feel.

Today's makers of westerns are more interested in rewriting history to suit the prejudices of modern times; it is the day of the revisionist historian — and the revisionist filmmaker. So be it. Someday, the men and women of a new era may bring back a traditional (or was it mythical?) approach to the western. Whatever the future holds, the western will never die. It will always exist, in some form, different though it may be from those of the golden age.

Just what constitutes that golden age is, of course a matter of opinion — and my opinion is represented by the films included in this book, covering the years 1929 through 1962. It is an opinion I have developed through a lifetime of love for the western, of cinema-going, of reading, of writing, and, in later years, of building up a comprehensive collection of western films on video so that they are there at my fingertips—all the great and not-so-great westerns to evaluate (or to sentimentalize over as the case may be). The evaluations in this book are mine, though I have quoted many well-known writers on the subject of western films.

I begin my coverage in 1929 because it represents the beginning of the sound era. For all of their interest, for all of their artistry or entertainment, to most people the silents are relics of a long dead age, an amusing incident along the road to the cinema we know today. Personally I enjoy silent films, including many silent westerns, but I can understand the viewpoint of the majority. Silent films are an art form of their own and deserve to be treated separately. However, the silent films of many performers and technicians are part and parcel of their overall careers and will be treated as such in this story.

There is also a practical reason to begin with the sound era: so much of the output from the silent days is unavailable to evaluate now. The record of western icons like John Ford, Tom Mix and William S. Hart contains huge gaps, and many players and artists who did not carry on into the talkie era are lost to view now, apart from some fleeting glimpse in a faded and scarred old print.

I end my coverage in 1962 because in that year, paradoxical though it may seem, three great western films were released amidst what was otherwise a lean year for western movies. Hailed at the time as a new resurgence of the genre, in retrospect these films turned out to be swan songs, for both old and new talent and for the traditional western itself. The decades since have witnessed the demise of a style, of a philosophy and of talent that had nurtured the western for so long.

In 1962 television westerns, by contrast, were reaching their peak of popularity, a peak that would carry on for some years. Though highly rated in their genre these TV westerns did not compare well with cinema releases. Budget constraints resulted in long dialogue scenes; attempts to please sponsors translated into an accent on family values; and overall the shows suffered from a lack of old-time action. But they captured audiences mesmerized by the magic box in the corner of the living room.

Meanwhile, the financial climate created difficulties for cinema westerns, which could no longer be produced cheaply. Not only that, but audiences had lost their taste for the B-western, morally upright cowboy. There was a cynicism in the air, reflected, as the '60s passed, in cinema production generally. Changes were in store — and not always in Hollywood. Producers went offshore to make westerns more cheaply — to Spain and Italy. And enterprising producers and players, many of them Italian, began turning out the "spaghetti westerns," hybrid affairs, often with American stars, that were increasingly violent and in reality a take-off of the genre.

In Hollywood, veteran western players and technicians were getting old and retiring. No new talent geared to the western film scene arose to replace them. The John Waynes and other popular, older Hollywood actors went on making westerns that were increasingly parodies of their former work. New, earnest producers with television backgrounds, accustomed to dealing with a sponsor-related production style, took over in Hollywood, new ideas flourished, violence predominated, and it all helped blast the traditional western off the screen.

Now and then, through the '70s and the '80s, some director or star would come up with a movie to approximate the old style western, but such films did not prosper. After 1962 there were no productions comparable to *The Man Who Shot Liberty Valance*, *Ride the High Country* or, to a lesser extent, *Lonely Are the Brave*, the three movies that gave hope and inspiration to western film lovers in that year. There were some close calls, but John Wayne's last film, *The Shootist*, in 1976 was probably as close as it got. Some will believe otherwise, but this is a personal view, and personal views are what this book is all about.

In fact, the book was written with the hope of providing a perspective sufficiently personal, sufficiently "real," to take one back to those heady days from the late '20s through the early '60s, a period of film production in which the western played sometimes a humble and other times a mighty role. And it is in Hollywood, the undisputed home of cinema for most of the last century, that our story unfolds.

1 9 2 9

The Sound Revolution

The western film was on the decline as the silent era ended. Considering it had only existed for 26 years, this seems now a very early demise, but the sound revolution in film making hit the western in a big way. For a while all outdoor movies appeared doomed as the crews struggled with heavy sound equipment inside the studio, not even considering a venture into the great outdoors. "The film cowboy is finished!" trumpeted the media, spurred on to this verdict also by the widespread interest in filming other outdoor escapades such as flying, then a sport capturing the imagination of thousands of spectators. This combination — sound technology plus up-to-date thrills and spills — pointed to the death of the old West, cn celluloid, anyway.

Remember that when silent western films were at their height, the real American West was just a stone's throw away in time. The last frontiers had stretched out into the early 20th century and there were still plenty of rural towns and settlements that looked just as they did in turbulent frontier times. Automobiles, despite the efforts of Henry Ford, had not yet reached to the very grassroots of American life. In the wide open spaces cowboys still rounded up the cattle in the time-honored way. The western films, starring the likes of G.M. "Broncho Billy" Anderson, Bill Hart and Tom Mix, had hit the heights of popularity at a time when the subject of those films was still a very living and vibrant memory. But by 1929 the young people of that day had been born into a new world, especially the urban populatior. Westerns still retained much of their popularity in rural settings but the urban sophisticates were living, as they saw it, in the vibrant present, and scorned these simplistic and unsophisticated manifestations from the past. The western film — the genre of the idealist, romantic Bill Hart, the daredevil adventurer Tom Mix, of Buck Jones, Fred Thomson, Ken Maynard, Tim McCoy, Art Acord, Hoot Gibson, Tom Tyler and many, many lesser cowboys (many real cowboys), of early directors such as D.W. Griffith, of John Ford and James Cruze and William Wyler, the western epic quality pioneered in 1923 by the *Covered Wagon* and in 1924 *The Iron Horse*, of that best of all epic westerns, Ford's 1926 *Three Bad Men*— it all seemed over. Bid adieu to the western, they said.

William S. Hart had said his good-bye with the classic *Tumbleweeds* in 1925. Hart's dusty, realistic approach to making westerns, balanced by his sentimental romanticism, was outdated by the circus cowboy Tom Mix, who had brought the popularity of hard riding, fun-filled action westerns to a new peak. But Mix had ceased production too; Fred Thomson, he of the meteoric rise to the top, had died. Buck Jones, solid, dependable, was off screen. Minor cowboy stars struggled on in inferior, still silent westerns seemingly locked in the dark ages. Of the major western stars only Ken Maynard and Hoot Gibson at Universal were still in the saddle as the first tentative part-talkies were made. However, two productions were underway in 1929 that would alter all perspective on the future of western film making. One was a major product, the other a minor affair that would, in its own way, have immense influence on the much-maligned and scorned over the years B, or series, western.

With the release of *In Old Arizona*, directed by Raoul Walsh and starring Warner Baxter as a very un–Henry style Cisco Kid, the prophets of doom were forced to think again. The sounds generated by sizzling bacon, gunshots and hoofbeats entranced the audience. Outdoor action could still be filmed with a silent camera and at a distance. When the sound equipment came in close the audience could all but smell the bloom of the desert flower. It was intoxicating. Audience response was immediate and favorable and Fox Studio rushed star Baxter into a similar role in *Romance of the Rio Grande*, no great western but again successful. Baxter himself was not that impressed; he didn't want to spend the rest of his career playing Mexicans! He would, however, return again to the Cisco Kid role, and why not? It won him an Oscar in 1929.

In Old Arizona proved that westerns could be made with the new sound equipment, but would they be limited to just a few major products, something special now and then? At about the same time as *In Old Arizona* was being made, a tubby silent screen cowboy-producer-director, one Leo Maloney, who had toiled hard for some years in the western field without reaching any great heights, had bought, borrowed, and otherwise acquired as much sound equipment as he could and embarked upon making a western of his own. *Overland Bound* was done on the cheap and very much a formula western. There were no pretentions about higher artistic aims. Maloney starred himself in the film, along with silent western stalwarts Wally Wales and Jack

Cowboy favorite of the early talkies, Ken Maynard, on Tarzan.

Perrin. When stitched together, the film was taken to New York by Maloney, who was desperate to find a distributor since he was now in debt. A distributor was found, the film released, and it captured the audience it had set out for, the unsophisticated, mainly rural population that lapped up the bootleg sound effects generated by *Overland Bound*, and paved the way for all minor westerns to now embrace the new medium. Leo Maloney did not live to see this. Celebrating in the grand manner, he overtaxed his heart and fell dead of a heart attack. Both as a cowboy player and as a producer-director, Leo Maloney would never have been but a minor player, but he has, through *Overland Bound*, a unique niche in western film history. He pioneered the sound B western. His co-stars, Wally Wales and Jack Perrin, struggled on into the '30s as western players for minor poverty row producers. Neither opted for other creative occupations in the genre, as Maloney had done, remaining steady, reliable players in their chosen field. The creative effort of Leo Maloney, for one moment (or about 60 minutes to be precise), upstaged them both.

Universal Pictures, under the auspices of Carl Laemmle, was the first to make tentative sound western production movies. Their Ken Maynard and Hoot Gibson films for 1929 were part-talkie. Both Maynard and Gibson were very popular cowboy stars. Both were circus-rodeo performers, fine riders and trick artists. Maynard's riding ability is said to only have been bettered by his own brother, Kermit, and that is hard to believe once you have seen Ken in action. Hoot Gibson was a less flamboyant, almost comic cowboy with an easygoing Will Rogers–style approach. Two of his 1929 films were part sound, *The Long, Long Trail* and *Courtin' Wildcats*. Sound slowed down the Gibson films. They had never been speedy affairs; that was not Hoot's style. Modern parlance would have him as a "laid back cowboy." The advent of sound made him appear even more laid back as scriptwriters inserted dialogue into scenes in which nothing happened. Hoot's wisecracking style was easy to listen to but audiences did tend to get restless. Also, the sound equipment remained static—and so did the film while it was operating. Even in Hoot Gibson westerns action was a keynote. Sound slowed his westerns down to a crawl. Maynard, on the other hand, in scenes out of reach of the sound equipment, kept his westerns fast moving. Dialogue did not do much for Ken, who never quite mastered it through his long career, the consequences being obvious as the years progressed. However, sound did give Ken a chance for one innovation that would have a major effect upon western films— the insertion of songs and music. *In Old Arizona* had pioneered this and Ken was eager to incorporate cowboy songs into his films. His 1929 releases *The Wagon Master* and *Señor Americano*, part sound, part silent, did this. It would lead to bigger things. Ken Maynard himself was an untrained, talented musician who could play fiddle and guitar and sang in what could be described as "an authentic cowboy voice." That means he didn't sing very well, but he was enthusiastic.

Not many westerns were made in 1929 but one more requires mention. This was the adaptation of Owen Wister's story and play *The Virginian* to the sound screen.

Hoot Gibson in an unusual photo of him wearing two guns.

Walter Huston and Gary Cooper in The Virginian *(1929), a Universal picture.*

The Virginian had been filmed as a silent in 1923 and was regarded as a literary classic. Time had dimmed that verdict, and time has also brought conflicting views on the 1929 definitive film version of the story. *The Virginian* was never a pretty story, and Wister, it appears, was obsessed with western justice, hanging in particular. The tale of one man having to have his best friend hanged and the so-called code of the West ("When you call me that — smile") is both tragic and grim. The dialogue fails to crackle, moving at a snail's pace. Cinemagoers in 1929, in awe of this new innovation, were more tolerant than later audiences. The gradual unfolding of a plot was more acceptable. Perhaps it was the gangster films of the '30s that inspired the fast talking, ever-action movies that even in today's age are called for. As television emphasizes, action is still the keynote. In 1929 sound, any sound, was novelty enough to hold the attention of an audience. Thus, today, the 1929 *Virginian* seems unbearably slow. Even allowing for this, *The Virginian* does not stand up as one of the classic westerns. Its scenes and setting are good, it has the freshness of photography that sound outdoor movies brought to the screen and, most of all, it has Gary Cooper, lean and laconic, in the role that more or less made legendary cowboy status. For all of its faults, strangely enough, this 1929 version still stands as the best yet filming of the Wister story.

The Virginian is a pioneer film, along with *In Old Arizona*, and, to a lesser extent Leo Maloney's *Overland Bound*, that proved the western movie could survive with sound and, indeed, was ideally suited to the new phenomenon. Film makers were still feeling their way, cautiously, into the new era as the '30s began, bringing depression, hard times for many, boom years for cinema and radio and a decade of resurgence for the western film that started out with a "bang," endured what might be called a "whimper" in mid-decade and finished off the era with a grand sweep of heightened artistic and commercial renewal.

1930

The Epic Returns

The year 1930 found the western film back on screen in full flow as makers became confident with the new sound technology. Buck Jones, George O'Brien and Tim McCoy joined Ken Maynard and Hoot Gibson in well-made, if formulistic, movies while lesser lights Bob Steele, Jack Perrin, Bob Custer, Buffalo Bill, Jr., Lane Chandler and Wally Wales churned out lower budget efforts, working for small, independent studios and producers who could not afford the gloss that Universal, Columbia or Fox could put into their movies. Jones, O'Brien, McCoy, Maynard and Gibson were lucky enough to work for the majors, the studios who could afford the budget that turned a formula series western into something approaching art.

It was the artistic aspect of making western films (and the commercial one of course — no film studio or producer did anything they didn't figure would make a profit) that excited people in the industry in 1930 when they found that sound could be incorporated easily into outdoor filming. This artistic aspect led to the making of the first sound "epics," a type of western not seen for some years. In the trail prints of *The Covered Wagon* and *The Iron Horse* came *The Big Trail* and *Billy the Kid*, one a long, sprawling wagon train tale, the other an attempt at a dusty, wide screen definitive account of true incidents in the real West. It must have been quite a blow to all concerned that both proved to be box office failures.

The Big Trail, filmed for wide screen and originally 150 minutes long, should have been another successful *Covered Wagon*. It is in fact a better film than *Covered Wagon* and the definitive wagon trail movie. Yet, after failure at the box office, it was virtually "lost" for years and indeed, it has only been in recent decades that it resurfaced and became available for the interested to peruse. Unfortunately, copies now available cannot capture the real splendor of the original, but only hint at it. It is still powerful and rewarding viewing and it is amazing to think that such a classic film could be lost and forgotten for so long, and relegated to history as a failure while a pedestrian silent film, *The Covered Wagon*, was revered to such an extent. *The Covered Wagon* is very important, in both film and western film history. But *The Big Trail* is the better film notwithstanding some inept acting and awkward dialogue scenes.

A young John Wayne, star of the United Artists release The Big Trail.

Why was *The Big Trail* a failure? There have been various theories, often involving the star, John Wayne. Wayne, who was introduced to director Raoul Walsh by John Ford, was relatively new to the screen. He had played "bits" in John Ford's work. He was inexperienced and awkward at times but had a youthful charm and his naturalness appeared to be just right for the rule of the young frontiersman. A fault in the film is the sub-plot of Wayne's search for a murderer, a sub-plot that often tends to overshadow the more interesting struggle of the pioneers crossing the Great Plains. Some analysts point to a lack of interest in frontier days by a jazz-age public thrown into a worldwide depression. A combination of depression and prohibition led to a "live now" attitude amongst the public and they wanted entertainment that reflected that. They got it with spectacular song and dance cinema, hard-hitting gangster movies and, eventually, the sugar-sweet world of Shirley Temple.

In many respects *The Big Trail* was ahead of its time. It was filmed for 70mm projection, which most cinemas could not accommodate. That and the other aspects mentioned above relegated John Wayne to B film production, eking out a living in the minor studios until John Ford took pity on him in 1939. By then *The Big Trail* was forgotten. It is, however, one of the great westerns and without a doubt the best work done on the great wagon trek west.

Billy the Kid was a more personal story but also filmed in wide open spaces, in this case New Mexico, and made for the big screen. A slow moving, beautifully filmed movie, *Billy* is both somber and realistic in its approach. Directed by King Vidor, it was meant as an accurate picture of the untamed West in the great cattle days. The story of the ill-fated and almost mythical *Billy the Kid* is romanticized and based on the totally inaccurate book from Walter Noble Burns. That said, the atmosphere of the times is powerfully projected — the bawling cattle herds, the dirty towns and saloons, the empty country and the grizzled, dirty men who inhabited it. What it lacks, as a film, is diversity. Everything unfolds at a distance, as if the director wanted us to be in awe of the land. These big scene images are powerful but one sometimes feels remote from the characters, where a close-up or two would draw us emotionally to them.

Another newcomer, Johnny Mack Brown as Billy the Kid, *MGM, 1930.*

The casting of Johnny Mack Brown as Billy is also a drawback. Brown would become one of the better of the series cowboy actors, but his gentle southern accent and manners do not convey the sense of the complex, neurotic character the *Kid* must have been. Johnny is just too nice. Worse, MGM filmed two endings; the one for American audiences saw Billy alive and well riding off for the border while the other, for European showing, has him shot down by Pat Garrett, as he actually was. The false happy ending does not blend well with the downbeat, broody nature of the entire film up till then.

Viewed today *Billy the Kid* is an uneven classic still to be enjoyed for its fine photography and atmosphere, and for showing that when a man has several bullets pumped into him, he dies in agony, crying out in pain. Also interesting is the use of a cowboy song at the opening shots of cattle plodding along, wagons rolling and said cowboy, one leg over his saddle, jogging in tune to "hi-ho, hi-ho, a lonesome cowboy's song...." Even at this stage it was apparent that music and cowboy songs would play an important part in the making of western movies.

Billy the Kid had been an MGM production and though it was not such a big failure as *The Big Trail*, it did not do the business expected, so Hollywood's glamour studio showed little further interest in making westerns, apart from the western-musical operetta *Montana Moon* starring Brown again, and Joan Crawford. The major studio doing its best for the West at this stage was Paramount. Not only did it resurrect the silent Zane Grey series, featuring now Richard Arlen and George O'Brien, but it also produced the first sound version of *The Spoilers* starring Gary Cooper, plus another vehicle for Cooper, *The Texans*. Over at Universal, besides their series western, the studio made the first sound version of *Hell's Heroes*, better known to us as *Three Godfathers*. In this sentimental and picturesque production, Charles Bickford, Raymond Hatton and Fred Kohler played three misfits who find and look after a baby in the desert. It had been a John Ford silent film and many see it as Ford's personal property. Ford made his own sound version in 1949 but critics have, with due respect to The Master, always felt that the William Wyler–directed 1930 version was the better.

Universal was busy because it also produced the screen's first sound western serial in 1930, *The Indians Are Coming*. The star was Tim McCoy, who was out of work after MGM showed no further interest in him once his silent series had ended. While setting the pattern for many a serial to follow, *The Indians Are Coming* also set McCoy's career back on track, this cowboy with the military bearing joining Buck Jones as a Columbia contractee in 1931. With its wagon train versus Indians and bad whites theme, *The Indians Are Coming* was a big hit. Universal would repeat the formula through most of its '30s serials, constantly using stock footage of raiding Indians drawn from silent days, sometimes as far back as Thomas Ince. The audiences lapped it up, even if one or two disgruntled Indians may have gotten weary of seeing themselves decimated week after week. But nobody, save a scarce few, cared what Indians thought in 1930. Colonel Tim McCoy was one of the few, even if today's liberal Indians see him as a paternalistic style figure who never treated his Indians as equals. McCoy, as mentioned, ended up in a good many series B westerns at Columbia.

Already at Columbia was Charles Buck Jones, a silent screen cowboy who, if never touching the heights of Tom Mix or the later Fred Thompson, had been very popular. Jones was a gritty, authentic looking cowboy star who could act a little and projected a noble if stoic heroic image. He cared about the films he made and about the West he depicted. Through his influence, his Columbia series of films from 1930 to 1934 stand as one of the best set of B westerns ever made, if not the best. Although a few were "flops" inevitable in such a large turnout, many are gems. Westerns were serious enough to appeal to adults, not just to children, filmed in excellent natural surroundings with good casts, and had strong stories and the solid presence of Jones himself who, on the strength of this work, rose to be top cowboy star of the screen by the mid–'30s. From his 1930 work *The Dawn Trail* stands out, with Buck as the local lawman attempting to avert a range war, the early scenes in a saloon having as much authenticity as any carefully made "epic" western.

Buck's rival as king of the screen cowboys for the early '30s was Ken Maynard, who was finishing off his Universal series with *Mountain Justice, The Fighting Legion, Song of the Caballero, Parade of the West* and *Sons of the Saddle.* These were all interesting features because Maynard had his own ideas about how a western film should be and, at that stage, Universal left him to his own devices. Ken, unlike Buck Jones, was no actor but his awkwardness on screen possibly endeared him to fans who saw a naturalness in the smiling, likable Maynard. Action, especially fast and fancy riding, was his specialty but Ken also liked to have complex plots (some too complex) and was continually interested in inserting music into his pictures. Fans liked his showmanship and in some ways he had an advantage over the more sober Jones. Ken projected a screen image of rugged innocence backed by integrity, manliness and awesome athletic ability in the saddle. Off screen it was a bit different. Ken Maynard was a complex, quick tempered, often brooding man with an increasing fondness for alcohol. At this stage it was kept under control but circumstances would change all that.

The bad times for the likes of Maynard started when Universal, going through one of its periodical financial crises, decided to ditch all series westerns for the time being. That meant that not only Ken Maynard but also Hoot Gibson was out of work. Gibson, who relied more on genial affability rather than guns, fists and action, had not been able to reproduce his silent screen popularity in talkies. The Gibson westerns were interesting and often amusing, but moved very slowly and lacked the hectic heroics of Maynard or the tough stolidity of Jones. Nevertheless, Gibson retained a following that would stay with him for a few more years until his particular style of easygoing western deteriorated under the slap-happy methods of poverty row productions.

The two other cowboy stars who worked regularly through 1930, although in a minor league, were Jack Perrin and Bob Steele. Perrin, a mature cowboy who had been around some time, had last starred in a silent Universal series. He was a big stolid man with a cheerful smile who rode a smart white trick horse, Starlight. During 1930 he appeared for various independent producers in titles like *Beyond the Rio Grande, Ridin' Law, Phantom of the Desert* and *Romance of the West.* Perrin was another non-actor and was clumsy in fight scenes but he rode well, and was sincere. Taking his attributes and weighing them up against his failings, it could be deducted that his future lay with the small indie companies rather than with major operators.

Bob Steele, on the other hand, was a still young man who had begun acting as a boy for his producer-director father R. N. Bradbury. Steele had more natural ability than Perrin, being a good horseman, agile fighter and believable as an actor, given good direction. His major drawback was in being a very small man and he had to work hard to make it convincing as he took on and knocked down villains much bigger than himself.

Amazingly, he got away with it by the sheer ferocity of his pretend fighting. Steele's work during 1930 was for Tiffany, not a major company, but not one of the very smallest, and which had, by the end of the year, signed on Ken Maynard, discarded by Universal. Maynard was bigger at the box office than Steele, and Tiffany put more into his pictures, but the Steele films, starting with *Near the Rainbow's End*, were adequate with Bob a popular figure.

At the close of 1930 the western film was once more at the crossroads. The lukewarm reception to *The Big Trail* and *Billy the Kid* (both, it must be noted, popular in Europe) cast doubts upon their worthwhileness to the major studios. The discarding of Maynard and Gibson by Universal was a telling point, even though Jones and McCoy had good contracts at Columbia. It appeared that most of the western film work was falling into the hands of the cheap independent producers whose artistic credentials were nil. The western serial seemed to have made a bit of a comeback for the Saturday matinee crowds and, looking at it from all angles, it was difficult to know whether the western was alive and kicking or on the decline. Over at RKO, formerly FBO in the silent days, they were working on a western film that would generate renewed interest in the genre.

1931

Best Film

The first, and only for almost 60 years, western film to win an Oscar as Best Picture of the Year was released in 1931—*Cimarron*. This RKO epic was truly that, unfolding a typical Edna Ferber saga in leisurely fashion and one would have supposed that its success would have ensured further western epics to follow. Surprisingly, this did not happen. It is difficult to understand why. Like the (much) later *Dances with Wolves*, which became the next academy winner, it is hardly representative of the western genre. More a great romance than a wild West yarn, possibly that is how audiences perceived it. Following the hero, Richard Dix, and his empire through into the 20th century, *Cimarron* was nowhere as good a western film as *The Big Trail* or *Billy the Kid*, but it succeeded where they failed. It appealed to both the romantic and the patriotic strain in American audiences and the director, Wesley Ruggles, is better at evoking sentiment than conveying a western atmosphere. The action highlight of the film is the big land rush, which is well done, joining Ford's *Three Bad Men* and Hart's *Tumbleweeds* in that regard, an exciting, massively executed rehash of the opening of the Cherokee Strip.

Richard Dix, he of the square jaw, and Irene Dunne were fine as the leads, but after 1931 *Cimarron* faded from sight and was seldom revised. It did not last the course of time, being a bit stodgy and boring outside its land rush pinnacle, but still retains a place in history for being the first western to win that Oscar. Hollywood waited almost 30 years to remake it and this 1960 version, although directed by a great artist, Anthony Mann, is even duller than the original, which does have, dated though it may be, some high spots. Once again an old black and white movie proves to be better than a glossy, wide screen color remake.

Paramount tried another wagon train western in 1931, although on a smaller scale than *The Big Trail*. *Fighting Caravans* had Gary Cooper starring but was dull. Interesting, but ultimately pedestrian despite nice desert locations, was *The Painted Desert*, not least because its star was a white-haired silent veteran who couldn't ride a horse, William Boyd. A lower-ranked player in the cast caught the eye — Clark Gable. Boyd was mildly pleasant but certainly did not look as if he could have made a career in westerns. Warner Baxter, academy winner of a few years back with *In Old Arizona*, was busy making more Cisco Kid material and also featuring in the first sound version of Cecil B. DeMille's *The Squaw Man*, a melodramatic stage piece that had run its race in silent days and should have been left there.

The year 1931 was really taken up by the resurgence of the series, or B western. Cowboy stars from the silent days began to creep back into the fold and the early '30s was the heyday of the cheap independent producer, shooting westerns on a shoestring budget and doing very well out of it, thank you. A cheap western, brought in for

From Columbia's 1931 Desert Vengeance, *leading cowboy star Buck Jones, on Silver.*

$5,000 to $10,000, would make a 100 percent profit for the producer, which was not big money even then but when you could churn out a film in five days, it wasn't bad. The bigger stars and studios, of course, invested more money even into what were B westerns. A Maynard, Jones or O'Brien western might cost $80,000 to $90,000 and would still, in those days, bring in a healthy profit. Westerns were, indeed, the bread and butter of the industry. Of course there were problems with a maverick like Ken Maynard, who given his head might go over budget to the tune of $20,000 or $30,000, but that's more applicable to the future and Ken's second stay at Universal in 1933–34.

Back in 1931 Buck Jones and Tim McCoy were turning out good quality series for Columbia, the superior ones being from Jones who was, in all actuality, a cowboy star superior to McCoy. Jones, with some say on what went on screen, made intelligent little westerns, the highlight for the year being the realistic and very downbeat *Desert Vengeance*, with Buck playing an out-and-out bad guy with some redeeming features. Jones, with popularity soaring, was beginning to ride far and wide above all contenders, even if he too had the odd failure — for example, when he played Joaquin Murieta in *The Avenger* and the strains of adopting a Mexican accent and romancing the girl got a bit beyond the old cowpoke.

The majority of cowboy players had to be content with minor producers and companies. Hoot Gibson had slipped into that category and riding with him were quite a crew: Bob Steele, Tom Tyler, Jack Perrin, Wally Wales, Bill Cody, Bob Custer and Buffalo Bill, Jr., all leftovers from the silent screen. Of this group Steele, with his boyish looks and spring-heeled action, and Tyler, tall, strong and menacing of voice, were probably the best.

Ken Maynard had joined Tiffany, a small studio. Though budgets were much lower, Ken was still in his prime, and this enthusiasm overcame undersized budgets. He was still slim in those days, athletic in the saddle and awkward with dialogue. His sheepish approach to romancing the ladies was fine with rural audiences — they would be sheepish too. Ken was still rivaling Buck Jones for the cowboy king title, simply through his own personality. There is no doubt that the Jones westerns were better, but there were those who found his often stony-faced acting a little bit too drab. They turned to Ken Maynard who, whatever else he may or may not have been, was never drab.

A couple of new faces were on the western scene, though both had been on screen before. Tom Keene was an interesting cowboy star employed by RKO, which was returning to the genre. Keene had been known as George Duryea (his real name) in non-westerns in 1928–29 before making a couple of independent oaters and being signed by RKO. What was most interesting about Keene, who became genuinely popular at that studio, is that he represented a new breed of western film star. Most of the previous cowboy stars had come from ranch, rodeo, circus or country backgrounds and acting was not their forte. Keene, with no western background, was first and foremost an actor.

Not only was Keene an actor, he wanted to further his acting career. Westerns were taken up purely as a short term monetary business. Keene actually looked good in the saddle and his films were superior to independent offerings, as they should be considering their source. As mentioned, he became more popular for a brief period than history remembers him. His employment pointed the way for other actors, players with real dramatic training, to take up westerns as an occupation. Silent screen cowboys suffered the handicap of having to learn to speak on screen from scratch and many of them were not that good at it. Sound required that bit more from a cowboy player. It was easy to cover up the fact that your cowboy was no great athlete, doubles did that, and long shots. It was harder to cover up a cowboy star's inability to read lines well. Sound saw the end of the dominance of real cowboys amongst western film stars. From now on they would come from acting, or a new departure within a few years, a musical background.

The other new old face was young John Wayne. After the failure of *The Big Trail* Wayne was required only for B grade pictures and was finding it hard. In 1931 he was at Columbia, where he was not happy, appearing as a second lead to Tim McCoy in a few pictures. He also made one with Buck Jones. It was a prelude to his being offered a contract by Warner Bros., which was then thinking about series westerns. It was the beginning of a long, hard slog for Wayne through the poverty row production houses. He endured it, however, and in the end fought his way back up to where he had virtually started, at the top.

Apart from those already in action, other silent screen cowboys were preparing to re-enter the scene. Rex Bell, a relatively young man and latecomer to the silent screen, and the more established Jack Hoxie were two of them. But the big news was that the king cowboy of the silent screen, Tom Mix, was on the verge of returning to the screen.

I have left till last for 1931 the westerns of George O'Brien. They were produced by Fox and they consisted of the finest group of series westerns produced at the time, probably better than those of Buck Jones overall. Jones had failures as well as hits, whereas the Fox–George O'Brien group was just about flawless. Filmed in beautiful surroundings, mostly based on Zane Grey tales, they were taut, action-packed, yet thoughtful B westerns. In fact, there is a point of view that they don't qualify as B westerns at all, being superior in production values and contents. The star, George O'Brien, was an actor from the silent screen who had been made famous by his association with director John Ford. O'Brien could act; he was also muscular and athletic. As a cowboy star he was possibly too good. His acting and his humor appealed more to adults and he never had the huge following of children that Mix, Jones and others garnered. O'Brien westerns such as *Riders of the Purple Sage* and *Rainbow Trail* are little classics of the western screen.

By the close of 1931 it appeared pretty obvious that, notwithstanding the success of *Cimarron*, the general public was not that much interested in the average western

Star of a good Zane Grey series at Fox, George O'Brien.

movie. Where the clientele for this type of film belonged was the rural areas and small towns. Big city sophisticates looked down upon the form and critics became increasingly ho-hum when reviewing the latest horse opera, or oater, as they would get to be called. In short, the western was not taken too seriously and hardly recognized as an art form. It should be noted that while this was happening in America, European audiences remained interested, seeing far more in the humble 60 minute western than their American counterparts did. The market was, however, in the States, and those who did enjoy westerns enjoyed them for their action most of all. High drama, too much romance and slowness in their westerns were not acceptable. Hollywood has always tried to give audiences what they think they want and so the small, low budget western film for the double bill began its growth. It was noticeable that a director like John Ford, who had in silent days almost specialized in westerns, stayed clear of them. It was also noted that these minor films, with very few exceptions, made healthy profits, much more so than artistic drama or big lush productions. They might not be prestigious, but by golly, they provided the quick bucks.

1 9 3 2

B Westerns in Abundance

Many western films were made in 1932 and these were predominantly B or series westerns, a few made by major studios but mainly by cheap independent producers. The major studios showed little interest in making big westerns and the general assumption was creeping in that westerns, along with serials, were for the unsophisticated audiences and not to be taken seriously. There appeared to be nothing new to be made on the subject, although Ken Maynard could be counted on to be a bit different, so the western became the "bread and butter" production. In its favor was that it invariably made money. Small time producers flocked to cash in on this, some of them with a genuine love of the western film for itself, others purely for the profit. Independent companies came and went with regularity — there was always somebody there with a few dollars eager to churn out another few films.

The only western of the year that could be regarded as artistic and worthy of genuine seriousness, among the non-series work, was Universal's *Law and Order*. Not meant as a major product, this unpretentious work was directed by Edward Cahn, who would produce no comparable work again. *Law and Order* was based on a W. R. Burnett novel, itself based on the Wyatt Earp–Gunfight at the O.K. Corral affair. Rugged stars Walter Huston and Harry Carey played the lawmen, with Raymond Hatton, Russell Hopton and Ralph Ince in a tale devoid of feminine characters. It was gritty and realistic, violent and non-sentimental, and was not a popular hit. Experts regard it now as one of the great westerns but it made no impression upon its release. It was very much in the W. S. Hart–silent John Ford–*Billy the Kid* mold. It lacked glamour at a time when glamour was the glitzy hallmark of Hollywood production, but today it stands out as a fine effort to portray the West as it was, dirty and dangerous and unrewarding.

More in the popular category was *The Conquerors* directed by William Wellman, somewhat similar in shape and intent to *Cimarron* and again starring Richard Dix. The story, more a historical romance, like *Cimarron*, than a pure western, unfolded from the frontier range into World War I with the hero's grandson joining the Lafayette Escadrille. It did better than *Law and Order* at the box office but was not another *Cimarron*, being ignored by the critics and academy.

Over at Columbia, Buck Jones was riding high with an ever-increasing fan club and worldwide fame. However it was his Columbia saddlemate, Tim McCoy, who made the B western "statement" of the year. Amidst his usual quota of well made but undistinguished B westerns, Tim McCoy was personally involved with one in particular, what seemed to be just another entry in the series called *The End of the Trail*— but one that was actually a personal statement by McCoy on the condition of, and relationship with, the American Indian. *The End of the Trail* today looks and sounds very old-fashioned. Time has marked it, the overacting brought on by years of playing in silent features, the heroic poses and the slimness of the budget causing hiccups in the flow of the narrative. It still stands as a powerful statement because, for the first time for some years, and the last time for many, it seriously questioned the actions of the white man, and government, in their dealings with the native people on the frontier. McCoy plays the army captain whose rival (Wheeler Oakman) has him accused of cowardice and dismissed from the service. With his young son he wanders the prairie, his son is killed, and the captain finds a home and peace among the Indian tribes. When conflict between white and red man breaks out again the captain tries to bring peace, and also points out to the conquerors of the plains that they have broken their word to the red man — more than once. Shot while interceding, McCoy's character dies, in the original filming, knowing that his death has caused white and red man to think again and try to settle their differences fairly. Unfortunately producer Columbia got frightened about the idea of a B cowboy hero dying on screen and insisted a happy ending be tagged on. Even with this cop-out *The End of the Trail* is an outstanding B western, and should be seen and assessed for what it is. McCoy had no big budget to play with, no endless millions of dollars and the players were just average contract actors and actresses on what they assumed was an every day job of work. Viewed in that light, *End of the Trail* is a powerful and well-meaning message film about a topic Americans still have not completely come to grips with. And it was definitely unusual in the midst of a series of average, formula B westerns.

Ken Maynard was still very popular and turning out low budget but action-filled westerns and Warners was making a series with John Wayne that had a reasonable budget plus stock shots from silent days, many of them from Ken Maynard films, thus Maynard was doubly in action. Warners, sticking strictly to a budget, would reuse the same footage of Maynard in a later Dick Foran series, so they really got their

Tom Mix returns to the screen at Universal in 1932.

money's worth out of it. Other cowboys riding the range were Tom Keene, Bob Steele, Tom Tyler, Rex Bell, Bill Cody, Jack Hoxie, Hoot Gibson, Lane Chandler and even Harry Carey, a veteran from way back. Some did well, but one whose return to the screen was disastrous was popular silent screen cowboy Jack Hoxie. Hoxie, who might be described as a "well-built man" (non-wellwishers claimed he was simply fat) had a catastrophic problem for someone trying to make it in sound pictures—he could not read or write. He soon faded from sight. But the biggest news in the western film field for 1932, complete with appropriate studio publicity, was the return to the screen of the silent "King of the Cowboys," Tom Mix.

Mix, who had spent two decades making silent westerns, returned to the screen for one reason only—money. He was getting on in years and there was some doubt about his capacity to rekindle the flame of yore. Universal, which had discarded Maynard and Gibson, was eager to try. Later critics and historians have tended to write off the Tom Mix westerns of 1932 and 1933 as an inferior product made by a man far past his prime. This is simply not true. As a B western series it is one of the best ever made, and Tom himself, certainly no youngster, is still agile and appealing. Much has been made of his speech and reading of lines. No Barrymore he, but he is not that bad. His voice is pleasant enough and if he has a fault it is a tendency to lack expression, to read his lines in a monotonous tone. Look at it this way, he loses nothing in comparison to Ken Maynard. Nine films were made, the best being the early ones. *Destry Rides Again* was a rather grim Max Brand story not really fitting the Mix image—so Tom simply played himself; it should have been titled *Tom Mix Rides Again*. *My Pal, the King* was a Ruritanian kingdom affair, lighthearted, with Tom more at home teaching the young king (Mickey Rooney) the pleasures of the cowboy and American way of life. Best of all was *Rider of Death Valley,* with a good story and entrancing desert photography from Tom's old silent screen cinematographer Dan Clark. Quality fell away a bit after that but *Texas Badman* was very good with atmospheric camera work and a villain with Napoleonic aspirations who must have inspired the scriptwriters of the 1935 *Bar 20 Rides Again* (and others). Seven of Tom's westerns were made in 1932. He had two more to do the next year but he was beginning to feel the grueling schedule of western film shooting, and now he had some more money and was eager to return to the circus life.

It is worth noting that, in 1932, among the bevy of handsome young men populating the Hollywood scene, some in leading roles, some supporting, some quite minor, were the likes of Gordon Elliott, Allan Lane, Charles Starrett and Johnny Mack Brown. All would become leading cowboy film stars, something that seemed unlikely at that stage. Brown was the closest to this, having played *Billy the Kid* and been in two other westerns, *Montana Moon* and the 1932 *Vanishing Frontier*, a minor effort of no great interest. He, like the others named, wanted to make his name as a dramatic actor, not as a western player. None of these men had a western background and it was a far cry from the days when Mix, Gibson and Jones had made their debuts.

You no longer had to be a cowboy — to be cowboy. And there were names that would become even more famous than those mentioned — William Boyd, Joel McCrea and one other gentleman, from Virginia, who in 1932 started his career on the western trail, namely Randolph Scott.

Zane Grey westerns had been, and were being, made by Fox, first with Richard Arlen, then with George O'Brien. In 1932 Paramount began to remake its own Zane Grey silent features and the actor chosen to star in many of them for the next few years was Randolph Scott. As with the films themselves, which were neither B nor A features but somewhere in between, so the star himself, a suave man about town in Hollywood, was an in-between western player. As a gentleman in a cozy domestic drama, a comedy or musical, Randolph Scott became more highly regarded with the sophisticates than through the Zane Grey westerns at Paramount. He was rated as a dependable player in whatever he did, a sort of junior Gary Cooper who, with his genuine cowboy background, had started as a western player but had shed that image to become a romantic idol.

The Paramount Zane Grey features, falling somewhere between the two classifications of westerns, were also neither very good nor very bad. They were tradesmanlike and used mainly by Paramount as a training ground for actors and actresses, directors and technicians. Shirley Temple made her feature debut in *To the Last Man*, one of the more austere and impressive titles of 1932.

1 9 3 3

Popular, but...

In 1933 western movies were popular, but perhaps not quite as popular as they had been in silent days. The audiences were becoming more select for such movies, being mainly rural and small town viewers. Mainstream western films would play in big centers less and less. At the most, they would be the lower end of the double bill. In the less urbanized areas they usually constituted a double bill of their own. It did seem as if they had found their niche and said niche did not include serious evaluation of the genre. Some major studios made westerns as their own 3 grade features, useful for training and keeping players and technicians occupied between major roles. The studios that specialized in westerns were small to minute businesses, many being fly-by-night outfits that made a series or two featuring a washed up cowboy star then disappeared — along with their star. Even so, many of the series westerns on offering were of a high standard, considering the budgets they worked under. They were still "formula" in plot and content as a rule and used players who had become associated with the genre, seldom used elsewhere or wanting to work elsewhere if it came to that. Most cowboy players were happy in their work, knowing that is where they belonged and getting pleasure, and a steady living, out of their occupation. There were some who had other aspirations, but once you worked in B westerns it was seldom you realized those. John Wayne was a notable exception but it took him long years of toil in the small studios before his rise to real cinematic stardom.

No "big" westerns were released in 1932 to interest the more jaded critics who scorned the unpretentious series oaters, unless one includes the MGM drama *Operator 13*, which was a Civil War story starring Gary Cooper and Marion Davies. Otherwise,

most interest centered on the last features of Tom Mix at Universal, which were inferior to the 1932 releases as both the studio and Mix came to the conclusion that he
had ridden far enough. Mix was tired, he had made enough money to put himself
back on the circus trail and he wanted out. Universal offered a new contract to Ken
Maynard, who had been making good, if budget constrained, westerns at Tiffany and
World Wide. Perhaps unwisely, Universal offered Maynard control over his pictures,
something both parties may have regretted later as the wayward genius that was Ken
Maynard invariably went overboard on budget to realize his enthusiasm. Ken did,
however, turn out interesting and entertaining features, none more so than his happy
Strawberry Roan, which, linked around the song of the same title, was a forerunner
of the musical western.

There may not have been any major westerns made, but apart from the Maynard films there were other very good series turned out, especially those of Buck
Jones at Columbia and George O'Brien at Fox. Buck Jones dominated the scene, at
that time exceptionally popular and making westerns of many styles, including the
outstanding 1933 entry *The Sundown Rider*. Jones could be deadly serious or lighthearted in his approach. Critics over time have come to the conclusion that his best
work was the "deadly serious"; Jones "lighthearted" tended to go overboard with
comedy bits that did not entirely suit him.

Tim McCoy was also still at Columbia but for unknown reasons the studio took
him out of the saddle in 1933 and into a series of action dramas set in modern times.
These were not bad, but probably lost Tim some of his audience, those who were
happy with him as a cowboy star. Columbia returned him to the West in 1934 but
he would never obtain the same following and was soon relegated to poverty row.
McCoy's autobiography hints that he was never entirely happy making B westerns
so the change to non-westerns may have been at his own request. If so, his hopes
were not realized because he would spend most of the next decade appearing in
cheaper and cheaper B westerns.

George O'Brien, in features such as *Robber's Roost*, *Smoke Lightning* and *The
Last Trail*, continued his superior work at Fox. O'Brien never cultivated the same
western following as did Buck Jones and others. Jones had that entire cowboy air
about him, on and off screen, and was particularly conscious of his impact on children. He not only played cowboy on screen but, like Maynard, off screen. George
O'Brien, although the epitome of the cowboy on screen, was just himself, an actor,
off, with a multitude of other interests besides western living. O'Brien's manner and
humor were adult oriented, even while appearing in a genre that had a huge children's following. In 1933 he, along with Jones and Maynard, were the best of the
screen cowboys.

Others had their following and Paramount continued its Zane Grey series that
was superior among B films if not quite of A stature. Randolph Scott, all Southern
charm in those days, was usually the star. Since most were remakes of silent features

much stock footage could be utilized, thus keeping the budget down. When Scott remade *Man of the Forest*, which had originally starred Jack Holt, Scott had to wear a thin mustache to link in with the stock scenes featuring Holt. Still, the quality of these mainly Henry Hathaway–directed westerns can be gauged from the cast listing of *Man of the Forest*, which along with Scott included Harry Carey, Buster Crabbe, Noah Beery and Guinn Williams.

John Wayne was at Warners, his material liberally spiced with Ken Maynard silent stock, and Tom Keene was still popular at RKO, where he tried to be somewhat different. Most of Keene's westerns linked the modern East with the wild West, and were fast moving and lighthearted. Keene looked likely to become a big cowboy star but he was one of those cowboys with other aspirations— he wanted to be a dramatic actor and anyway, RKO

Popular cowboy star Tom Keene in 1933.

was not, at that stage, a consistent western film maker. They terminated the Keene series and, for a while, made one-off westerns of basically B stature, starring the likes of Richard Dix or Harry Carey, before embarking on seriesdom again later in the '30s.

Hoot Gibson had lost popularity and was making slow, cheap features for producers like Allied and First Division. He was struggling with both his professional and personal life, but it was a shock to his fans when within a couple of years he disappeared from the screen, nobody wanting the amiable, cheerful, non-violent cowboy with the face that, as one critic wrote, "looked as if it had been lived in." That was still to happen, but in 1933 he struggled on less and less earnings while still enjoying a flamboyant private life style. Bob Steele, Tom Tyler and Rex Bell had popular followings but it was hard going for them in less than salubrious features. Bill Cody was off screen, between assignments, and Jack Hoxie's comeback was painful. Watching Jack lumber his big way through a cheap production, trying to cope with dialogue, it was hard to believe he had been a top cowboy in silent days— but he had. It is hard to defend series such as Hoxie's. Hard core B western fans "like 'em all," even the totally inept Reb Russell, who was superb on a horse but the worst actor of all time. For some, however, though they love the old B western, it takes fortitude to endure many of these Z grade '30s offerings, with their clumsy sound, pathetic acting and technical calamities— players appearing where they shouldn't be, bits of unrelated dialogue on the sound track and stunts that don't come off. It can be done — by suspending disbelief and laughing, these turkeys can generate good fun. At the same time it is sad to see once respected cowboy stars like Hoxie, Ted Wells and others relegated to such productions that allow them no chance, even if they were capable of taking it. What it does prove of course is that being a cowboy star in silent films was a different affair than being one in talkies. It took a while for that to sink in for some hopeful producers.

Which brings us back to Ken Maynard. The fact is, Ken, at his worst, was not much better than Ted Wells or Reb Russell. He could be, and often was, a terrible actor, with no idea of the meaning of his lines and given to ad-libbing, results of which were not much better. But Ken, for all of that, had some dynamic appeal. Not only was he a superb rider and showman but his sheer exuberance, when he was enjoying his work, came through to audiences. Ken had that indefinable star quality, call it charisma if you will. He also had a fertile and romantic mind and when in control of a project could come up with some pretty entertaining work — or disastrous, as the mood took him. Ken was a law unto himself, as he proved at Universal where his work was never dull and the westerns he made there are probably his best remembered. His interest in cowboy music continued, often with him singing and playing the fiddle. Around this time he also made some historically interesting recordings.

As 1933 closed Maynard was riding close on the heels of Buck Jones and George O'Brien for the cowboy crown. He had everything going for him and would have been a good bet for favoritism in 1934, all things being equal.

1934

Jones as "King"

Little western production occurred in 1934 outside the series western, unless one includes *Viva Villa!* at MGM with Wallace Beery, a sentimental account of the Mexican revolutionary story. The year was more notable for the continued success of Buck Jones who, after Ken Maynard fell from grace at Universal, was undisputed "King of the Cowboys." Jones completed his Columbia series and then accepted an offer from Universal that involved him in production work on his own pictures, as well as the occasional directing job. Buck was less self-indulgent than Maynard and Universal had more confidence in him. He began his contract with popular and well-balanced pictures like *Rocky Rhodes* and *When a Man Sees Red*. Jones was also at this time becoming king of the chapterplay, his work in that field, which still was respected, having begun in 1933 with *Gordon of Ghost City* for Universal, one of the best western serials ever made. He continued, once at that studio, with *The Red Rider*, almost equally good. Buck Jones, dedicated to his task, honest and foursquare, was the ideal of the youth of America and many other parts of the world by 1934, having taken on the throne left vacant by Tom Mix.

His rival, Ken Maynard, ran into problems at Universal, where his relations with Carl Laemmle and his son, who ran the studio, were not good. When Ken turned in a bizarre feature called *Smoking Guns*, utilizing, among other things, home movies from his crocodile hunting in South America, relations between them boiled over and Ken, unable to contain his quick temper, walked out. He walked into a deal with Mascot, a lowly studio run by Nat Levine, who specialized in serials. For them he made the serial *Mystery Mountain*, which proved very popular even if Ken contributed

From the Universal serial Gordon of Ghost City, *Buck Jones chases a villain on horseback.*

less than he should have to it. By this time Maynard was drinking heavily and he was often late or absent from shooting. Mascot did the best it could around him and took the opportunity of giving two radio singers, Gene Autry and Lester Burnette, small roles to test their suitability. Ken had also signed with Levine for a series of features. Only one was made, a good one directed by David Howard, *In Old Santa Fe*, one of the best westerns Ken made. But he was still surly and uncooperative much of the time and Levine fired him, taking a chance on elevating to stardom the radio singer Autry, who had a musical interlude in *In Old Santa Fe* with his pal, Lester Burnette. Ken Maynard had also "sung" in the film but his voice was dubbed, probably by Bob Nolan of the Sons of the Pioneers. Autry, popular on radio, had bombarded Nat Levine with requests to try him on screen and Maynard's troublesome ways forced Levine to give it a go, thus leading to the real birth of the singing cowboy, whatever the efforts made up till then in that direction by others—including Maynard himself.

One of these abortive singing affairs was at Monogram where John Wayne, not wanted by Warner Bros., had begun what would be a long running series of quite cheap, but enthusiastic, B westerns. In *Riders of Destiny* Wayne played "Singing Sandy," a lawman who warbled in moments of stress, such as when he was gunning for a varmint in the street. Wayne, who could not sing, was dubbed, but the voice doing the dubbing wasn't the most melodious. The idea was dropped. Wayne rode on, often in the company of Yakima Canutt and George Hayes, through more traditional adventures dubbed "authentic looking" by fans. Monogram shot its films in the western country because it had limited studio facilities. They looked dusty and atmospheric, but direction, acting and sound reproduction often let them down. Robert North Bradbury, father of Bob Steele, directed many of these — as well as his own son's films. Bradbury, an enthusiast if limited in talent, did the best he could with slim budgets. He often, after downing a suitable amount of alcoholic refreshment, liked to film sentimental, poetical endings, watching his son, or some other cowboy, ride off into the sunset with a tear in his (Bradbury's) eye.

During 1934 George O'Brien concluded his high-class Fox contract with titles *Frontier Marshal* and *The Dude Ranger*. *Frontier Marshal* was yet another adaptation of the Wyatt Earp story. This version would furnish the script copied for the Randolph Scott feature of 1939 and also Ford's *My Darling Clementine* of 1946. They were all based on the (imaginative) book by Stuart Lake, giving the Earp version. O'Brien then signed with producer Sol Lesser, though these films were still released through Fox. They involved westerns and non-westerns over the next few years before O'Brien joined RKO in 1938 for a final series of superior westerns.

Bill Cody, always looking rather underweight, was back on screen in a series for Spectrum that was variable while Bob Steele, Tom Tyler, Jack Perrin, Reb Russell and Wally Wales were all active, all in very cheap productions. They all, even the hapless Russell, had some following. Tim McCoy had returned to westerns at Columbia, but they were only average and it was obvious that the studio was looking for fresh cowboy blood. Columbia would try a multitude of fresh cowboys over the next few years; it was a continual shuffling in and out.

Of interest was the work of another Maynard, Ken's brother Kermit, with an independent group, Ambassador Pictures. Kermit had followed his brother west and appeared in a few silent westerns as "Tex" Maynard. He was reputed to be as good, if not better, at riding than his brother, something he showed constantly at Ambassador. His acting and appearance were more constrained than Ken's; in fact it could be said that his personality was a little lacking. In comparison with his brother he was pallid, which is no doubt why Kermit did not flourish past this one series from whence he dropped to character acting for many years. The difference in his series was that he played a Canadian Mountie, but presumably response was lukewarm because before the series ended in 1936 he had reverted to plain American cowhand. Kermit's films, though respectable in B western terms, suffered from the common

Busy cowboy favorite Bob Steele.

denominators of the poverty row productions—lack of polish through tight budgeting, no musical backgrounds, inept dialogue spoken by actors who were prolific players in cheap productions and never improved their meager talents, and directors who had no time to take care. He lasted longer than many, did Kermit Maynard.

Zane Grey features continued at Paramount, with Randolph Scott, later replaced by Larry "Buster" Crabbe and Tom Keene when Scott was given more dress suit dramas to play in. Scott must have been invaluable at Paramount because he could perform in any type of film. Paramount did not have Zane Grey all to themselves. RKO also produced westerns based on the Grey stories, notably *West of the Pecos* in 1934, starring the manly Richard Dix, no longer a big name but not a series player either. Dix could handle a variety of roles but through the rest of the '30s and early '40s his strong, rugged he-man style was at its best in westerns.

Western serials continued to be popular, with Mascot (*Mystery Mountain*) and Universal (*The Red Rider*) the two participating studios. Universal's were bigger and more ambitious while Mascot, limited of funds, went in for constant action and way-out plots and characters. They also, for a while, utilized animal actors like Rex the Wild Horse and Rin Tin Tin the famous dog (and son of). In those serials the male lead, often a western player like Bob Custer, was rendered relatively incompetent when side by side with the animals, who usually displayed more wit and intelligence than the humans.

It was a quiet year in 1934. Hollywood's cowboy stars got on with doing their thing and audiences who related to their efforts turned out in big numbers while those who did not relate left them alone. In some ways it was the last of the old-time western, series style, because in 1935 new highways and byways suddenly appeared that turned the B or series western upside down. As of yet though, there was no sign of a revival in the big screen western, the epic or serious study of the western myth. That would take longer to revive.

1935
The Coming of Cassidy— and Autry

Annie Oakley was one of the very non-series westerns produced during 1935, and it was meant to be a major movie. It was pleasant, with Barbara Stanwyck, then new to westerns, giving the first of many fine performances in the genre, but no more. History, as usual, took a back seat as Hollywood's version of a western lady hit the screen. Most notable was the director, a young George Stevens. Stevens would become a leading Hollywood director and would return to westerns only once in his long career — if one excludes *Giant* from being called a "western." Stevens' return gave us one of the greatest ever westerns, *Shane*, some 18 years later.

In the world of series westerns major events took place during the year. What might have been the most major, but in the end wasn't, involved the return (again) to the screen of Tom Mix. Mix again needed money and Mascot lured him back to appear in its serial *The Miracle Rider*. There is debate over *The Miracle Rider*. Some historians rate it one of the best of serials; others write if off as rubbish. It was typical Mascot, cheap, but fun when you suspend disbelief. Mix also took the role because the serial had a good story of patriotism that he felt was good for young children. At least, so he said. As history knows Tom Mix was a joyful and prodigious liar, to put it mildly, with a love for spreading valiant tales about his own exploits. He may rightly have cared for what the youngsters of America were watching on screen — after all, he would not be the only cowboy star who began to believe his own publicity about himself — but the fact of the matter is he did the Mascot serial mainly for the money.

And whereas at Universal Mix still had looked good, two years later the years were really beginning to tell. He had to be doubled regularly (which would have been common serial practice anyway, to save money) and he simply looked old. Still, the fans were faithful. *The Miracle Rider* was Mascot's biggest revenue producing serial. This time Mix retired from the screen for good. He only had a few more years to live.

Mascot did not have much longer to go either. Herbert J. Yates persuaded Nat Levine, head of the studio, to amalgamate with Monogram Pictures under a new banner, Republic, to be run by Yates. Levine, who never regarded himself as a businessman, was happy to let Yates take over. It was a significant move for western pictures because the newly formed Republic would almost immediately start producing them in large numbers—and good ones. Soon the names "Republic" and "series westerns" would become synonymous, as it would with fast action serials. Republic never would become a major studio; "the little studio in the valley" they called it, notwithstanding Herbert Yates' ambitions. They remained best at producing westerns and serials and their efforts to make bigger budget product never quite came off, except

Singer Gene Autry became the first screen "singing cowboy" at Republic in 1935.

when a major talent like John Ford was involved. As of now, 1935, one of their first moves was to take up Levine's Gene Autry contract. After Ken Maynard had departed Levine had starred Autry in a serial, *The Phantom Empire*. It was a weird mixture of western, modern radio and futuristic underground kingdom modes and Autry was oddly out of place on screen, totally unable to act, clumsy and unathletic looking. Yet amazingly, possibly because of the Autry voice, *The Phantom Empire* was a huge success. Levine hastily signed him up for more and with the new merger, Autry became the property of Republic Pictures. It was under the Republic Pictures banner that the first full "musical western" featuring a "singing cowboy" was released that year. *Tumbling Tumbleweeds* starred Autry and his friend and sidekick Lester "Smiley" Burnette, a low comic but talented musician.

Joseph Kane, on the verge of a long and fine western film career, directed and *Tumbling Tumbleweeds* was a potent mixture of traditional western action plus many songs, including the hit title song. Autry himself was still awkward on screen, and would remain so for a while before settling into a strange metamorphosis where he played Gene Autry on screen and played the role faultlessly.

Republic also inherited John Wayne through the Monogram merger. His pictures, still budget westerns, took an immediate upswing and became more ambitious, the first signs that Wayne might be on the way up. Besides nurturing its own cowboy stars, Republic would soon also take over distributing series made by producer A. W. Hackel and starring Bob Steele and Johnny Mack Brown.

At about the same time Levine-Mascot-Republic was initiating the Autry westerns, Warner Bros., out of western production for a while, had its own idea

Johnny Mack Brown as he appeared in his first Universal serial, Rustlers of Red Dog, *1935.*

of a singing cowboy series. Historians have pointed out that there was too close a gap between the initial Autry and Dick Foran releases for one to have copied from the other. The same idea had come, about the same time. The difference was in the formula. Levine had chosen an authentic country style singer in Autry, his soft Texan twang being easy on the ear. Autry was already a big seller of records. Warners went for an actor and musical comedy–light opera style singer in Dick Foran. While Republic, after an initial feeling of the way, based its singing cowboy in a never-never world of a modern and a traditional west, Warners, like imitators to come, made its musical westerns straight — as traditional western films set in the 1880s. Foran, and similar cowboys to come, had a fine voice, but wasn't a known voice or a country and western voice. Foran, who was a capable player, actor and genial character, did well, but never rivaled Autry's surge of popularity. This lesson was not heeded by many producers who followed up with their singing cowboys in the Foran mold.

While still on singing cowboys and to show that producers are slow to learn from their errors, when John Wayne came under the Republic banner and his first western with the new logo, *Westward Ho!*, was released, cinemagoers were treated once more to a "singing Wayne," with Big John seated around the campfire with other waddies vocalizing for all his worth. Once again, of course, he was dubbed. And after this time the mistake was not repeated.

While these momentous events were taking place, over at Universal Buck Jones was still indisputable king of the cowboys. Jones, tough, agile and honorable, turned out classy B westerns like *The Crimson Trail*, *The Ivory Handled Gun* and *Stone of Silver Creek*. He had a hand in production and was never afraid to experiment with ambiguous endings and twisted plot lines. Unfortunately, as the Universal series proceeded Jones was inclined, like Ken Maynard before him, to overindulge his artistic imagination. He did not, like Maynard, go crazy with the budget but it seemed that any cowboy star given his head would overindulge. Even as late as 1960 we can see what happened when John Wayne produced his own *Alamo* and, of course, modern film stars (not strictly western) are notorious for self-indulgence. The old Hollywood producers and directors had no time for actors getting involved with the production side of filming — and they had a point. Buck Jones also had a failing he shared with the great director John Ford — he overindulged his sense of humor. However, it must be noted that Jones was hugely popular at this time with both children and adults.

Tim McCoy, popular for some years, had left Columbia and was on the downhill trail, making much cheaper westerns for an outfit called Puritan Pictures. McCoy, who liked to masquerade as a Mexican or gypsy and overact wildly, still had a following. His replacement at Columbia was Charles Starrett, and Columbia was also proposing a series with one Bob Allen, who had supported McCoy in a few of his later westerns. Neither Starrett nor Allen had any western background; they were professional actors with ambitions. Starrett, tall and handsome, was reluctant to take up westerns whereas young Bob Allen was eager to do a stint as a cowboy. He had watched McCoy working and felt that he, Allen, could do as well as "this old man," an arrogant attitude that boomeranged, because Allen did not do as well as that "old man." Meanwhile Starrett had donned dark clothing, a large white Stetson and spotless flowing white kerchief, and astride a snow white mount had starred in *Gallant Defender*. It proved popular. Among the supporting cast, singing over the credits and in the film itself, was an up and coming western group called the Sons of the Pioneers, one of their number being a young, very slim Len Slye, of whom more would be heard.

George O'Brien continued to turn out medium budget features of impeccable quality like *When a Man's a Man*, *Thunder Mountain*, and *Whispering Smith Speaks*. In the last named O'Brien's delightful touch with humor was never more evident in a lighthearted film whereas *When a Man's a Man* was a serious affair with surprisingly little violence and a villain of mild proportions, who ends up, quite justifiably, free.

Paramount continued its Zane Grey series with Larry "Buster" Crabbe, Tom Keene and others. In the hands of lesser directors than Henry Hathaway these had become more B-oriented features but were still good. Harry Carey was finishing off

New cowboy star Charles Starrett.

some cheap westerns in which the main problem was Harry himself — he was obviously too old to be a romantic lead, and a father figure as a hero could come off in the soon-to-be Hopalong Cassidy series, but it did not fare well in poorly crafted poverty row westerns. Bob Steele, Tom Tyler and Johnny Mack Brown toiled away, Steele and Brown for lowly Supreme, and A. W. Hackel. Both would eventually come under Republic. For Brown it was his first western series. After starting out with MGM as a potential big star, he had drifted down the ladder to appearing in a Mascot serial, *Fighting with Kit Carson*, and had a moments of glory with Mae West, but by 1935 was firmly immersed in series westerns, something from which he would never recover. Eventually it dawned on Brown, as with other cowboy actors, that appearing in westerns was not such a bad occupation and he became satisfied, enjoying himself and his career.

An interesting sidelight to the year that would eventually involve bigger things was the use on screen of characters from a popular western author, William Colt MacDonald. These were the Three Mesquiteers, an obvious takeoff of the Three Musketeers, with characters Tucson Smith, Stony Brooke and Lullaby Joslin. *Law of the .45s* was a cheaply made feature using just two of the characters, Tucson and Stony, as played by Guinn Williams and Al St. John, an unusual combination considering that both would go on to become popular comic sidekicks. Williams, large and amiable (on screen), had played cowboy lead in a few films but St. John was a bit player who would end up, with whiskers suitably enlarged, as the famous "Fuzzy." More popular and widely circulated was RKO Radio's *Powdersmoke Range*. This was billed as "the Barnum and Bailey of Westerns," listing a huge cast of current and former cowboy players, mostly lower-trade ones. Harry Carey starred with Bob Steele, Tom Tyler (playing the first of his interesting "villain" roles), Hoot Gibson and Guinn Williams. The last two named played Stony and Lullaby, with Carey taking the Tucson part. Named down the cast list were Wally Wales, William Desmond, Buffalo Bill, Jr., Buddy Roosevelt, Art Mix, Franklyn Farnum, William Farnum and Buzz Barton, all familiar to western film devotees. *Powdersmoke Range* is a nostalgic favorite but, oddly enough, it is a slow, rather dull film with Tyler taking the acting honors. The people who took most notice of it were at Republic Studio. They decided to make their own Mesquiteer film, for 1936 release.

Jack Perrin was working that year, as was Reb Russell in his final pictures. They were not good, but even worse was a film called *The Phantom Cowboy* made on what must have been a world record low budget and surely a contender for worst western ever made. The plot, acting, sound and direction were so bad that words are inadequate. This turkey starred Ted Wells, a respectable silent screen cowboy who is made to appear totally inept in *The Phantom Cowboy*. He couldn't have been that bad but poor Ted never got another chance. There is talk that a further western was made by the same producer with Wells starring but thankfully it has disappeared into limbo.

Both Maynards, Ken and Kermit, were working in 1935. Kermit was making his

Mountie films at Ambassador and, to Ken's chagrin, doing quite well. The brothers did not get along well and Ken was always jealous of any Kermit success, especially as he was relegated to appearing for producer Larry Darmour, who released through Columbia. This was not as bad as it might appear. Darmour's budgets hovered around $60,000. Within a few years Ken would be working for outfits with shooting budgets of $15,000. Directed by longtime action technicians Al Herman and Spencer Gordon Bennett, Ken's features such as *Western Frontier*, *Western Courage* and *Heir to Trouble* were not too bad. Ken himself was putting on weight but still looked quite athletic. Off screen he was a continuing problem, arguing with producer and director, wanting things his way and getting drunk when crossed. Sadly, Ken was distancing himself from respectable producers by his actions. On screen he was still popular. The Darmour westerns accentuated Ken's musical talents, for what they were. Ken was enthusiastic with his fiddling and singing, but his talent was limited.

A minor western of the year worth mentioning for a strange reason is the Commodore feature, directed by William Berke, *Toll of the Desert*. This cheapie starred Fred Kohler, Jr., son of the noted heavy and for most of his own career a villain or bit player. It was poorly produced and badly acted, yet a respected film historian, the late William K. Everson, selected it as one of his ten favorite B westerns in the reprint of *Hollywood Corral*. This astonished the editors, not surprisingly so. I guess Everson used *Toll of the Desert* as an example for all those cheap, shoddy B westerns made that, if you have the capacity to relax and enjoy them, have a certain fascination. Bad movies do delight in a strange way; just look at the work of Ed Wood.

Finally for this year—the subject of the title of this chapter. "Hopalong" Cassidy had been a popular fictional figure for many years. The author, Clarence E. Mulford, who had sold only sporadic screen rights to this character in the silents, was persuaded by producer Harry "Pop" Sherman to relinquish them to him. Sherman wanted to produce "authentic" westerns. He had trouble getting the right actor to portray Cassidy. James Gleason is said to have been his first choice. Finally the role went to washed up romantic star William Boyd, prematurely white haired, handsome, but unable to ride a horse and a well known womanizer and drinker. In his eagerness to get work Boyd promised to give up the drinking and hard living. The first film based on Cassidy came out in 1935. Called *Hop-Along Cassidy*, it was well done, capturing a (romanticized) vision of how life was on the Bar 20 ranch, using Mulford's characters but adding an old geezer called "Uncle Ben." Uncle Ben's brutal shooting by Kenneth McDonald provoked the famous ending when, all of a sudden, frantic background music announced the saddling up and riding for vengeance of the Bar 20 and other ranchhands. As Hopalong Cassidy, Boyd affected his own rather strange outfit, definitely not that of a working cowboy. He hated horses and fell off one early on and broke his leg, thus causing delays but giving the actor an authentic limp. For any future films he promised he would learn to ride. *Hop-Along Cassidy* led to two more 1935 titles, *The Eagles Brood* and *Bar 20 Rides Again*. They were good, Sherman was working through Paramount and budgets were reasonable. Boyd got to where he could sit a horse, and the support cast, including Jimmy Ellison as the romantically inclined Johnny Nelson, was good. Notably, the role given to George Hayes as "Uncle Ben" in the first film spawned further use of that actor. By *Bar 20 Rides Again* he was "Windy," alive at the end and joining the Bar 20 crew. A famous trio was born with Boyd, Ellison and Hayes. Hopalong Cassidy was there, it seems, for a while. For just how long, nobody had any idea.

1 9 3 6
The Return of the Epic

Epics, or at least, large scale westerns, returned to the screen in 1936, led by Cecil B. DeMille's *The Plainsman*. Other titles came from Paramount (*The Texas Rangers*) and Universal (*Sutter's Gold*), and MGM had a rush of western blood to the head, producing *Ramona, Three Godfathers, Robin Hood of Eldorado* and *Rose Marie*. *Ramona* and *Rose Marie* are peripheral westerns only, but *Robin Hood of Eldorado* was a romanticized study of Joaquin Murieta played by Warner Baxter and directed by William Wellman. *Three Godfathers* was another remake of the Peter B. Kyne story, last filmed as *Hell's Heroes*. This 1936 version had the unlikely trio of Chester Morris, Lewis Stone and Walter Brennan, but was well done. *Sutter's Gold* was a rather expensive "flop," lacking action and star players, but *The Texas Rangers*, directed by King Vidor and starring Fred MacMurray, Jack Oakie, Lloyd Nolan and Jean Parker, was entertaining and expansive.

Paramount also made *The Trail of the Lonesome Pine*, the first major outdoor film in color. Sentimental though it is, *Lonesome Pine* is good to look at and Fred MacMurray (again) and Henry Fonda gave good performances, along with B stalwart Fuzzy Knight. However, it struggles to be recognized as a western. But then so should that year's *Last of the Mohicans*, set well before the "West" as it is generally recognized was colonized. Still, the wide ranging criteria for what is or is not one of the genre usually lets "colonial" history in and the 1936 *Last of the Mohicans*, released by United Artists and directed by George Seitz, was good, perhaps the best of all the versions, in pretty color and starring a stoic and heroic Randolph Scott.

Bing Crosby, fast becoming a popular item, ventured onto the musical-comedy

49

Cecil B. DeMille's 1936 epic The Plainsman *with Gary Cooper, Anthony Quinn and James Ellison.*

range in 1936 in *Rhythm of the Range*, perhaps most notable now for western film fans as an early chance to see the Sons of the Pioneers. Films geared more toward A class than B were *Yellow Dust*, with Richard Dix, square jawed as ever, and Jack Holt's *End of the Trail*—the same title as Tim McCoy's 1932 film and from the same studio, Columbia, but completely different with its grim story and ending of hero Holt being hung.

The major cinematic event of the year, however, remained *The Plainsman*. DeMille had "epic" in mind from the start and it must be said that *The Plainsman* proved popular and made money. Seen today, it is a plodding and rather dull film enhanced only by the performances of Gary Cooper as a determined but gentlemanly Wild Bill Hickok and Jean Arthur as a wildly unlikely Calamity Jane. DeMille, who liked to present "authentic historical moments and mementos," gives ultimately an innocently sentimental picture of America's past and shows no interest when the big action scenes come up for filming. They are mostly done by process screen, painfully obvious. In the cast as Bill Cody is James Ellison, then playing Johnny Nelson in Pop Sherman's Hopalong Cassidy series. Ellison does quite well and must have had dreams of a developing career because he left the Cassidy series soon after, something he may have later regretted because little came his way and his career ended up back in B westerns of the cheapest variety.

If *The Plainsman* proved anything in retrospect it was that Paramount did medium budget features (like its Zane Grey series) and B westerns (such as the Hopalong Cassidy run) better than it did A films. With *The Plainsman* doing good business, though, it did not seem apparent at the time. Paramount, like MGM, was a studio that over the years would turn out numerous sober and painstaking features without ever quite capturing the essence of even the western myth. There were the odd exceptions of course, but they were not that frequent.

The studios that dealt in B or series westerns were churning them out at a great pace in 1936. The advent of new cowboy stars, the continued popularity of established ones and the singing cowboy phenomenon all helped to fuel the demand for minor westerns. Serials too were at a new peak with Buck Jones still king at Universal, joined by Johnny Mack Brown who would make four entertaining, if repetitious, western serials at that studio. Brown's first had been the excellent *Rustlers of Red Dog* (his best) in 1935 and he would be back again in 1937, 1938 and 1939. Meanwhile Buck made *The Roaring West* in 1935 and *The Phantom Rider* in 1936. Neither were as good as his earlier ones but he was so popular it didn't matter. From the ashes of Mascot, Republic had picked up the chapterplay torch with a very good first western entry in *The Vigilantes Are Coming*, starring its bright new handsome action star Bob Livingston. An independent group, Stage and Screen, even got into the act with *Custer's Last Stand* but proved unable to match the quality of the bigger producers. It was about the last farewell for a sporadic western lead, Rex Lease.

There was now no doubt that Buck Jones at Universal was top cowboy. George O'Brien was making interesting but not hugely popular works for independent producer A. C. Hirliman, and Ken Maynard had slid out of contention. Jones tried more and more for interesting and different plots and situations in his westerns, not always with success. *Empty Saddles* was good, as was *Sunset of Power* but something good could be said of all his films, and sometimes something bad. His big challenge now as leading cowboy star came not from previous contenders but from newcomers like Boyd and Starrett and, most of all, the singer Gene Autry.

Gene Autry in 1936 took an amazing leap up the ladder of popularity and at the end of the year was third cowboy at the box office. By the end of 1937 he would be Cowboy No. 1, all to the teeth-gnashing bewilderment of rivals and critics who found nothing much right with the man. He was short, not particularly good looking, though decidedly amiable, he couldn't ride very well, or fight very convincingly and his screen adventures seemed set in a ludicrous "West" of horses and baddies, plus

Robert Livingston, as "The Eagle," is held by John Merton and Bud Osborne while heavy Fred Kohler gloats in this scene from Republic's 1936 serial The Vigilantes Are Coming.

motor cars, Tommy guns and songs at the drop of a sombrero. Yet the audiences loved it. Historians have analyzed it as being for the same reason viewers loved Shirley Temple and Astaire and Rogers—for pure escapism. The thirties were tough times for ordinary folk. They flocked to the cinema as the best and cheapest form of entertainment (with radio) and they wanted to escape for an hour or two from their hard, dull, ordinary lives. Autry, the likable Texan with a big smile and a song for any situation, gave them a dream world where right triumphed over wrong because it was good. The worst things could be overcome with a song and smile, a little bit of riding and fighting—but essentially the song and smile. Gene Autry sold records by the million, was on radio and film and made personal appearances. As a character says in one of his later films (*The Old Barn Dance*, 1938), "That cowboy's got something these folks like."

In 1936 films like *Red River Valley*, *Comin' Round the Mountain*, *The Singing Cowboy*, *The Big Show* and *The Old Corral*, Autry's mysterious charm proved irresistible and the huge profit Republic made on Autry pictures was the base upon which Herbert Yates built his empire.

Autry's rivals were not so lucky. Dick Foran has already been mentioned. His Warner westerns continued with the likes of *Song of the Saddle, California Mail* and *Treachery Rides the Range* and they were good westerns. But Foran's two or three songs per picture sung in his breezy baritone did not capture nearly the public adoration Autry enjoyed. Foran remained popular because his westerns were old style and fast moving. With producers frantically looking about for cowboys who sang, two small companies came up with theirs. Spectrum, which had employed Bill Cody, dropped him in favor of Fred Scott, an opera singer who displayed no horse savvy to begin with but obviously learned to ride reasonably well. Spectrum did not have the budgets to add much gloss to its westerns so all depended upon Scott. He had a very fine voice but it was not a country and western voice and though musical purists admired his dulcet tones, cowboy fans were

Close behind Autry came singing cowboy number two, Dick Foran.

not so impressed. Fred Scott, often dressed in black and toting two long-barreled Colts, did generate enough enthusiasm to stay around for a few years. He was helped for a while by having Al St. John, still pre–Fuzzy, as sidekick. St. John proved popular and for some years worked prodigiously in minor westerns.

Grand National made a deal with producer Ed Finney in 1936. Finney had signed up a radio and stage singer from Texas, Woodward Ritter, called by one and all "Tex." Ritter looked cowboyish and had a most unusual baritone-bass voice. He was one of those singers you "either liked or disliked," there were no half measures. He was something of an expert on real cowboy music; he had made a few records and appeared in the early version of *Oklahoma!* called *Green Grow the Lilacs,* also the title of the song he would ever be associated with. Ritter also had a way of putting across drinking songs like "Rye Whiskey." Finney thought highly of him so Grand National took the chance.

Beginning with *Song of the Gringo,* Ritter would prove popular. His singing certainly sounded "authentic" and he had an easygoing, likable personality. Grand National, though, did not have the budgets that could have lifted the Ritter westerns up to challenge Autry and his 1937 releases would suffer from this. Tex Ritter himself remained a popular performer and would carry on to become the third longest surviving singing cowboy of them all. His westerns, though, did not follow the Republic-Autry

The first Hopalong Cassidy "trio" in 1936, Jimmy Ellison as Johnny Nelson, George Hayes as "Windy" and William Boyd as Cassidy.

never-never land formula, and with a couple of exceptions remained firmly fixed in the old West.

More singing cowboys would be thrust upon the screen before too long, but there were other non-singing westerners, some old hands, others new and challenging. Hopalong Cassidy, in the form of William Boyd, was the fastest rising star. Boyd had been a leading player for DeMille in silent days but this was a brand new career for him. His 1936 westerns, *Call of the Prairie*, *Three on the Trail*, *Heart of the West*, *Trail Dust* and *Hopalong Cassidy Returns* were superior product with good stories, still based on Mulford originals, good casts and winning performances from Boyd, whose avuncular playing on screen carefully hid the fact that he hated horses and children. The story goes that Boyd was at a baseball game with his friend Buck Jones when a horde of youngsters besieged them for autographs. Boyd swore at them and Jones quietly told him, "Remember, Bill, these kids are your audience." Boyd learned and in public and on screen he was a good enough actor to hide his natural instincts. He also realized that he would have to learn to ride, and this he did, though he never became more than a passable horseman and avoided the animals whenever he could. Boyd, with the young Ellison and George "Windy Halliday" Hayes as sidekicks was on the way to the top in westerns. The very best of a good bunch of 1936 films was *Hopalong Cassidy Returns*, with Boyd, in those days still wearing his guns tied down and making no bones about shooting an opponent dead, falls in love and kisses the dying Evelyn Brent at the end — something that in a few years would be unthinkable for Hoppy to do.

At Columbia Charles Starrett was doing well, although he thought at the time that he would do a year of westerns and then return to drawing room dramas. Films like *The Cowboy Star* and *Code of the Range* were well done. Columbia product, after Buck Jones, was always formula, but they had more polish than the independents could muster. Starrett was told by the studio that he was doing so well they intended to keep him in westerns a bit longer. Little did he know how much longer.

George O'Brien was not on screen as much as before, but he did in 1936 make a respectable version of *Daniel Boone*, with John Carradine a malicious Dirty Simon Girty. Other old timers like Tim McCoy, struggling in cheap Puritan films under director Sam Newfield, and Hoot Gibson, with no series at all, waited upon events. Gibson did turn up in a secondary role in the amusing *Last Outlaw*, a John Ford story that starred Harry Carey as an amiable old timer released from jail and struggling to come to terms with the modern world. It's a pity it wasn't directed by Ford, but it was still fun, giving Tom Tyler another snarling villain role and introducing Fred Scott, who would go on to star at Spectrum. In the film Carey and Gibson make it pretty obvious they do not think much of "singing cowboys."

Ken Maynard, out of sorts with most people, turned out four final Columbia-released Darmour productions, *The Cattle Thief*, *Heroes of the Range*, *Avenging Waters* and *The Fugitive Sheriff*. Though Ken could still charm on screen, and rode well, some of the work was shoddy, notably some pathetic flood scenes in *Avenging Waters*. Ken dressed as a peddler and making a little music in *The Cattle Thief* was about the best of the bunch.

Johnny Mack Brown, Bob Steele, Tom Keene, Rex Bell (whose greater claim to fame would be that he married Clara Bow and became governor of Nevada) and Kermit Maynard were all busy in average to bad productions. Brown, working for A. W. Hackel, looked impressive and his future seemed assured, with his serial work at Universal, for a long tenure in westerns. Steele was always busy while Tom Keene, having failed to make the dramatic acting hit he had hoped for with *Our Daily Bread*, had returned to westerns. Rex Bell had made an interesting but cheap group of four films with Buzz Barton and Ruth Mix, daughter of Tom, the previous year and was at Grand National. He had the makings of a good cowboy star but never really got the breaks.

Back at Columbia Bob Allen looked good in cowboy clothes; he could act and

Short-lived (on screen) Columbia cowboy Bob Allen.

he appeared in six westerns all with *Ranger* in the title. The studio never really gave him a chance because production was woeful. A more forceful personality might have overcome that but Bob Allen was nice and too mild. His series came to a quick end in 1937. John Wayne at Republic was growing in stature but the real success story there, after the Autry miracle, was the birth of the Three Mesquiteer series.

As previously mentioned the Mesquiteers had been dabbled with but not persevered with. Republic bought the rights from author MacDonald and began with a trio comprising Ray Corrigan, a muscular serial star of *Undersea Kingdom*, known as "Crash," handsome and promising Bob Livingston as Stoney and well known comic sidekick Syd Saylor as Lullaby. *The Three Mesquiteers*, directed by Ray Taylor, was an average western not creating too much notice. Republic tried again with *Ghost Town Gold* and made one cast change. Max Terhune, a gentle comic and ventriloquist, replaced Saylor. Whatever magic Terhune added is sometimes hard to analyze, but he did. This trio hit if off—as did *Ghost Town Gold*. The two action stars, Corrigan and Livingston, were also better dressed than in the first film, and things just seemed to click into place. Joseph Kane directed and that also helped, since Kane was a far more talented director than Taylor. Although Terhune was supposedly the comic of the trio, it was the exchanges between Corrigan and Livingston, often rivals, that provided most humor. This would continue for the series notwithstanding that off screen the two disliked each other intensely. Republic would never give the Mesquiteers the budgets it gave Autry but the series would grow in popularity to become another good money earner for the studio.

The series western was at a crossroads in 1936. Veterans scorned the newfangled singing cowboy and announced firmly that it was a fad that would not last. They watched in horror as Gene Autry sang his way into the hearts of a nation and the world. Millions of fans just sat back and enjoyed this new brand of western, newfangled and all. The old timers were right, it didn't last, not forever, but the singing cowboy survived as long as the entire life of series westerns and from 1937 onward one of that breed would always be top cowboy star at the box office.

1937
Never So Many Westerns, but....

The spurt of production by major studios from 1936 did not carry over into 1937. The year is notably barren of major western productions except for MGM's Wallace Beery vehicle *Badman of Brimstone*, entertaining enough but lightweight, and the one "epic" western attempted, *Wells Fargo*, another Paramount effort. Like so many major Paramount efforts, *Wells Fargo* fell short of its mark, far short in fact. Directed in ponderous style by Frank Lloyd, *Wells Fargo* had "this is an epic" written all over it. It is a painstaking and dull march through the history of that company, episodic and lacking tautness and punch. Vain efforts at "humor" from lugubrious Bob Burns add nothing and any interest generated is solely from the solid and ever-dependable Joel McCrea performance. It was McCrea's first real western and showed he had a natural aptitude for playing a frontiersman. However, apart from sporadic roles, he went back to drama and light comedy for some years before turning finally to westerns full time, one of the most satisfying decisions made in Hollywood. Adding interest, Frances Dee, his wife in real life, played the heroine. *Wells Fargo* also put Johnny Mack Brown back in a major film, but his role is minimal and he gets killed off before too long.

So for western fans 1937 was a stream of some excellent, many competent and some awful B westerns from what was becoming a huge variety of cowboy stars. By 1937 just about everybody who was really anybody in westerns was on screen, with a few notable exceptions to come. It was also a good year for western serials. From

Frank Lloyd's ponderous 1937 epic Wells Fargo, *with Joel McCrea there on the freight wagon.*

Universal came a good Johnny Mack Brown film, *Wild West Days*, and from Republic *Zorro Rides Again*, an action classic, plus what may be the best western serial ever made, *The Painted Stallion*. *The Painted Stallion* was partly filmed on location in Utah and locked splendid. It also introduced a young director, William Witney, still in his 20s, who would go on to become one of the few real artists among series western directors. Ray Corrigan, on duty from the Three Mesquiteers and dressed in becoming buckskin, was a strong lead and the female role was more important than usual and in the hands of Julia Thayer, also known as Jean Carmen, an otherwise unremarkable B western heroine. As the pivotal rider of the painted stallion Thayer had a role few western leading ladies were lucky to get and made the most of it. Even romance was hinted at by the end of the very satisfying *Painted Stallion*.

From the galaxy of cowboy stars working that year the big four were Buck Jones, William Boyd, Gene Autry and George O'Brien. And the big one by the end of the year was Gene Autry. Republic released seven Gene Autry westerns in 1937, from *Roundup Time in Texas* (which was actually set in Africa) to *Springtime in the Rockies*.

Three cowboy stars, Ray Corrigan, Hoot Gibson and Wally Wales, now playing character parts under the name of Hal Taliaferro, on guard in Republic's classic 1937 serial The Painted Stallion.

One of the in-between titles was *Public Cowboy No. 1*, and that was in fact how things were. Backed up by sidekick Smiley Burnette, who became popular in his own right, good casts and able direction from Joseph Kane, Autry rode away from the opposition. He never did learn to act, never became an outstanding rider, often looked pudgy and was one of those singers who, though his records sold in millions, could not really sing very well. Dozens have tried to work that one out and come up with reasonable solutions, but no matter. Smiling, singing Gene and his horse Champion were top of the western tree and would remain so, only stepping down by choice to join the services in wartime. There is a magic about Gene's Republic westerns of that period never quite recaptured in later years. They were ludicrous, fascinating and sheer enjoyment. The sophisticates were never won over but that does not surprise. The majority, the ordinary public, you and I, sat back and enjoyed it. And we would do so for many a year.

One of the strange aspects of the time was that although Autry had made singing cowboys all the rage and many were now riding the range, of the top four cowboy stars three were non-singers. All at some stage allowed western music to be performed in their films—Jones and Boyd, who appeared to be soul mates on this issue, reluctantly, and O'Brien because he appeared to quite enjoy it, though no singer himself.

Buck Jones was still very popular and it is amazing to now realize that his career would suddenly drop away from under him within a year. He made a mistake in 1937. When his Universal contract closed, the terms he wanted from the studio for another were not acceptable, so he left. Universal, no doubt much to Buck's disdain, replaced him with a singing cowboy. Jones made a deal through Columbia but, apart from *Hollywood Roundup*, which was set in a modern studio with Buck as a double and stand-in and Grant Withers as bigheaded cowboy star, the results were mediocre. Buck was still making westerns as 1937 ended, but only just.

Boyd, as Hopalong Cassidy, continued to go from strength to strength. After *Borderland*, at 82 minutes possibly the longest ever series western, Jimmy Ellison was replaced by tall, lanky Russell Hayden, playing Lucky Jenkins. Hayden immediately fitted in and proved popular. Boyd, Hayden and Hayes rode on through *Hills of Old Wyoming*, *Rustlers' Valley*, *North of the Rio Grande*, *Hopalong Rides Again* and *Texas Trail*, all superior B westerns directed by Nate Watt (perhaps the strongest of the Cassidy directors—under him Boyd turned in his best acting), Lesley Selander and, briefly, David Selman. Howard Bretherton had been the other early director and he did a good job too. Of all the cowboys, Boyd as Cassidy chased Autry the hardest.

George O'Brien had moved to RKO Radio during 1937. It was here that he would put together, with director David Howard, one of the strongest and most enjoyable sets of B westerns ever made. While that was on the way, there was only one western release from O'Brien in 1937, *Hollywood Cowboy*, a typical fun-filled 60 minutes. George was actually topped in the year's cowboy listing by Warner Bros. singer Dick Foran, but that could not be taken seriously because, after a couple of westerns the Foran series had been discontinued by the studio, a great shame because Foran had been liked. His films, with his booming but enjoyable voice, had become increasingly staked with stock footage as Warners lost interest. Also, while Foran had been making westerns his studio had liberally used him in other roles, creating some confusion. Now they gave away series westerns for good. Foran would stay with them a while but make no progress and within a couple of years had moved to Universal, which also misused him, slotting him into a bewildering variety of roles including westerns, where he really looked at his best. With Foran now out of contention George O'Brien was technically number four cowboy.

How had the other singing cowboys fared? Tex Ritter was the most popular. His Grand National films were cheap but carried by Ritter's strength. *Trouble in Texas*, *Sing, Cowboy*, and *Mystery of the Hooded Horsemen* were the best for 1937, the first named featuring a young Rita Cansino (Hayworth). Ritter's cause was not helped by his gaining first Horace Murphy, and then Snub Pollard as a pair of moronic sidekicks.

At this stage Ritter dressed in a sober fashion, carried two guns, sang genuine cowboy songs and rode a white horse, White Flash. He was a mixture of the authentic and showy cowboy. Later, the need to keep up with Autry and Co. meant the introduction of fancier gear and more popular songs.

Fred Scott never made any top ten listing and his Spectrum westerns were primitive at times. Scott, who had a nice personality, carried them along and even muted his opera-style voice a bit as time went by, trying to sound a bit more "country." His films such as *Roaming Cowboy* and *The Singing Buckaroo* were watchable because Scott was pleasant, and Al St. John a useful sidekick.

While Universal was advertising to replace Buck Jones (and testing Len Slye of the Sons of the Pioneers, who didn't get the job) Monogram had been looking around for a singing cowboy too. Monogram had been reformed after the original merger with Mascot into Republic. The Monogram people were not happy there and split from Herbert Yates, reforming their old company. Their product would continue to be B series and naturally they needed to join the modern trend and avail themselves of a singing cowboy. Their choice was another stage-trained singer with a big voice, one Jack Randall. Randall was good looking, had this big voice and could ride a horse, though he never liked them. Westerns were not exactly what he wanted to do but he had not been getting far in Hollywood so he thought that a stint as a star, even if in "oaters," would help him gain recognition. What so many aspiring actors who became cowboy stars failed to realize in those days was that once you were a cowboy, Hollywood producers looked upon you as the lowest of the low and your chances of anything but minor roles elsewhere became very limited. Jack Randall was also the brother of Republic star Bob Livingston, Randall being the family name. His first film, directed by the enthusiastic but limited Robert North Bradbury, was *Riders of the Dawn*, a most interesting little western. Monogram put a bit of extra money into it and took care. It had a good story and action, plus a chase scene over salt flats that may have influenced John Ford for his later *Stagecoach*, if he (Ford) ever saw it. There was also a powerful climax with the villain getting killed by a bolt of lightning. Drawbacks were some B quality acting and an uncertain Jack Randall. Randall had a good speaking voice but tended to hurry his lines and not get much meaning into them. His singing when riding along was badly filmed; close-ups revealed no relationship between Jack's lips and the words. And his big, slightly quavering voice was just not western — western as radio and recording listeners knew it. At the end of 1937 Jack Randall's future was unsure.

That was not so for Universal's new singer. Real name Leland T. Weed, he was renamed Bob Baker. His first film, *Courage of the West*, was good. Baker looked comfortable in his large white Stetson and fancy Autry-style shirt and he sang not with the twang of Autry but with an easy sounding natural voice. Baker was helped in his first film by excellent performances by veterans J. Farrell MacDonald and Harry Woods and a bright young director, Joseph H. Lewis.

At their peak in 1937, Republic's Three Mesquiteers are, left to right, Ray Corrigan, Max Terhune and Bob Livingston.

    Besides its Autry series Republic had produced a good John Wayne group in 1936. Wayne then left the studio for a while to star in an action, but non-western, series at Universal, as well as a "oncer" at Paramount, *Born to the West*. *Born to the West* also featured Johnny Mack Brown, who had completed his Supreme-Republic work and was about to embark on a career at Universal where he was already a serial favorite. *Born to the West* was an average B western, nothing more, made notable for future release by having Alan Ladd in a small role. John Wayne would soon be back at Republic, where he would stay, with regular outings to other studios "on loan" for many years, along with Autry and later Roy Rogers, Republic's big standard bearer.

    Popular at that studio were the Three Mesquiteers. The trio of Livingston, Corrigan and Terhune generated a breezy affability in lighthearted adventures full of action like *Hit the Saddle*, *Heart of the Rockies*, *Gunsmoke Ranch* and *Wild Horse Rodeo*, the last named containing a musical interlude by new contract singer Dick Weston, formerly Len Slye, later Roy Rogers. The Mesquiteer films cheerfully bounced about between times, never taking themselves seriously and providing sparkling entertainment.

Over at Columbia Charles Starrett was doing well. He looked impressive and modern, his films were very much formula scripted but fast and furious and Columbia used a good stock company including Jack Rockwell, Edward LeSaint, Alan Bridge, Norman Willis and many others. Starrett had some interesting leading ladies in 1937, Barbara Weeks, Rosalind Keith, Peggy Stratford and Iris Meredith. At the close of the year someone made the decision to use Meredith as Starrett's regular leading lady, and also use the same heavy from film to film, Dick Curtis. They were good but as one or two writers have noted, the feeling that one had seen the same movie before grew and grew with each release. A positive gain was the signing of a singing group at the end of 1937, the Sons of the Pioneers. An unusual, and good, factor of the Starrett westerns was that Charles was given no comic sidekick; Pat Brady of the Pioneers filled in there. Also in for a while was another singer, Donald Grayson, but he was unremarkable and soon dropped. Starrett, by the close of 1937, had become eighth cowboy on the box office listing, which doesn't sound great, but he would remain a fixture on the list through many years while others came and went.

Grand National, by the close of 1937 a struggling small studio, tried a new series that year. Although Kermit Maynard's Ambassador group had not been greatly popular, Grand National unveiled a Canadian Mountie series using a radio character called Renfrew. The difference was that their Mountie sang. Another big voiced baritone, James Newill, had a dimple, a smile, and no western expertise. He admitted later that he could not ride a horse when the role was offered him, but he learned. The Renfrew series came to an abrupt end when Grand National went out of business in 1938, but Monogram picked up the pieces.

At Paramount the Zane Grey westerns continued, often starring Larry "Buster" Crabbe, now a familiar face as serial icon Flash Gordon. The best of the Zane Grey features, highly regarded by many critics, however, starred Gilbert Roland, *Thunder Trail*. Tom Keene, another Zane Grey regular, finished his independent "historical" series and moved to Monogram for a brief stay of four films. Tom Tyler was another familiar face still making a living in cheap westerns, in 1937 for Victory Pictures. Tyler tried hard but the material was awful. The fact that he survived attests that he had a following. Tyler would prove to be long-lasting, taking on new leases of life farther down the track. Rex Bell was finishing off his short, promising but ultimately uninspiring cowboy career at Grand National early in 1937.

Two more singing cowboys emerged that year. Fox got into the act with a radio singer, tall, lean and looking a bit like Gary Cooper, Smith Ballew. Ballew sang pleasantly, had no great personality and, only through the superior distribution opportunities of Fox, got into the top ten cowboys for the year. Fox was under no illusions after five westerns, though, and early in 1938 dropped Ballew. Ballew would be seen again, briefly, in the '40s, singing in some Johnny Mack Brown Monogram features. The other singing cowboy was unique and barely noticed. Herb Jeffries was black, and his films were made with all black casts. It was an interesting experiment

O iver Hardy and Stan Laurel in the marvelous Way Out West, *a 1937 MGM release.*

but had no wide distribution or future at the box office. Jeffries was a historical curiosity.

Firally for 1937, mention must be made of the funniest western of the year and one of the most endearing of all time, Laurel and Hardy's *Way Out West*. Most comedians "went west" at some stage of their career but few with the charm the enduring couple managed as they bumbled and sang their way through this still delightful western farce. Years later their recording of "The Blue Ridge Mountains of Virginia" would top the charts. Whether soft-shoeing, singing or trying to break into a saloon in the night with disastrous results, the funniest and most loved comedy pair of all time are irresistible.

1938

B Westerns Everywhere

The trend of vast numbers of B or series westerns being produced and very few major ones continued in 1938. One of those few included Paramount's *The Texans*, starring Randolph Scott and supposedly an epic journey western, but actually built around stock shots from earlier trail epics and dominated by Joan Bennett with never a hair out of place or speck of dust on her dress, even in the most dire of mud or dust-ridden surroundings. Michael Curtiz made a serious *Gold Is Where You Find It* without arousing much interest. George Brent and Olivia de Havilland were featured and in a small part was a young Tim Holt. Gary Cooper contributed a weak western comedy, *The Cowboy and the Lady*. Apart from that, the sophisticated theaters showed Jeanette MacDonald and Nelson Eddy cavorting out West in *Girl of the Golden West* and crooner Dick Powell as a *Cowboy from Brooklyn*, hardly serious western fare. A little known small western was made by Warner Bros. *Valley of the Giants* was notable mainly for the interesting cast of a young Wayne Morris, Claire Trevor, Alan Hale, Donald Crisp, Frank McHugh and Charles Bickford. Mainly it was business as usual for the "cowboy stars" and by 1938 they were quite a mob.

Gene Autry had an interesting year. He was doing very well, as was his studio, Republic. Autry figured that Republic undervalued him and threatened for a while to take action if something was not done about it. Republic had, in 1937, quietly advertised for another singing cowboy. The position was won by Len Slye of the Sons of the Pioneers. Renamed Dick Weston, he sat about doing a few bits of song. After *The Old Barn Dance*, (in which Weston sings a song) Autry disappeared to parts south. While his and the studio lawyers wrangled, the newcomer was rushed into

Number one cowboy Gene Autry with co-star Jean Rouverol in Western Jamboree, *1938, at the height of his career.*

Under Western Stars, meant for Autry. His name was changed to Roy Rogers and he was given a nice looking palomino, formerly Golden Cloud, now named Trigger to ride. *Under Western Stars* proved popular on release; even hard-bitten critics viewed it favorably. But both Republic and Autry knew that Gene's worth was greater and they came to agreement. Autry came back and was soon given, as well as a pay raise, bigger budgets, longer running times, more songs and even production numbers that turned his films more and more into musicals rather than westerns. The public lapped it up and Gene's popularity soared even higher. There is a moment in *The Old Barn Dance* when Gene, Smiley and their boys have ridden into a country town and stop to advertise their performance that night at the local barn dance. Gene sits on Champion and quietly sings "Rocky Mountain Rose" as locals flock to gather around from all over town. They are enraptured. Now this is acting on the part of extras, but there is truth to it. Somehow, as he drawls out the song in that familiar way, something of the innocent, almost shy charm oozes across between singer and listeners. Now Gene was not, in real life, shy or innocent, and he was no actor. That he could put across such emotions speak of his high rating as a "performer." When all is said and done, that's what he was—a performer, an entertainer and really good at that job. While Gene went back to work in films like *Gold Mine in the Sky*, *Man from Music Mountain* and *Prairie Moon*, Republic had another success in Roy Rogers under contract. Rogers was slim (too slim, some said, to combat the heavies he had to face in films), agile and eager to learn from the wranglers on the set how to ride and fight well, sang in a sweet tenor and, most of all, could really act a bit. Republic decided wisely not to make him, at this stage, another Autry. After his first film his other features for 1938 were traditional westerns with some songs and they were good. A plus was that *Billy the Kid Returns*, *Come On Rangers* and *Shine On Harvest Moon* were directed by Joseph Kane, Republic's best and formerly Autry's director. Autry's loss was Rogers' gain and Kane would guide the young cowboy through some 40 odd films before moving on to bigger things. Autry's directors became more at ease with song and comedy than western action, although an action expert like B. Reeves Eason would sometimes be given a title. Finally matters reached a compromise with George Sherman, who could manage both song and action capably, and who never could understand how his star, Autry, conjured up the magic audience response that he did. Years later when interviewed, Sherman was still shaking his head in wonder.

Until Rogers soared into the list in 1939, three other singing cowboys were among the 1938 top ten, and two of them, Smith Ballew and Dick Foran, had stopped making westerns, leaving only Tex Ritter as a real contender. Of the first eight places, only seven were filled by non-singers, adding fuel to the argument that the singing cowboy never quite swept through Hollywood westerns as some detractors point out.

Although Buck Jones finished an average series at Columbia and made no other films that year, his name and fame held him in high regard and thus high up on the listing, at number three. Number two was William Boyd, immensely popular as Hopalong Cassidy in a series still produced by Harry Sherman and released through Paramount. More and more the Cassidy role had changed from the steely gunman of earlier films with the sudden smile and hearty laugh to an avuncular figure both to his sidekicks and the audience, especially young boys who were highlighted more and more in Cassidy films. Calm, level-headed and noble of sentiment, Cassidy was portrayed by Boyd as the father figure of them all. It became a slightly boring concept but the westerns were excellent and audiences loved Hoppy. Off screen Boyd had become a model of decorum, had happily married, for the fourth time, to actress Grace Bradley and it proved a lasting union. Off screen Boyd remained a big drinking man but he hid that side of his life from the public. He was not, of course, the only one, but others did as he did and had the wit, and good sense, to divorce their private life from their screen one.

Sadly, one cowboy who could not manage this was former big star Ken Maynard. Ken, portly now, was drinking heavily and off screen, when on tour, even in public gave vent to his bruised feelings. He was known to lash out at little boys he did not like, and he didn't seem to like them at all, or shoot up a town when disgruntled. Nobody ever quite knew what Ken was disgruntled about in life, but whatever private demons haunted him, they played their roles out where people could not help but see them. Those who did not, and they remained many, still liked Ken on screen and that meant he was able to work, but only for cheap producers. The mainstream film makers would have nothing of him. In 1938 Ken was working for a dying Grand National on $15,000 budgeted pictures like *Whirlwind Horseman* and *Six Shootin' Sheriff*. It is recorded by Jon Tuska that those films raked in $100,000 each, so someone made a good profit. Not Ken, who was on a straight salary. Amazingly, the overweight and out-of-condition old star could still look good on his wonder horse Tarzan and he would continue in front of the cameras into 1940. He couldn't make any top ten though, and at number four was the often underrated George O'Brien.

With a nice, nasal and amiable singing sidekick, Ray Whitley, at his side O'Brien had begun his last group of westerns at RKO Radio. This is a series many rate as the best B western series of all time. O'Brien's light touch, his ability to handle action (and stunts at times) himself plus superior casts and direction from David Howard made *Gun Law*, *Border G-Man*, *The Painted Desert*, *The Renegade Ranger* and *Lawless Valley* a stream of superior B westerns, every one a gem. *The Renegade Ranger*, besides O'Brien and Whitley, had a young Tim Holt and Rita Hayworth in the cast. More than any other cowboy O'Brien with his humor and his way with the ladies had an adult following probably bigger than his youth one. Unlike the three stars ahead of him in the top ten list, O'Brien did not play the cowboy star off screen as Jones always had and Autry and Boyd came increasingly to do. This probably also cost him, certainly in publicity and overall popularity. O'Brien didn't mind; he was happy at his work.

Number five cowboy position on the top ten went to a trio, the popular Three Mesquiteers at Republic. They had continued on in the same cheerful vein through *The Purple Vigilantes*, *Call the Mesquiteers*, *Outlaws of Sonora*, *Riders of the Black Hills* and *Heroes of the Hills* before Bob Livingston, increasingly agitating for non-western dramatic roles, got his wish. He was replaced by John Wayne as Stony Brooke. The films he made in 1938 with Corrigan and Terhune, *Pals of the Saddle*, *Overland Stage Raiders*, *Santa Fe Stampede* and *Red River Range*, are regarded as top rate but Wayne was never quite comfortable as a Mesquiteer. He didn't have the on-screen rapport with Corrigan that Livingston had, and the two were similar in style and build. Still, the trio remained very popular.

Bob Steele (seven) and Charles Starrett (six) were the two other cowboy stars who made the list. Steele's placing was the most surprising because he was working for cheap producer Hackel. However, Hackel was releasing his films through Republic and the greater exposure they got gave them an advantage over other independent

Columbia's first western serial was 1938's The Great Adventures of Wild Bill Hickok, *and here star Gordon Elliott (soon to be known as "Bill" Elliott) looks to be in some danger.*

productions. Steele himself, the small man with the flying fists and acrobatic horsemanship, was good giving titles like *Paroled to Die, Thunder in the Desert* and *Durango Valley Raiders* some punch not normally associated with director Sam Newfield.

Starrett earned his placing. His Columbia westerns, formula all, were clear and sharp and Starrett was forceful. His films were populated by what virtually became a Charles Starrett stock company—Iris Meredith, Dick Curtis, Ed LeSaint, Bob Nolan and the Sons of the Pioneers—but it had not yet begun to pall. In *West of Santa Fe, South of Arizona* and *On the Colorado Trail*, the Starrett films remained good entertainment, helped by the singing of the best group in the business—ever—the Sons of the Pioneers.

After Columbia had let Bob Allen go, a pity in a way because Bob may have made it given good budgets and guidance, the studio tried former silent cowboy Jack Luden, but Luden did not have it. He was colorless and the sight of a cowboy hero playing the harmonica as his specialty looked ludicrous. (Ken Maynard played one now and then, and Roy Rogers did once, but the harmonica seemed to be Luden's one set piece.) More successful was Columbia's entry in the serial field, to join Universal and Republic. They made a very popular chapterplay, *The Great Adventures of Wild Bill Hickok*, and for the Hickok role chose a tall, rather austere looking

Newcomer Bob Baker, Universal's first singing cowboy, on his horse Apache.

actor who had been around for almost a decade, essaying small to medium roles including some villainous parts in Gene Autry and Smith Ballew westerns. He had also had a good guy role in a Dick Foran western before turning to baddie in that series. He was Gordon Elliott. With twin pistols, butts placed forward in their holsters, Elliott made an immediate impression. Producer Larry Darmour immediately took him under personal contract, to release through Columbia. *Hickok* had made a new cowboy star and the man known now as Bill Elliott began a series starting with a plausible account of the Wyatt Earp–Tombstone story called *In Early Arizona.*

Colonel Tim McCoy, after a year off screen, was back in a series at Monogram. McCoy still looked good and his presence held the series together. Typical were *Lightning Carson Rides Again*, *West of Rainbow's End* and *Phantom Ranger*. Monogram, like Republic, had a busy cowboy schedule. Jack Randall continued in *Stars Over Arizona* and *Danger Valley*, which were good, but his singing did not go down too well. Slowly Monogram cut that back until, in *The Mexicali Kid* of this same year, Jack became an ex–singing cowboy. His films were about six minutes shorter but that did them no harm because they moved at a good clip and if not breaking any records Randall appeared to be doing quite well.

For its singer Monogram now recruited Tex Ritter (and producer Ed Finney who had Ritter under personal contract). Ritter's Grand National features had become short on everything and his first few pictures at Monogram, *Starlight Over Texas*, *Where the Buffalo Roam* and *Song of the Buckaroo*, were an advance. Ritter was personally popular and Monogram and Finney tried to give him novel script ideas and good outdoor scenery, but the restricted budgets told. The Ritter westerns were variable, with some excellent parts but too much stock footage to help keep within budget, plus the abysmal comedy of Murphy and Pollard.

Another singing cowboy, now ending his short career in 1938, Fred Scott.

At Universal Bob Baker continued a series that was nice, but short on action. Baker, pleasant and amiable, lacked a forceful personality and the studio inexplicably failed to give him strong support. He rode well and looked as if he could handle action well enough but was seldom given the chance. His stories ambled along pleasantly, nice songs and all that, good heroines (often Marjorie Reynolds) but little excitement. *Black Bandit* and *Guilty Trail* were two particularly likable entries though suffering from the same blandness.

Tom Tyler was still fighting the odds at Victory Pictures, Fred Scott was making Spectrum westerns which, once Fuzzy St. John had gone, lessened in quality though Scott himself was pleasant. Cowboys Jack Perrin, Reb Russell, Rex Bell, Bill Cody, Jack Hoxie, Buddy Roosevelt and Kermit Maynard, had departed the range as stars and were often as not working as bit players in other westerns. Old time Harry Carey too was about at the close of his starring career. He made a good western for RKO, *The Law West of Tombstone*, which had an interesting cast including Tim Holt, Evelyn Brent, Ward Bond and Allan Lane. Hoot Gibson was filmless and, as the year ended, even the great Buck Jones was without a starring series.

One-off westerns were made by one-off people, such as Gene Austin, a popular singer whose name, sounding suspiciously like one Autry, was sure to bring in a few curious cinemagoers. Austin's only starring western, *Songs and Bullets*, was enough

Republic's classic 1938 serial The Lone Ranger. *That's Chief Thundercloud, as Tonto, holding the Ranger's guns while Ranger Lee Powell goes into action.*

to prove even to an optimistic producer like Harry Fraser that no future lay in that direction.

On the other hand, success in 1938 went with serials, including the already mentioned *Great Adventures of Wild Bill Hickok*. Universal completed another Johnny Mack Brown, *Flaming Frontiers*, good fun as always, and Republic told for the first time on screen the legend of *The Lone Ranger*. This was a smash hit, even though the studio tampered with the radio and story format to give its own version of the masked rider. The star was an unknown Lee Powell and Tonto was played by Chief Thundercloud. Republic was soon at work on a sequel as 1938 closed.

1 9 3 9

Stagecoach, *Plus...*

What a great year 1939 was for film making and especially Hollywood. While Europe headed blindly into another war, the East reeled under Japanese militarism, and Stalin's tyrannical grip on the Soviet Union tightened, Hollywood, in a burst of creative energy, turned out great movie after great movie from *Gone with the Wind* to *Wuthering Heights*, from *The Wizard of Oz* to *Mr. Smith Goes to Washington*. And the western was not ignored amidst the riches. John Ford directed three excellent films that year, *Young Mr. Lincoln*, sincere and touching, *Drums Along the Mohawk*, a color "colonial" western of beauty, and *Stagecoach*. It was *Stagecoach* that, years later, is still remembered as the premier event of the western film year. This literate and superbly cast and directed movie brought the western film out of artistic darkness, gave us one of the great all-time cinema delights and sparked a revival in the genre's fortunes. More top class A westerns were produced in 1939 than there had been for many a day. *Stagecoach* was the greatest, but Ford's own *Drums Along the Mohawk*, DeMille's *Union Pacific*, George Marshall's humorous *Destry Rides Again*, Alan Dwan's *Frontier Marshal*, Henry King's *Jesse James* and Michael Curtiz's *Dodge City* were all near-classics in their own way. The year also gave us the diverting sight of gangsters James Cagney and Humphrey Bogart in western gear in *The Oklahoma Kid*, a Warner Bros. novelty if ever there was one. MGM made two big budget pictures that didn't even sound like westerns, *Let Freedom Ring* with Nelson Eddy and *Stand Up and Fight* with Robert Taylor and Wallace Beery. Neither Eddy nor Taylor looked at home in westerns although Taylor would prove, with maturity, to be a good western lead in later years. But then, MGM never could make really good westerns.

73

Of the major westerns mentioned, *Jesse James*, with Tyrone Power and Henry Fonda playing Jesse and Frank, was very well made but a dubious historical whitewash of the famous bank and train robber. Henry King handled it well. *Frontier Marshal* told the Wyatt Earp story and starred Randolph Scott (who was busy — he was also in *Jesse James*). It was a straightforward remake of the 1934 title and much of it would reappear in Ford's 1946 version. Ford's *Drums Along the Mohawk*, starring Henry Fonda, lovingly recreated the colonial period, spoiled only by leading lady Claudette Colbert's frenetic performance. *Dodge City* was a sprawling epic, "big on action and color" as historian Michael Pitts describes it. Errol Flynn was never more dashingly heroic and was partnered by the lovely Olivia de Havilland, not for the first or last time. *Destry Rides Again* introduced the (then) unlikely James Stewart to the western. Stewart, tall and gangly, with his stuttery drawl and perplexed expressions seemed totally out of place in the West, which was the purpose of the film, a light-hearted remake of Brand's novel and meant foremost as a vehicle for Marlene Dietrich. Today the film does not stand up so well, although it has some great comic moments and Stewart is enjoyable.

Cecil DeMille's artistic credentials may have been questionable but he knew how to win over audiences. Big romantic adventures that were historically based served him well. *Union Pacific* of 1939 is probably his best, ahead of *The Plainsman* and not including his silent work. It is really a remake of Ford's *The Iron Horse*, using some of the scenes from that silent feature and adding in a DeMille combination of a stalwart, honest hero (Joel McCrea), a sprightly Irish lass (Barbara Stanwyck with an exaggerated Irish accent), a smiling good-bad man (Robert Preston) and a no-good bad guy (Brian Donlevy). A great spectacle, *Union Pacific* is not a great film but it surely entertains and is typical DeMille.

Both *Dodge City* and *Union Pacific* made more money on initial release than *Stagecoach* but there any similarity ends. *Stagecoach* is a great film, a great western. Based on Guy de Maupassant or not, the Ernest Haycox story was molded by writer Dudley Nichols and re-molded and twisted back and forth by director John Ford to fit his conceptions. Ford, an Irish-American, had directed western stars Harry Carey, Tom Mix, Buck Jones and Hoot Gibson in silent films before becoming famous with *The Iron Horse* in 1924. After *Three Bad Men* in 1926 he made no more westerns, being regarded as one of the outstanding directors in Hollywood and too good for horse operas. His artistic pretensions rose higher in the '30s with expressionist works like *The Informer* and it was a surprise when he went to work on another western in 1938. With Nichols' screenplay, the photography of Bert Glennon and a little help from Yakima Canutt and his stuntmen, Ford turned out, for release through Walter Wanger and United Artists, a quickly (by the standards of great movies) filmed 97 minute long saga of a stagecoach full of diverse travelers wending its way through Indian country toward a final showdown for one of them, the Ringo Kid, in Lordsburg. Although stars like Gary Cooper had been considered for the film, Ford took a chance

John Ford's 1939 classic Stagecoach *featured George Bancroft, John Wayne and Claire Trevor in a United Artists release.*

on his former protégé and now Republic B actor John Wayne to play the Ringo Kid. Wayne got second billing behind heroine Claire Trevor and was encircled by a cast that included Thomas Mitchell, George Bancroft, John Carradine, Andy Devine, Donald Meek, Louise Platt, Berton Churchill, young Tim Holt and Tom Tyler in the pivotal role of Luke Plummer, doomed to be shot down in the streets of Lordsburg by the Kid. Wayne has little dialogue; it is his presence as filmed by Ford that tells. The famous chase across the salt flats and rescue by the cavalry is exciting and imitated to the cliché level, but the showdown in Lordsburg is the artistic highlight, Ford's use of lighting, cutting, music and cast being exquisite. *Stagecoach* is a great western with the credentials to be in the contest for greatest western of them all. And, as with many great movies, it is a simple black and white masterpiece.

Series western fans were well catered to, though it was now notable that with the exception of George O'Brien, who had never actually been a full cowboy star in

Warner Eros.' big western of 1939, Dodge City, *has Guinn Williams behind bars while Errol Flynn and Alan Hale eye him dubiously.*

the silents, the new breed dominated. Old timers Harry Carey, Hoot Gibson and, horrors of horrors to his still-many fans, Buck Jones were no longer starring. Jones in 1939 was relegated to a film as a down and out boxer, *Unmarried*, about as far from the West as he could get.

Gene Autry was about to reach his peak, which, next year would result in his being voted number four on the Hollywood all-star top ten listing, not just cowboys. Autry was clear winner of the cowboy poll. His westerns had become more elaborate and Gene himself was more confident in his role and singing at his best. Some of the awkward charm of the first few years had gone but audiences seemed not to mind and his fans grew and grew, all around the world. In 1939 he toured Britain and Ireland to tumultuous crowds. *Mexicali Rose*, also a big hit song, *Colorado Sunset* and *Blue Montana Skies* were his three best films of the year.

Number two cowboy at Republic was Roy Rogers, who was given good budgets in a series of Joe Kane–directed historical westerns, with the exception of *Wall Street Cowboy*, which did include good action and outdoor scenes and the unique pairing

A scene from one of Gene Autry's best westerns, Blue Montana Skies, *1939, showing villain Harry Woods, Champion, Gene and Smiley Burnette.*

of Raymond Hatton and George Hayes as Roy's sidekicks. *In Old Caliente, The Arizona Kid* and *Saga of Death Valley* were good westerns, and Roy, after having a good partnership with Ray Hatton, was even more at home with George Hayes, who had left the Cassidy series and joined Republic, a big loss to one and gain to the other. Rogers had also enjoyed a flourishing romantic pairing (on screen) with Mary Hart, formerly Lynn Roberts and later Lynne Roberts. Roy Rogers soared up the cowboy popularity listing during 1939.

Republic was still turning out respectable Three Mesquiteer westerns. Wayne, Corrigan and Terhune began the year but Wayne and Terhune quickly dropped out. First was Terhune, replaced by Raymond Hatton as another Joslin, Rusty. Wayne, who had made a big hit with *Stagecoach,* was obviously destined for greater things and he finished off 1939 with *New Frontier* along with Corrigan, who was not happy about being relegated all the time to second fiddle. Corrigan had negotiated a contract for himself at Monogram to make a new trio series, and Terhune was to join

New young singing cowboy Roy Rogers in one of his 1939 releases.

him there. As 1939 came to a close Republic had to virtually remake the Three
Mesquiteers. They retained Hatton as Joslin and brought back Bob Livingston, who
had not made much of note away from westerns, as Stony and added a completely
new character, a Latin Mesquiteer in the form of Duncan Renaldo. This new trio
began with *Kansas Terrors* and *The Cowboys from Texas*. Admittedly, some of the
magic had gone from the Mesquiteers as 1939 closed.

    To complete its year Republic also released two standout serials in *Zorro's Fight-
ing Legion* and *The Lone Ranger Rides Again* with Bob Livingston as the Ranger and
Chief Thundercloud again as Tonto. By 1939 Republic was producing the slickest,
most action-filled and zest-packed B westerns of all.

    William Boyd was still riding high as Hopalong Cassidy in well-made features
that appealed, as did George O'Brien, to adults and not just younger people. By now
any relationship between Mulford's original characters and stories had been abandoned. Mulford grumbled but the regular royalty checks he received from Harry

Sherman kept him relatively happy. A blow to the series came after *The Renegade Trail,* third 1939 release, when George Hayes left to join Republic. Sherman, director Lesley Selander and Boyd tried Britt Wood and, in one-off, even Sydney Toler, as sidekick without great success. It was the end of 1940 before Andy Clyde emerged as a viable replacement for Windy Halliday. Though Toler was out of place, the film *Law of the Pampas,* directed by Nate Watt who returned to the series for this one project, was the best 1939 entry.

At RKO George O'Brien, usually with Whitley but later Chill Wills, was busy turning out really good B westerns, *The Arizona Legion, Trouble in Sundown, Timber Stampede, The Fighting Gringo* and best of all, *The Marshal of Mesa City* (a little classic) and *Racketeers of the Range.* The last named was bright and breezy and set in modern times with cattle rustlers using trucks to do their dirty work, just like those in Autry's Republic world. It also showed in medium close-up O'Brien doing stunts like transferring from horse to train. It seems inconceivable that O'Brien, seemingly at his peak, would virtually close down his western film career in a year.

Universal B westerns had picked up after the slow, amiable Bob Baker series ended with *Phantom Stage.* Poor Bob, not for the first time, doesn't even get to finish off the villain in the end — his sidekick, George Cleveland, does that. Johnny Mack Brown completed a final serial, *The Oregon Trail,* good but using too much stock footage from earlier efforts, then began what would be a long running Universal series. Baker stayed around as saddle pal, along with comic Fuzzy Knight, who got very tiresome, but Brown dominated the films. Baker got to sing a song or two and help Brown in the action but that is all. In one, *Oklahoma Frontier,* Baker even got killed off half way through. Beginning with *Desperate Trails,* the series was superior, with Brown often dressed in the black buckskin outfits he had worn in Universal serials, still slim and agile and especially good in fisticuffs scenes.

Columbia still had Charles Starrett looking good and ambling through routine adventures that were slickly produced. The soundly professional cast knew what to do and so Iris Meredith, Dick Curtis, Nolan and the Pioneers backed Starrett up expertly. Starrett even changed his black outfit with the white Stetson and flowing white kerchief now and then for black hat and checkered shirt. This was notable because apart from that and the Pioneers' songs, one Starrett was pretty much like another. So at the close of 1939 Columbia took new cowboy Bill Elliott under personal contract as an antidote. Elliott had been making his westerns for Larry Darmour, good and interesting mainly through the unique personality of Elliott himself. Elliott's western of the year, *Taming of the West,* thus came directly under the Columbia banner with Bill playing "Wild Bill Saunders." Also during the year Columbia used Bill in another serial, a good one, *Overland with Kit Carson.* If full of mindless action at times, *Kit Carson* was shot on location and looked good, as did Bill in his buckskins with his two guns now reversed fully for the backhand draw. As Bill Hickok, in his first serial, Bill had worn the guns more for the cross draw and in his

A new team at Universal in 1939, Bob Baker, Fuzzy Knight and Johnny Mack Brown.

early features had adopted the traditional butts backward for the regular draw. Now he developed his own unique "gimmick" that would only be abandoned briefly during his A series at Republic. The serial *Overland with Kit Carson*, besides Bill's dominating role, is notable also for a good performance from Trevor Bardette as "Pegleg," the maniacal baddie. Bardette, in an oft underrated career, would play outstanding roles at Republic as a regular heavy, occasional good guy and, later in life, character player in numerous major productions. In a world of heavies where Charlie King, Roy Barcroft, Harry Woods, Dick Curtis, Jack Ingram and many others are rightly revered, Trevor Bardette is often overlooked, but he was one of the best.

Grand National was swiftly fading into the sunset but along the way it tried a few last minute desperate measures. One was to star a lady, singer Dorothy Page, as a "singing cowgirl." Page looked nice, sang well and could ride a horse but the whole thing was made meaningless when her leading man had to perform all the action to apprehend the villain in the end. It just didn't work; the world was not ready for women to take over such tasks. Grand National also tried a radio singer, Art Jarrett, in company with Lee Powell (later Lone Ranger), and Al St. John but results were lamentable. Finally, for one film, it was another radio star, Tex Fletcher, who played guitar left-handed (which was different) but had nothing else to offer worth filming. Grand National finally expired.

That leaves Monogram which, for all of its existence, would struggle on as a lowly cousin to Republic. One thing in Monogram's favor is that, with its B westerns, it never resorted to studio exteriors as Republic did. However, producer Ed Finney, personally supervising the Tex Ritter westerns, did. Too often his Ritter films strove for historical settings and big scenes that the budget just could not handle, so Finney resorted to stock shots. It was a pity because they marred otherwise good Ritter features like *Westbound Stage*; *Roll, Wagons, Roll* and *Riders of the Frontier*. Tex looked good, and if you liked his singing style you were enraptured by his unique voice. If you didn't, well... Ultimately the popularity of Ritter westerns rested with Ritter himself. His number seven spot in the cowboy list for the year tells its story.

Monogram also had Jack Randall, a reluctant cowboy player, turning out snappy-titled (running times were often only 50 minutes), non-singing westerns like *Trigger Smith*, *Drifting Westward* and *Across the Plains*. Randall was not rated highly but in retrospect his work was quite good, though he never seemed completely comfortable. For a man who disliked his job he managed to look capable in the saddle. Monogram also picked up the Renfrew series from Grand National, so James Newill was working at that studio.

Cheap outfits like Victory, which produced some Tim McCoy westerns that year, and Metropolitan, which employed Bob Steele, were on the way out in 1939. Metropolitan would last into 1940. Respected historian Don Miller wrote of one Bob Steele Metropolitan film that it consisted of "roaring ineptitude." That Miller, who loved

By 1939 popular singing cowboy Tex Ritter had been in the saddle on screen for four years. Eventually he would become the third most prolific singer behind Autry and Rogers as far as screen appearances are concerned.

and was kind to B westerns, should label a film so speaks volumes. Yet one new company was formed in late 1939, aiming to make action features and mainly westerns at low cost. This was Producers' Distribution Corporation, PDC, which would soon change its name to PRC, Producers' Releasing Corporation. No doubt PDC-PRC meant well but there, in the '40s, new levels of ineptitude in the making of western films would be reached.

The year concluded with the western movie at its peak, popular to all audiences and around a world increasingly beset by conflict. Hollywood, with its own country not at war, saw itself as the world's purveyor of happiness and entertainment meant to take people's minds off the agony around them. Western films were very much part of that production.

1940
Gene Autry's Year

There were some good major westerns made in 1940 but the main western event of the year has to be that a simple B western cowboy star, Gene Autry, was behind only Mickey Rooney, Spencer Tracy and Clark Gable on the complete Hollywood male box office listing. Republic, and Herbert Yates, must have been especially proud. In the history of this box office listing only one other B cowboy, Roy Rogers, would ever get on that exclusive list, and never higher than number ten. The fact that Autry's western films for 1940 were not his very best does not matter. As far as the fans were concerned, anything starring him and Champion was "must see" material. *Melody Ranch* was his big feature of the year. With a running time of 60 minutes (one minute more than Rogers ever managed) and featuring Jimmy Durante, Ann Miller, George Hayes, Barton MacLane, Vera Allen and Horace McMahon, it was pure musical comedy on a western ranch setting. As later with Rogers, a lot of to-do was made about Ann Miller kissing or not kissing Gene on screen. People have short memories, especially studio publicists — Autry had been kissed on screen quite a few times in his first few years, as Rogers would be in his.

While Autry rode far ahead of the field, Roy Rogers, a studio saddlemate, continued his climb up the ladder to reach number three on the western poll, behind Gene and William Boyd. George O'Brien was fourth, Charles Starrett fifth, Johnny Mack Brown sixth, Ritter seventh, Three Mesquiteers eighth, Bill Elliott was tenth and at number nine, proving his personal contribution to the Autry film success, was Gene's sidekick, Smiley Burnette. Rarities on the poll would be the placing of Burnette and Hayes in the future, along with the one woman to get there, Dale Evans.

A scene from the best western of 1940, the unsung Westerner, *directed by William Wyler. Pictured are stars Gary Cooper and Walter Brennan.*

Where were the old-timers? The cowboy stars who a bare decade before had thrilled the audiences, where were they? Off screen, dead (in the case of Tom Mix) or plodding along in dire production circumstances for the last prevailing poverty row studios. More of that later.

The Westerner was the best western film of the year. Not greeted with much enthusiasm at the time, it has endured while others have faded and can now be seen as the classic western it was, and is. Directed by William Wyler, who had long experience in the genre, *The Westerner* is a dusty, austere, unsentimental view of a rugged frontier where life is short and not worth too much. Gary Cooper, at the time a "heartthrob" through features such as *Beau Geste*, made a welcome return to the western and gave his best ever performance as the laconic but quick-witted cowboy who dices with death and Judge Roy Bean (Walter Brennan) in the midst of a saloon full of what might be described today as "hoons." Brennan got the honors and Oscar but Cooper was just as good.

The other best western of the year oddly enough also got no great reception,

Star Jean Arthur in the midst of the fight in Wesley Ruggles' 1940 Columbia epic Arizona.

possibly because the motivating character was a woman and there was no strong male lead. *Arizona* is a beautifully filmed epic about the founding of the state, directed by Wesley Ruggles and starring an ebullient Jean Arthur, perhaps a little too overpowering for some. Ruggles is not strong on the action scenes where other directors would have done a much better job, but he faithfully recreates the atmosphere of frontier times in old Tucson. William Holden is nice as the male lead but dominated by the fiery Arthur; probably the role needed a Cooper to carry it off. *Arizona* has faults that preclude it from being a great western, but it is very good, entertaining and can be watched again and again.

Errol Flynn, all dash and smiles, appeared in two big scale westerns, both directed by Michael Curtiz and released by Warner Bros. *Virginia City* had a great cast (Randolph Scott, Miriam Hopkins, Alan Hale, Guinn Williams and Humphrey Bogart) as well as Flynn and was action and romance all the way in a repeat of his success in *Dodge City* the previous year. *The Santa Fe Trail* was meant to be more serious with its story of John Brown, played by Raymond Massey and under the direction of Curtiz and with Flynn as star, but soon became another action-fest. Flynn's favorite leading lady, Olivia de Havilland, returned for this one, cast with Alan Hale, Guinn Williams and a young Ronald Reagan, joined by William Lundigan and Van Heflin in important roles.

The James Brothers having been a screen success, Universal made *When the Daltons Rode* with Randolph Scott, Kay Francis (a rare western appearance), Brian Donlevy, Broderick Crawford, Andy Devine, and George Bancroft. Action, directed by George Marshall, won out over thoughtful plot but it was well done, and not as sympathetic to the outlaws as *Jesse James* had been. Then, *When the Daltons Rode* did not have two sweet-faced leads like Power and Fonda. Speaking of whom, Fonda returned as Frank James in Fritz Lang's *Return of Frank James*, which was sober and grim in parts, Fonda of course being a great actor. Even so his performance was almost topped by the fabulous John Carradine in another of his almost-over-the-top interpretations, this time as Bob Ford. Carradine, who could be a real "ham" at times, was always great playing a sniveling, cowardly no-good.

The Return was made by Fox, which also did a big screen *Mark of Zorro*, all gloss and charm from Tyrone Power, who was fine as the fop but needed lots of assistance for the action scenes. It was a lighthearted look at the legend with humor and drama dominant and, dare it be said, not as exciting as a Republic serial based on the same character. Another Fox film, *Brigham Young*, was meant as a genuine tribute to the pioneering spirit and Henry Hathaway created some great scenes but probably the heroics of a Mormon group and its leader, played memorably by Dean Jagger, did not appeal to many cinemagoers. Tyrone Power was a weak lead, Linda Darnell a bit too much and the splendid supporting cast (Brian Donlevy, Jane Darwell, John Carradine, Mary Astor, Vincent Price, Jean Rogers, Ann Todd) could not turn matters around. As a film *Brigham Young* is impressive and worth seeing.

Republic, home of two of the three leading cowboy stars, also essayed a move into major production about now. A budget of more than a million dollars produced *The Dark Command*, a 97 minute retelling of the Quantrill sacking of Lawrence and affairs therein, directed by Raoul Walsh and starring John Wayne, in his new-found status as an A grade actor. *The Dark Command* was actually very good and probably the best A picture Republic ever produced. The success of *Stagecoach* was cashed in on by pairing Claire Trevor again with Wayne, and Walter Pidgeon adding status. Billed fourth was Roy Rogers in a serious dramatic role as Trevor's young hotheaded brother, a role that proved young Rogers could really act and adding to his worth to the studio. If *Dark Command* was a surprise and welcome success, even more surprising was the box office return for Paramount's *Geronimo*. Directed by Paul Sloane (western fans may well ask, "Who?") and starring Preston Foster and Ellen Drew, the film consisted mainly of stock footage of Indian fights; Geronimo, played by Chief Thundercloud, barely entered the picture and the reasons for its success are puzzling. Perhaps the "Geronimo," ever present but never seen, in *Stagecoach* the previous year attracted customers. If so, they must have felt a bit cheated. "Trite" was the verdict of historian Michael Pitts.

Back at Republic every effort was being made to please the fans. *The Adventures of Red Ryder* was an action-packed serial, directed by serial duo William Witney and John English and introducing a new star, Donald Barry, from here on known as "Red," much to his dislike. He didn't have red hair and only played Ryder once, but it stuck. Barry, a short, quick-tempered man with genuine acting ability, was immediately rushed into his own series of westerns. Barry was another reluctant cowboy who wanted to be a dramatic actor, but his first films were very good, especially *The Tulsa Kid* with scene-stealer Noah Beery playing a restrained and sympathetic role. Republic still produced Three Mesquiteer titles, eight of them in 1940, five with the trio of Livingston-Renaldo-Hatton and then three with a new trio, Livingston–Bob Steele–Rufe Davis. This latest trio, beginning with *Under Texas Skies*, was closer to the original although little Bob Steele as Tucson Smith was a long way down from big Crash Corrigan. This trio's second 1940 title, *The Trail Blazers*, turned out to be the name of a rival series at Monogram a bit later.

At this time Monogram had unveiled its own rival to the Mesquiteers, a trio called The Range Busters, which bore a remarkable Mesquiteer resemblance, not surprising since Ray Corrigan and Max Terhune were two members. Third spot was filled, a mark of the times, by a singer, John "Dusty" King. King was tall, good looking and sang nicely but was colorless. However, the trio seemed to enjoy themselves in *The Range Busters*, *Trailing Double Trouble* and *West of Pinto Basin* in what was always a cheaper version of the Mesquiteers.

Also at Monogram were Tex Ritter and Jack Randall. Ritter continued to be popular in films *Pals of the Silver Sage*, *Rainbow Over the Range*, *Arizona Frontier* and *Take Me Back to Oklahoma*, to name a few. The films themselves continued to have the same old problems but Ritter held them together. At least his sidekicks were a slight improvement, being angular Nelson McDowell and Arkansas Slim Andrews. Neither was in the Gabby Hayes class but they were better than Murphy and Pollard before them. Jack Randall's work tailed off into mediocre as Monogram obviously lost all interest in him. Some of his last westerns, *Covered Wagon Trails* being typical, were downright pitiful. Randall was not happy, Monogram had no interest in renewing his contract and that was that. Monogram, which installed and dispatched cowboy stars with great abandon, soon had others lined up.

At Universal Johnny Mack Brown had taken over as a solo star after a few more films with Bob Baker, who disappeared seemingly without a trace but who in fact hung around Hollywood a while playing various bit parts and one almost-starring role that didn't pan out. Brown's westerns, directed mainly by Ray Taylor, had action and bruising fight scenes and a bit of romance. If titles like *Ragtime Cowboy Joe* and *Bury Me Not on the Lone Prairie* sounded melodious, that was mainly to encompass Fuzzy Knight's (dubious) musical talent and those of singing cowboys like Jimmy Wakely's

Don Barry (complete with red wig) was star of Republic's 1940 adaptation in serial form of The Adventures of Red Ryder. *Tommy Cook was Little Beaver.*

At the end of the cinema trail in 1940 was Jack Randall, who began as a singing cowboy and ended up minus songs as an action one.

Rough Riders and Lucille Walker and the Texas Rangers. Brown even remade the classic 1930s western *Law and Order*, but the script, although based on the same source, W. R. Burnett's *Saint Johnson*, was a strictly B grade.

Universal also turned out a good western serial in 1940, *Winners of the West*. The star was former singing cowboy Dick Foran, now at Universal doing a range of action roles, only one feature being a western. Foran looked good in the serial and it seems a pity, for western fans, that Universal did not use him more in that genre. Other serials of the year, apart from Republic's *Red Ryder*, already noted, were Columbia's *Deadwood Dick*, which suffered from lack of a star "name," and Republic's second, *King of the Royal Mounted*, introducing as a star for the first time long-struggling actor Allan Lane.

PRC (PDC) westerns proved to be cheaper than Monogram's, which were very cheap indeed. Tim McCoy did a series for them, Tim's last as a solo star. The last entry, *The Texas Marshal*, introduced a radio singer, Art Davis. McCoy left after that and Davis hung around, soon to be offered more work at PRC. Like many cowboy radio singers Davis had dabbled in western films for a while, working for Gene Autry and having a role in the inept independent film *The Adventures of the Masked Phantom* in 1939. PRC also had Bob Steele in a series in which he played a law abiding Billy the Kid. Before the last of these quickies had been released Steele had escaped and gone to Republic to join the Mesquiteers. PRC signed Larry "Buster" Crabbe, by now on hard times and remembered both as a swimming champion and serial king Flash Gordon, to replace him.

George O'Brien concluded his work at RKO during 1940. After *Triple Justice* he quietly packed up his bags and left the studio. It seemed a shame when O'Brien was obviously still in his prime. O'Brien was interested, as war approached, on resuming his military career. Also his westerns, never cheap to make, had been taking less at the box office than before. O'Brien himself was still very popular but RKO figured it had a young man at the studio whose westerns would cost far less (mainly because his salary was much less) than O'Brien's and bring in a healthy profit. O'Brien and RKO seemed to have parted on amicable terms. The new cowboy star was Tim Holt, son of Jack, a good rider who could act but looked very young. RKO gave him Ray Whitley as a singing sidekick and Emmett Lynn as a comic for *Wagon Train* and *The Fargo Kid* in 1940. A biggish budget went into *Wagon Train*; *The Fargo Kid* was noticeably cheaper, as subsequent Holts would be.

Columbia had both Charles Starrett and Bill Elliott in the top ten listing. Starrett's westerns continued to have that "stock company" look about them. It was noticeable when one of the company had time off, as when Lorna Gray replaced Meredith as leading lady for *Bullets for Rustlers*, and one of the two best Starretts for the year resulted. The other "best" was titled *The Durango Kid*, Starrett assuming the role of a masked rider for justice who reveals his identity at the end and settles down with heroine Luana Walters. Walters was another welcome change. The Durango Kid having been used, he was discarded, seemingly a "oncer." Some years later, in 1945, someone at Columbia thought of him again....

After four "Wild Bill Saunders" westerns Bill Elliott became officially "Wild Bill Hickok" on screen for his subsequent Columbia career. The Wild Bill Saunders titles had been good; Iris Meredith appeared to have left Starrett and become Bill's permanent leading lady and the change of name made little difference in the quality of the films. Bill had Dub Taylor as sidekick. Taylor was a talented man but his hick style humor at that stage was hard to take. The only change in subsequent entries was that Iris Meredith disappeared.

Last but by no means least of the successful 1940 cowboys was William Boyd playing Hopalong Cassidy through his sixth year. The quality of these Paramount-released westerns remained good; the weak spot in them was that Britt Wood was inad-

Always a joy to watch on screen, George O'Brien surprisingly retired in 1940 after an enjoyable RKO series, but returned for a few minor roles after the war.

equate as the comic member, no substitute for George Hayes. In *Three Men from Texas*, the last 1940 title, the answer was found in the form of silent screen, Scottish born comedian Andy Clyde playing California Carlson. Clyde blended in well with Boyd and Russell Hayden and the Cassidy series was back on track.

In all, 1940 was a year of good quality A and B westerns and of much success. There were sadder aspects on the western film front. The death of Tom Mix in an automobile accident was one of them. The lack of room for the likes of Buck Jones and Hoot Gibson on the screen was another. One of the saddest sights of the year was the final, or what seemed very much like the final, screen moments of a former great cowboy star, now grossly overweight and playing in shoestring budget pictures for Colony, directed by Sam Newfield. This was Ken Maynard. Once the proudest and fittest of cowboys, athletic and dashing, Maynard was now decidedly what is called "a shadow of his former self," if a substantial shadow. His final three westerns for 1940, *Death Rides the Range*, *The Phantom Rancher* and *Lightning Strikes West* were not what Ken's fans of yesteryear would have recognized. It was a true Hollywood story in stark Hollywood tradition, the washed up star who had contributed to his own downfall. But old cowboys never die…. Ken wasn't quite finished yet and would be heard from, and seen again, on screen.

Nineteen-forty had been quite a year.

1941

The Return of Buck Jones

After two vintage years for major westerns, 1941 was not as inspiring. The main western event of the year was the return to the screen of Buck Jones after what his fans thought was an incredible absence. Jones, approaching 50 now, was featured in two serials during the year, one a minor affair from Columbia called *White Eagle* that rephrased a feature film he made in 1932. The other, more impressive, was the Universal "million dollar serial" *Riders of Death Valley*, much hyped by the studio and falling short of expectations. Actual star of the serial was Dick Foran, while Buck was featured along with Noah Beery, Jr., Lon Chaney, Guinn Williams and Charles Bickford as the heavy. General opinion is that much of the "million dollars" went on salaries. It is good enough, as western serials go, but no better than many others. Most importantly for Buck Jones was a contract, through his good friend Scott Dunlap, with Monogram to appear in eight Rough Riders westerns with trio companions Tim McCoy and Ray Hatton. The Monogram westerns were a far cry from Buck's days at Columbia and Universal in the '30s but he was back on screen and that was the important factor to his fans, and for him. The Rough Riders series, beginning with *Arizona Bound* and *Gunman from Bodie*, were greeted with respect and film historians have been kind to them, but are really not classy B westerns. Jones and McCoy (and the ever reliable Hatton) make them of interest but plots are mundane, action is limited and stereotyped and supporting players go through the same motions as they would a thousand times. Buck Jones looked older and acted older and without the realism of earlier years. Gimmicks like chewing gum when ready for action were childish innovations and the old, austere, grim Buck Jones was not that evident. Also, though

The big serial event of 1941 was Universal's Riders of Death Valley.

the films were labeled "trio" westerns, there was no doubt that Buck, and horse Silver, were the stars and McCoy played second fiddle. McCoy got along fine with Jones but would never be content endlessly playing a secondary role. He had been a big star himself and after eight Rough Rider films was looking for a way out. But that was in 1942....

Best big western of the year was Fritz Lang's *Western Union*. Sprawling and in color, it looked good, had sincere performances from the likes of Dean Jagger (and an inept one from Robert Young) and, most of all, inspired work from Randolph Scott in the type of role that would become familiar from him in the '50s. In *Western Union* he was a good-bad man, rugged, with a touch of humor and an air of fatefulness, dying in the end to save his friends and bring justice.

Belle Star (in which Scott was placidly mild, obviously walking through the role) was in glorious color too but Gene Tierney was an annoying and petulant Belle and the only interest lies in the score by Alfred Newman, which uses the same tune, the

Monogram's trio of old timers, Buck Jones, Tim McCoy and Raymond Hatton, in Arizona Bound, *1941.*

"Ann Rutledge theme," that is so poignant in Ford's *Young Mr. Lincoln.* Here it intrudes because one immediately thinks of Ann Rutledge rather than Belle Starr. Suitably, Ford would use it himself again in the 1962 *Man Who Shot Liberty Valance,* a film that "farewelled" the golden years of Hollywood westerns.

Bad Men of Missouri was another whitewash job for old outlaws, in the form of the Younger brothers, released by Warners. Stars were Dennis Morgan and Jane Wyman and of interest is the casting of a young Wayne Morris, who never dreamed that one day he would star in what is now officially known as the last B or series western, *Two Guns and a Badge,* in 1954. There were some medium budget efforts like Universal's *Badlands of Dakota* and Fox revised its Zane Grey schedule, starring a young lead, George Montgomery, in *Last of the Duanes* and *Riders of the Purple Sage.* Montgomery had been one of the "Ranger suspects" in the great 1938 serial *The Lone Ranger,* and had appeared in small roles with Roy Rogers. He appeared to be a good

Randolph Scott, far left, in action in Fritz Lang's 1941 Western Union, *from 20th Century–Fox.*

cowboy prospect but Fox saw more in him and elevated him to roles in non-westerns.

MGM dabbled in westerns, providing Wallace Beery with the vehicle *The Bad Man*, typical Beery escapism, and Clark Gable with *Honky Tonk*, glossy and ultimately, empty. Its main effort though was to remake *Billy the Kid*. David Miller directed in gorgeous color but the film was a pale shadow of the 1930 effort, Robert Taylor being totally miscast as the Kid.

The steadiest contribution to the west came in 1941 from the work of the lowly series cowboys, from the strangely mingled musical world of Gene Autry to the classically stereotyped, but entertaining, Columbia product. Along the way were more humble efforts from Monogram and the cheerfully inept world of PRC. Although some of top cowboy Gene Autry's films went overboard on matters non-western, at their best, with the likes of *Sierra Sue* and *Back in the Saddle,* a happy medium of old West action, singing and modern elements was obtained. A worrying situation for Republic was that, when war came at the end of the year, Autry made noises about joining up. Republic had been starring its number two cowboy, Roy Rogers, in a series of excellent historical westerns directed by Joe Kane. In 1940 Rogers had played young Buffalo Bill, young Bill Hickok and others. In 1941 he was Jesse James, in a double role, and various lawmen and the like in *Robin Hood of the Pecos*, *Sheriff of Tombstone*, *Nevada City* and others. With Autry's plans revealed the studio hastily changed the whole direction of Rogers' westerns for the last entry of 1941, *Red River Valley*. They updated it to the modern West, as in Autry features, put Roy in fancier gear, added more songs and hired the Sons of the Pioneers from Columbia to feature with Roy. They were ready for Autry's intended departure.

In 1941 Bill Boyd still clung to the number two box office position for westerners but he was being sharply challenged by Rogers. The Hopalong Cassidy westerns that year looked good under Lesley Selander's direction with *The Doomed Caravan*, *In Old Colorado*, *Border Vigilantes* and *Pirates on Horseback* culminating in a 77 minute long *Wide Open Town* that was impressive, but not so much so when you realized it was just a remake of *Hopalong Cassidy Returns*, and not as good. Even more than that, *Wide Open Town* saw the departure from the series of Russell Hayden. From Hayden's remarks later in life it seems that working with Boyd was not always the easiest and, in fact, Hayden declared he would "never have done it again." Andy Clyde stayed on and a new "Johnny Nelson" was added in Brad King for the rest of the year. King had none of Hayden's appeal and it was a weak spot of the Cassidys, only nullified by the continued excellent quality of production.

Republic continued its Don Barry and Three Mesquiteers series. The Barry westerns remained fresh and exciting with *Kansas Cyclone* the best of the year, but the Mesquiteer items began to lose their following. It was inevitable, after so many years and changes of personnel in the trio. Bob Livingston finally gave Stony Brooke away after a long run and left Republic for a while. He was replaced by Tom Tyler, who had made something of a comeback by starring in Republic's *Captain Marvel* serial. The trio of Tyler, Bob Steele and Rufe Davis saw 1941 out with *Outlaws of the Cherokee Trail*, *Gauchoes of Eldorado* and *West of Cimarron* and did inject some new life into the Mesquiteer series. Incongruous, after the original casting of beefy Ray Corrigan as Tucson Smith, was Bob Steele in that role and the big Tyler as Stony, but no doubt it would have been too complicated to have swapped them around.

With the departure of the Sons of the Pioneers from Columbia the Charles Starrett series changed. For a brief while Starrett played a character called the Medico, a doctor, but Columbia ran into copyright problems. In mid–1941 the studio hired Russell Hayden, who had left the Cassidys and co-starred him with Starrett. Their films were full of action, if not much plot. Starrett by now must have been resigned to the fact that he was a cowboy star, and prepared to see that through. The quality of his westerns faltered in the '40s and he might have faded from the screen earlier if a new idea had not been introduced in 1945. But that's a way down the trail....

Apart from moments such as in *Son of Davy Crockett* when Elliott's stark grimness

Bill Elliott (formerly Gordon) was busy and popular at Columbia in 1941.

comes to the fore when he forces two outlaws to drink tainted water, the Bill Elliott series at Columbia had lost momentum, so the studio hired Tex Ritter, late of Monogram, to co-star with Elliott. It proved a happy arrangement; Elliott and Ritter went very well together in what would be about the best co-starring series ever made, starting with *King of Dodge City* and *Roaring Frontiers in 1941*. Ritter had just finished his Monogram–Ed Finney contract. His last western there, *The Pioneers*, was awful, full of stock footage and little else, but he made up ground with his series at Columbia with Elliott.

Monogram had its Range Buster series doing quite well. Corrigan, King and Terhune never had the polish of Republic's Mesquiteers but they formed a likable group in a series of mild adventures, often played for laughs. Monogram also used Tom Keene, who had been off screen for some time, in a series in which Keene was the main, if only, asset. Keene films like *Wanderers of the West* had nice titles but little else to recommend them. Monogram was more concerned about its Rough Riders series, which it hoped would be the big attraction.

Universal and RKO Radio both used just one cowboy star each. Johnny Mack Brown was up there with the leading cowboy stars and his Universal group had polish and plenty of action. Action was Brown's forte, although Universal made sure there was some music in his westerns, performed both by sidekick Fuzzy Knight and western singing groups like the Kings Men, the Texas Rangers, and the Eddie Dean Trio. *Man from Montana* was Brown's best 1941 western and during the year he had a good part in an A budget feature, Abbott and Costello's *Ride 'Em Cowboy*, playing second fiddle to Dick Foran in the romance stakes. Apart from Foran and Brown one other (former) cowboy star was in the picture, Bob Baker — but Baker only had a non-speaking bit as a bus driver.

The Tim Holt westerns at RKO were pleasant and much tighter budgeted than the George O'Brien films had been. *The Bandit Trail*, *Six Gun Gold* and *Thundering Hoofs* were good, with Ray Whitley often prominent and, in *Thundering Hoofs*, former singing cowboy Fred Scott singing a song. Lee "Lasses" White had replaced Emmett Lynn early on and was placidly amusing.

Elliott's co-star in eight excellent little westerns at Columbia in 1941-42, Tex Ritter, is seen here with White Flash and double.

The "other" B western studio, PRC, churned out mediocre groups starring Buster Crabbe and George Houston. It also had some trio westerns in the pipeline ready to go in 1942, and one unusual grouping. In 1941, though, the studio relied upon Crabbe to impersonate an unlikely Billy the Kid (he'd taken over from Bob Steele) and Houston an even unlikelier Lone Rider. The Crabbe westerns co-starred Al "Fuzzy" St. John, who would be given his head in several entries that centered more on his comedy than Crabbe's heroics. A certain degree of popularity must have followed the honestly hard working Buster Crabbe because he stayed at PRC for several years while others came and went about him. As Fenin and Everson wrote in their groundbreaking *The Western* (1962), PRC westerns were rushed through so quickly that there was no time for retakes. They write, "The scripting was also of an equally carefree order, it being sufficient for the villain to brush up against the hero, snarl 'I don't like your face!' and launch into an otherwise unmotivated fist or gun fight." It is always difficult to pick out individual PRC westerns because they were all much alike. Its "Lone Rider" group was evidently meant to cash in on "the Lone Ranger," although their Rider, George Houston, did not wear a mask. (Later, Bob Livingston, playing the part after Houston, would wear a mask for some films. Since Livingston had played the Lone Ranger in a Republic serial this was a more obviously blatant attempted association.) Houston was a strange choice as cowboy hero. He was an opera singer who had played in a few low budget pictures, including a 1938 one-off western for Grand National, *Frontier Scout*, playing Wild Bill Hickok. Houston's ambition was to make enough money through films to form his own opera company. As the Lone Rider he was given the busy Fuzzy St. John as sidekick. The films were no worse or no better than normal PRC output and Houston, a tall man, appeared totally disinterested or amused by the whole proceedings. It was difficult to tell which, since he kept much the same expression throughout. If you liked good singing it was possible to enjoy his bursts into prairie song in his booming opera style. The one thing that lingers in the mind about the Lone Rider westerns is George Houston hammering out the theme song ("I'm the Lone Rider, ridin' down the trail....") behind the credits and ending. It has a certain surrealistic quality about it.

If 1941 had not been a great year for major westerns, there was certainly plenty of choice for followers of the humble series western. As America joined in the world war, entertainment by way of lighthearted film forms and entertaining troops became more important, and cowboy stars would play a prominent part in both of those.

1942

Business as Usual

There were some great movies produced in Hollywood (and elsewhere) in 1942. None of them were westerns. The year was barren of really good large scale westerns; about the only one that had "epic" written all over it was William Wellman's *The Great Man's Lady* starring Joel McCrea and Barbara Stanwyck and that was rather dull and boring. Wellman, a fine director, had not quite yet made his mark in the western. It would come, with his later efforts being his best. In *Union Pacific* Barbara Stanwyck had played a sweet, if tough, Irish gal; here she was, well … Barbara Stanwyck, and her more domineering character rather overwhelmed the placid McCrea. Besides, audiences were not yet ready for the Barbara Stanwyck style of western lady — strong, domineering, often ruthless. As with director Wellman, her time would come.

Universal remade *The Spoilers*, big and noisy but lacking depth. The brawl between Wayne and Randolph Scott was expertly done by the stunt doubles. Mainly the film was a showcase for Marlene Dietrich, legs and all. Universal also offered *Men of Texas*, a large B western with non-westerners Robert Stack and Broderick Crawford, routine stuff, as was Republic's major western effort with John Wayne, *In Old California*. Richard Dix made his now usual minor A western, *American Empire*, for which the title promises far more than the average budgeted film can offer. The "vast cattle empire" Dix runs looks suspiciously minor. More satisfying was Dix's United Artists release, *Tombstone*, yet another version of the cleaning up of that town. Harry Sherman produced this in his search for something better than Hopalong Cassidy. Sherman was weary of Bill Boyd's placid interpretation of the character and longed to produce more authentic westerns. *Tombstone* was not one, but it entertained.

A 1942 remake of The Spoilers, *with Randolph Scott, Marlene Dietrich and John Wayne.*

More small budget, one-off westerns came from Warners with *Wild Bill Hickok Rides*, Wild Bill relegated to being played by Bruce Cabot, a declining player, and from RKO *Valley of the Sun* about crooked Indian agents and Geronimo, played by Tom Tyler in a break from Republic. Starring Lucille Ball, James Craig and, unlikely enough Sir Cedric Hardwicke, *Valley of the Sun* was promoted by RKO as "bigger than anything since *Cimarron*," a ludicrous claim. Writers Phil Hardy and Michael Pitts simply call it "dull." More enjoyable was Joe E. Brown out West in *Shut My Big Mouth* for Columbia. A stellar supporting cast was added by the studio and behind Brown were Adele Mara, Lloyd Bridges, Forrest Tucker, Victor Jory, Don Beddoe, Earle Hodgins, Russell Simpson, Joan Woodbury, Ralph Peters, Noble Johnson and Chief Thundercloud to help give it that western flavor.

Fox had seemingly, the previous year, attempted to nurture a new cowboy star in George Montgomery but he was considered too handsome and useful and kicked "upstairs" from B grade westerns. In 1942 Fox tried again with a football star, Jim Kimbrough, in the Zane Grey story *Lone Star Ranger* and in *Sundown Jim*. As a football player, he was no doubt fine, but as an actor, even a B westerner ... forget it. Fox seemingly gave up trying to find another George O'Brien and from then on westerns it made were "oncers" usually starring non-westerners, or someone bigger than a B cowboy, anyway.

So what 1942 came down to was really "business as usual" with the smaller studios and producers turning out their series features with the various cowboy stars then popular. The list of top ten box office cowboys at the end of 1942 looked, by now, familiar. In order, they were Gene Autry, Roy Rogers, William Boyd, Smiley Burnette, Charles Starrett, Johnny Mack Brown, Bill Elliott, Tim Holt, Don Barry and the Three Mesquiteers. Gene Autry was also number seven in the Top Ten Money Making Stars of 1942, overall. Smiley Burnette's fourth placing — a western comic ahead of most steely jawed cowboy stars — was amazing, but even more amazing would be his eventual elevation, by 1943, to number three, with George Hayes right behind him at number four. Hayes would even reach number two in 1945, thus showing the immense influence mere "sidekicks" Burnette and Hayes had in B westerns. Neither player has received his just tribute from writers on the western; both deserve full biographical coverage. Hayes has been treated with some respect by historians, but Burnette generally written off as "tiresome." The statistics of his popularity speak otherwise and to dismiss him as such is belittling of one who had genuine talent, even though it was rarely utilized correctly. Certainly no review of the successful movie careers of Autry and Rogers should fail to pay tribute to the help (and just how much is difficult to estimate) given both by Burnette and Hayes. Fact is, one could watch a mid–'40s Roy Rogers western, see up there on screen this mass consisting of Rogers himself, horse Trigger, sidekick Hayes, leading lady Evans plus Bob Nolan and the Sons of the Pioneers and be excused for wondering if Roy Rogers was a corporation.

Another point about the 1942 top ten westerners involves Brown and Elliott. During the year Elliott was finishing off, and Brown beginning, co-starring series with singer Tex Ritter. Both were obviously popular, and Elliott and Brown got on the top ten list — but not Ritter. Just how much did Ritter contribute to the popularity of Elliott and Brown? Sadly, even though Ritter was plainly an equal co-star to Elliott, at Universal with Brown he was definitely the junior partner, and distributors obviously considered him so for both series, with Elliott and Brown getting the votes. Ritter deserved better, his contribution both as singer and as action cowboy to the Elliott series being immense. This Columbia group, consisting in 1942 of *Lone Star Vigilantes*, *Bullets for Bandits*, *North of the Rockies*, *The Devil's Trail*, *Prairie Gunsmoke* and *Vengeance of the West*, gave up only one failure, the odd (for the series) *Vengeance of the West*, with Elliott suddenly dropping his Wild Bill Hickok role to play Joaquin Murieta and Ritter, as the ranger after him, suddenly having a much smaller part. It was a strange one.

Tex Ritter, after a comfortable stay at Monogram, was on the move, first to

Columbia and then to Universal. His co-star Elliott was also moving, to Republic for a series beginning release in 1943. In the meantime Columbia extracted another serial from Wild Bill. *Valley of Vanishing Men* had a great title and a marvelous behind-the-credits sequence of captured men straining and struggling to turn a tiller while Wagner booms out in the background, but was not in the class of Elliott's first two Columbia serials. It was hurried and less photogenic. An example of the hurrying, some would say shoddiness, I find it amusing, is when one of the cast who had obviously worked with Bill frequently speaks to him and, instead of calling him "Bill Tolliver," his name in the serial, refers to him as "Bill Hickok." They left it in, either because they missed it or thought it a bit of fun.

Ritter had joined Johnny Mack Brown, popular at Universal but needing, the studio felt, a new touch. Ritter was it. The studio, and Brown presumably, saw Ritter in the earlier Bob Baker role, just backing Brown up. Even though the first entry, *Deep in the Heart of Texas* (noted by some as the best in the series, but nowhere near that) seemed to suggest this with Brown being dominant, by entry two, *Little Joe the Wrangler*, the Ritter personality had exerted itself and Tex played an increasingly important role in the series. But he never could supplant Brown as the star. Brown got the girl and the lead role, and Ritter got the more interesting role where he was able to exude far more personality than Brown could in his conventional hero part. Most notable is entry three, *The Old Chisholm Trail*, where Tex, in a great black outfit with two guns, plays a flashy gambler cum gunman. Added fillip in this title is that Tex gets to sing two songs, rather than the lonely one he was usually allocated. This is one of the mysteries of the series—after hiring a singing cowboy Universal gave him little chance to sing. They also hired the Jimmy Wakely Trio for the entire series, sidekick Fuzzy Knight usually barked out a song and even heroine Jennifer Holt sang. And Ritter, the most interesting voice of all, was allowed one song per picture. That's one of the many reasons I consider *The Old Chisholm Trail* the best of the series—Tex singing twice!

Charles Starrett and Russell Hayden continued their partnership in what Don Miller calls "seven rip-snortin', brawlin', shootin' saddle sagas." He also notes that production values were "cheesy, not to say sloppy." *West of Tombstone, Lawless Plainsmen*, and *Down Rio Grande Way* all looked much the same, and comic and musical Cliff Edwards, who had been at RKO with Tim Holt, completed a sort of trio. Starrett remained popular and Columbia must have considered Hayden so, because they gave him his own series for 1943. He was probably cheaper than Elliott or Ritter.

Tim Holt, youthful and popular, had continued at breakneck speed turning out RKO westerns. Breakneck because Holt wanted to join the services and RKO wanted as many films "in the can" as could be generated before he left. Thus Holt's later 1942-43 releases have a hurried look. Cliff Edwards replaced Ray Whitley, probably because Whitley used his back-up group and that cost more. Holt also made non-western appearances about this time, in Orson Welles' *Magnificent Ambersons* and

Partners at Universal in 1942: Johnny Mack Brown, Tex Ritter and Fuzzy Knight.

the quickie *Hitler's Children*, and his future was debatable. He seemed to be a good enough actor to make a career for himself in non-westerns. For now, he was off to war.

Also off to war was king cowboy Gene Autry. His later features for Republic in 1942 included good *Home in Wyomin'* and *Call of the Canyon* and a painfully patriotic *Bells of Capistrano* with a blatant flag-waving conclusion which was, in all fairness, the order of the day. Gene went to war still under Republic contract and would be away for four years. Republic had readied Roy Rogers. Backed by Gabby Hayes and the Sons of the Pioneers, he was placed in a group of excellent westerns, midway between the early Autry style and the big, showy 1940–42 Autry fashion. Stories were good, there was action, romance, nice Pioneer songs and an easy camaraderie between Rogers, Hayes and the Pioneers that showed under Joe Kane's direction and supervision. *Man from Cheyenne, South of Santa Fe, Sunset on the Desert, Romance on the Range, Sons of the Pioneers, Sunset Serenade* and *Ridin' Down the Canyon* stand out as a superior Rogers period. Just one film of that year, *Heart of the Golden West*, made sounds that promised a change for the future. It was longer, there were show

Top box office cowboy and about to join the forces, Gene Autry in Stardust on the Sage, *1942. Louise Currie and Bill Henry are pictured with him.*

tunes, dancers and black singers. There were even two sidekicks in Hayes and Smiley Burnette, who, with Autry gone, Republic was not quite sure what to do with. *Heart of the Golden West* still had action and was fun but ominous signs were there. Herbert Yates had been thinking....

Republic could also be proud that both of its other series, that of Don Barry and the Three Mesquiteers, were in the top ten. Barry was always of good value with gritty little westerns like *Outlaws of Pine Ridge* and *Arizona Terror*. Barry also kept badgering his producers for better roles in non-westerns. Republic gave him *Remember Pearl Harbor*, where he dies a gallant death avenging just that in an improbable scenario. The Mesquiteers were getting to be a bit "old hat" but Tom Tyler had injected new life and was performing and looking better than he had for years. During the year, after *The Phantom Plainsman*, the trio made its last change, with Jimmy Dodds replacing Rufe Davis for *Shadows of the Sage*. The Mesquiteer series lingered into 1943 but Republic felt it needed new faces and had hired Bill Elliott during 1942.

Popular Republic star Don Barry in 1942.

William Boyd remained near the top of the polls but only one Hopalong Cassidy film was made in 1942. Paramount had grown weary of them and Harry Sherman had to seek new distributors. He found them in United Artists and production started up again on *Undercover Man*, an unpretentious title for an unpretentious Cassidy western. Saddle pal Brad King was replaced by Jay Kirby. Kirby, of slight build and little personality, played Johnny Travers.

At PRC westerns were produced like sausages. Buster Crabbe and Fuzzy St. John had found a niche and kept riding. George Houston boomed out "I'm the Lone Rider" until, at the 11th entry, either he or PRC grew tired of the whole thing and abandoned it. During the series Dennis Moore, known as "Smokey," had steadily climbed from bit player to young saddle pal for Houston. Moore was shorter, but had more western personality. Houston died in 1944 of a heart attack. PRC thought it over and finally decided to try the Lone Rider again. The studio hired from Republic the more interesting Bob Livingston and the new series got underway with *Overland Stagecoach*. Fuzzy St. John was still there, as was Dennis Moore, but he and Livingston appeared similar so there was no further room for both. Moore went to join the Range Busters at Monogram.

PRC, busy as beavers (or as St. John, who was just about everywhere), had two other series during the year. One produced six cheap westerns and was a trio known as "The Frontier Marshals." What was unusual about them was that they consisted of two country and western singers, Bill Boyd (not Hoppy) and Art Davis, and one straight cowboy, Lee Powell. Boyd and Davis were supposed to be responsible for music, what passed for comedy and backing up Powell — which also passed for comedy. They were inept but likable. Powell, he of the good voice who had been the original Lone Ranger, kept a stony face throughout, probably because it was his only one. The productions had nice titles like *Along the Sundown Trail*, but were rubbish. Six was all even PRC could contemplate. Lee Powell joined the marines and was killed in the Pacific. Finally PRC started another trio, "The Texas Rangers," with *The Rangers Take Over*. It looked a bit better than the Frontier Marshals and PRC would persevere until 1945 with the Rangers. The original trio was Dave "Tex" O'Brien, who had been around for some time, James "Jim" Newill, an ex–Renfrew star and comic Guy Wilkerson, who would be a finalist in the "unfunniest B western comic of them all" contest. But O'Brien and Newill, who were real friends off screen, had an easy and relaxed relationship that was the main virtue of the group. Newill sang a few songs along the way.

Over at Monogram things were a bit rocky too. The Range Busters, after some moderate entries like *Boot Hill Bandits* and *Texas Troubleshooters*, split up, Corrigan leaving the group after producer problems. Dave Sharpe, stuntman extraordinaire, replaced him in *Texas to Bataan* (obviously not a "historical" western) and for two and a half more films into 1943. The "half" will be explained in the section for that year.

The Rough Rider series finished after *West of the Law* in 1942, when Tim McCoy left to rejoin the military. Buck Jones continued with Ray Hatton in *Dawn on the Great Divide*, and old timer Rex Bell as featured. Before the film had been released Buck Jones was tragically dead in the Coconut Grove nightclub fire in Boston. Monogram looked for a new cowboy star. It was a tragic business, the death of Jones, even more so than that of Tom Mix two years before. Mix had obviously left the picture business and seemed a name from the past. Jones was very much alive and active and looking forward to a few more years as a screen cowboy. Then, 1942 was a year of worldwide tragedy on a vast scale with few countries untouched by hostilities. Hollywood was the dream factory that helped a little to make the tragedy momentarily forgettable. Western movies were a part of that.

Colonel Tim McCoy at the close of his career in 1942.

1 9 4 3

Republic's New King

This was the year Roy Rogers became King of the Cowboys, according to Republic Studio and the annual top ten box office poll. Gene Autry fans disputed this as a "no contest." They had a point; let's just say Rogers topped the poll and Republic, as part of a big publicity campaign on the cowboy, starred him in a picture called *King of the Cowboys*. The bigger budgets spent on Rogers' films were evident in the casts and crowd scenes, the big musical numbers that increasingly were inserted (including the Robert Mitchell Boy Choir) and longer running times. Even so, *Idaho*, *King of the Cowboys*, *Song of Texas* and *Silver Spurs* were still superior entertainment with plenty of fast western action. Smiley Burnette continued as Roy's sidekick through *Silver Spurs* but Roy's last for the year, *Hands Across the Border*, introduced Guinn "Big Boy" Williams. It also, at 72 minutes, introduced Hoagy Carmichael songs, which did not suit the Sons of the Pioneers or Roy, and big fiesta scenes. That it was a horse story centered on Trigger kept the western element to the fore, just. Republic knew best though. What would become western musical comedy extravaganzas suited the larger public taste and audiences who would not normally go to a B western flocked to see Rogers.

There were some interesting major westerns made, but none could claim greatness. Howard Hughes made his *The Outlaw*, a story of Billy the Kid mainly shot to show off Jane Russell's bosom. Jack Beutel, who played Billy, became a Hollywood afterthought and the more professional Thomas Mitchell and Walter Huston could not save the day. *The Outlaw*, of course, ran into censorship problems and never did receive wide release. More serious and worthy was William Wellman's *Ox-Bow*

111

Incident, an indictment of lynch mobs. It was stark, filmed mainly on studio sets and never had a chance of impressing the public. Henry Fonda, Dana Andrews and a fine cast all played earnestly but the film was lacking in the human touches that bond an audience and true art. It was not the subject matter or the starkness; Wellman's work was fine, but somehow fell short. It remains a worthy attempt but flawed work of art.

More conventional and mildly successful were *The Apache Trail*, from MGM, *The Kansan*, a Sherman–United Artists film, *In Old Oklahoma*, Republic's John Wayne "special," and *Frontier Badmen* from Universal. John Wayne also made a comedy-western at RKO with Jean Arthur, *A Lady Takes a Chance*. Probably the best received western of the year was Columbia's *The Desperadoes*, an old-fashioned "shoot 'em up" directed by Charles Vidor with a cast of Randolph Scott, Glenn Ford, Claire Trevor, Evelyn Keyes, Edgar Buchanan and Guinn Williams. Joan Woodbury, a versatile B actress who also made many A features, usually playing mid to small roles, was also in *The Desperadoes*, called by Michael Pitts "well made and quite entertaining."

William Boyd retained a leading spot in the cowboy poll after 1943, even though the Hopalong Cassidy westerns were nowhere near as good as they had been. *Hoppy Serves a Writ* and *Bar 20* were the best, and in the latter George Reeves took over, very briefly, as young partner. More interesting, in many of the 1943 titles was a badman named Robert Mitchum, who began to attract attention. Things improved further with *False Colors* and *Riders of the Deadline* when Jimmy Rogers joined Boyd and Clyde, oddly enough, playing himself. Rogers was the son of the famous Will, was mild and had a pleasant, warm, slightly humorous personality. He never took the place of Russell Hayden (or James Ellison), but was better than the others.

Bill Elliott, at Republic, made eight action-packed westerns that helped his popularity soar and made him Republic's number two cowboy. With the star billed as "Wild Bill Elliott," the series co-starred George Hayes and Anne Jeffreys. Jeffreys, very attractive with a nice voice, didn't really have much to do but Hayes was at his cantankerous best. The series began with *Calling Wild Bill Elliott*, probably the first time a cowboy star had his own name in the title. Other entries, including *The Man from Thunder River*, *Bordertown Gunfighters*, *Wagon Tracks West* and *Death Valley Manhunt* were just as good as the first. In *Wagon Tracks* Tom Tyler, his role as Stony Brooke finished, was listed high in the cast playing an Indian. The last two of Elliott's eight were actually released in 1944 while Elliott, still at Republic, had moved onto another role.

The Don Barry series continued to be of quality, including *Days of Old Cheyenne*, *Dead Man's Gulch*, *Black Hills Express*. Those directed by John English, including the last two mentioned, stood out. Lynne Merrick, an attractive blonde, had featured with Barry for a while. She was replaced by Helen Talbot, and a child player named Twinkle Watts was added to the cast. Barry could have done without her. A plus was comedian Wally Vernon, an unlikely Bronx comic out West — but it worked. Vernon had a nice dry touch.

Henry Fonda and Harry Morgan in 1943's Ox-Bow Incident, *directed by William Wellman at Fox.*

Tom Tyler was the last to play Mesquiteer Stony Brooke at Republic in 1943.

The Three Mesquiteers, after *Riders of the Rio Grande*, were disbanded. It has been a long ride. Jimmy Dodd went to television, Tom Tyler mainly to supporting roles but Bob Steele was still active and joined the Trail Blazers at Monogram. Replacing the Mesquiteers was Eddie Dew, who had appeared at RKO in Tim Holt films, mainly as a heavy. Dew was pleasant enough and sang mildly but his two starring westerns, *Beyond the Last Frontier* and *Raiders of Sunset Pass*, made no impact and Republic hastily dispensed with Dew's services. Even the casting of Smiley Burnette with Dew had not helped. Republic induced Bob Livingston to move back from PRC, which took little persuasion, and thought further.

At Universal, after some years of steady Bob Baker–Johnny Mack Brown–Tex Ritter material, changes came. Brown and Ritter finished off their excellent group with *Tenting Tonight on the Old Camp Ground* (which must be a candidate for longest ever title), *Cheyenne Roundup*, *Raiders of the San Joaquin* and *The Lone Star Trail*. Many have rated the last one, *Lone Star Trail*, the best, partly because Bob Mitchum was in it and had a memorable fight with Brown, but I place the other three ahead of that. In *Raiders of the San Joaquin*, Ritter, whether consciously or not, played the clichéd good-bad role by wearing a white hat when he is an upstanding hero and the minute he is branded as an outlaw (which of course he isn't) switching to a black hat. With the series completed it was not Ritter but Brown who left. Monogram sought him as its Buck Jones replacement. Before the last of the Universal films were in releases, Monogram had hurried out *The Ghost Rider*, *The Stranger from the Pecos*, *Six Gun Gospel* and *Outlaws of Stampede Pass*. The Monogram features did not have the class of the Universal ones, but Brown was still good, if showing signs of putting on weight, and they gave him Ray Hatton as sidekick, a happy pairing that would last for many a film and year.

Tex Ritter believed he had his own series now at Universal. He made one film, *Arizona Trail*. Universal clung to its policy of having a supporting cowboy, along with Fuzzy Knight, by putting Dennis Moore in the picture. Ritter now took the Brown role. However, he had an accident before another picture could be started. Universal hastily replaced him with Russell Hayden. Hayden's agent had a clause inserted that said the studio had to employ his client for a few more roles. So when Ritter came back he found Hayden co-starring with him. This would be early 1944 and nobody was happy about it, Ritter or Universal, although Hayden may have thought he came out of it well enough.

At Monogram the Range Busters' ride finished. They had ambled on for three years but never captured the audience as the Mesquiteers had. During the filming of *Haunted Ranch* David Sharpe was suddenly called to serve in World War II. Getting around this by, in the film, stating he had been called up for Teddy Roosevelt's Rough Riders, the studio replaced Sharpe for the rest of the film with old-timer Rex Lease. This was a stand-by action and Ray Corrigan, who himself owned a part of the Range Buster series, returned. For whatever reason John King then left, and when Max

Terhune opened his eyes he had Corrigan and Dennis Moore as pals for the last films, which concluded with *Bullets and Saddles*. (John King was back in, briefly, in the second-to-last film, *Black Market Rustlers*, but one suspects that it had been filmed earlier.) Monogram had hired a top ten cowboy in Johnny Mack Brown and to conclude its 1943 activities it began another series with some old-timers, just like Jones and McCoy. One difference was that Ken Maynard and Hoot Gibson, lured back to the screen, were not in as good condition as Jones and McCoy had been. It seems that both intended to diet and lose weight when offered the work, but then found out the salary offered and scorned the idea. So into *Wild Horse Stampede* rode a rotund Ken Maynard and a well-worn Hoot Gibson. Alan James, who had worked with Maynard without too much difficulty before, directed. The film was cheap, but fun, as Maynard and Gibson played it lightly. Betty Miles, a fine equestrian, was an added attraction and a kind of trio format was suggested by the third billing of Bob Baker, returning to the screen after a spell of three years (and some bit and serial work). But for some reason Baker was not allowed to sing and the role he was given, as a bookworm law officer hating the idea of guns, was anything but heroic. Some sources say Maynard resented Baker and made life difficult for him, but whatever the reason, it was a waste of a talented cowboy who drifted away into obscurity apart from some non-speaking roles in the Hopalong Cassidy series. The Trail Blazers, for that is what they were called, rode on through *The Law Rides Again* and *Blazing Guns* before producer Robert Tansey decided some help was needed and hired Bob Steele to form a real trio. Steele had been around a long time, he was a veteran, but he still looked young and considerably more active than Ken or Hoot. Once again stories state that Maynard didn't get along with Steele. Maynard, who was continually moaning about something, didn't get along with anybody much so Bob shouldn't have felt isolated.

Columbia was left with Charles Starrett after Russell Hayden finished his series of eight (in which western swing master Bob Wills co-starred) and wandered off to other pastures. The Starrett westerns had reached their lowest point, an hour of sometimes mindless riding and fighting with the hero as upright and staunch as ever. Arthur Hunnicutt was used as a sidekick until Dub Taylor replaced him. Western musical groups came and went as support until in late 1943 Jimmy Wakely arrived with his aggregation and stayed around for a while, Wakely's parts getting bigger as producers considered his worth as a cowboy player increased. It would lead to Wakely getting his own series at Monogram.

PRC continued to grind out cheap westerns. They were so cheap they made good profits, so PRC went happily ahead. As long as B westerns remained cheap to make, they were in business. The Lone Rider series with Bob Livingston went nowhere in particular except Livingston went back to Republic, thus freeing Al St. John (a real busy Fuzzy) to concentrate on Buster Crabbe's Billy the Kid series. Some people were dubious about a hero playing one who was, when all was said and done, a real life killer and outlaw so, at the end of 1943 Billy became Billy Carson and Crabbe would

An overweight Ken Maynard near the end of his film trail in 1943.

PRC's longest-running cowboy star, Larry "Buster" Crabbe.

grind out more features, right through until 1946, amazing really, considering the overall quality.

The Texas Rangers (Dave O'Brien, Jim Newill and Guy Wilkerson) got through the year too. It's difficult to know how after seeing *Bad Men of Thunder Gap*, *Return of the Rangers* or *Boss of Rawhide*. Newill's western contribution was limited even if he sang nicely, Wilkerson existed seemingly in state of limbo and maybe O'Brien, a good action player and cheery personality, carried them through. Fennin and Everson, in their famous book, put it this way: "The westerns of PRC ... were shoddy, cheap, carelessly made, badly photographed and ineptly directed." Seeing them now, in a more tolerant state of mind, the authors may have agreed with me that, though what they say is true, the PRC westerns can be fun. It does require that certain state of mind when watching them.

1 9 4 4

Tall in the Saddle

Since *Stagecoach* and perhaps *Dark Command*, John Wayne's films had been larger scale but unremarkable. Republic was trying to elevate his roles with westerns that were essentially minor scripts with 20 minutes extra running time. His roles outside the studio, excepting the pleasing *Shepherd of the Hills*, had also been mundane. So it was good in 1944 to see Wayne back in an action western again, *Tall in the Saddle*, at RKO. Directed by Edwin Marin, *Tall in the Saddle* was a good blending of B action and A story as Wayne battled with old friend Ward Bond and heroine Ella Raines.

The major western for the year was William Wellman's *Buffalo Bill*, a glossy and over-hyped version of the great man's story centering on extreme heroism and little else. In the guise of Joel McCrea, Cody was a quiet, manly, almost introverted man of the plains, quite unlike the jovial showman history portrays. It was typical McCrea but hardly Cody. Still, it looked good, especially with Maureen O'Hara in color. Thomas Mitchell played the commercially minded Ned Buntline.

Studios were more interested in dashing war films than westerns in 1944 so once again the main output came from the smaller producers with their cowboy series. The year also seemed to mark the demise of the Hopalong Cassidy series after so many years. With *Forty Thieves* the unit closed down, Harry Sherman having lost all interest. Lesley Selander directed this last UA production. William Boyd was left in a difficult situation. He had become so immersed in the Cassidy character that there was simply no chance of him being offered anything else. While keeping busy with personal appearances Boyd tried to get the money together to purchase the film rights to Cassidy with the aim, eventually, of producing his own films.

119

While Boyd languished the Roy Rogers stature grew higher. *The Cowboy and the Senorita*, *The Yellow Rose of Texas*, *Song of Nevada*, *San Fernando Valley* and *Light of Old Santa Fe* continued the new formula with up to 78 minutes' running time, production numbers and, from the first film of the year, a new leading lady for Rogers in Dale Evans. Roy's leading ladies had been good, and he had made more than one film with several of them. Evans, sexy yet maternal, fitted in with the boyish, smiling Rogers image and she became part of the team comprising Rogers, herself Gabby Hayes (who had rejoined the series with *Lights of Old Santa Fe*), the Sons of the Pioneers and Trigger. The sheer fun this group seemed to be having generated a like response from audiences. Rogers was never, even after the return of Gene

William "Hopalong Cassidy" Boyd in 1944.

Autry, to relinquish his hold on the number one cowboy spot until the poll closed.

Republic revived the Red Ryder role, used only once in the 1940 serial, and cast Bill Elliott in it. Elliott simply continued his "Wild Bill" characterization with all the gimmicks—Red Ryder became Wild Bill, or vice versa. With young Bobby Blake as Little Beaver, the films were good, sharp action productions so nobody minded whether Bill played Red or Red played Bill. Alan Barbour called the entire Ryder works at Republic "23 hours of action." George Hayes was able to return to the Roy Rogers pictures. Republic, after giving Bob Livingston a few pictures with Smiley Burnette, found its new cowboy star in Sonny "Sunset" Carson, a very tall, young cowboy who could ride well, fight with vigor and read lines with little meaning in a high-pitched Texas voice. The public, especially in the Deep South, who took him to their hearts, didn't mind his lack of thespian talent. Sunset Carson rode and smiled, and fought and smiled, and fought and smiled some more. The professional Republic casts around him did all the rest. At first worried about his impact, Republic actually starred Burnette in *Call of the Rockies*, *Bordertown Trail*, *Code of the Prairie* and *Firebrands of Arizona* with Carson supporting him, a unique situation. But Carson soon caught on and was given his own films. Smiley Burnette was left with nowhere to go, so he went. To Columbia.

The last Don Barry western was released in 1944 and Barry, thankfully at the time, was elevated to non-westerns. The studio decided to replace him with another cowboy and went for contract actor Allan Lane, tall, handsome and star of four Republic action serials. Lane inherited Wally Vernon for a while, which was fine, and child player Twinkle Watts for the series, which was not, but Lane looked suitably western and manly in *Silver City Kid*, *Stagecoach to Monterey*, and *Sheriff of Sundown* as the series continued into 1945.

At Columbia Charles Starrett was helped by Dub Taylor and singer Jimmy Wakely in *Cyclone Prairie Rangers*, *Cowboy from Lonesome River* and *Saddle Leather Law*, among others. Starrett also starred in a "special" during the year, *Cowboy Canteen*, Columbia's cowboy version of Warners' *Hollywood Canteen*. Tex Ritter was brought in for that one, along with numerous singing groups (including the Mills Brothers) and heroine was Jane Frazee, who would become a well-known Republic player. More and more Starrett appeared to be going through the motions, but he had a following. His co-star in *Cowboy Canteen*, Tex Ritter, was still looking for a contract and found it at PRC, lowest of the low. PRC felt that its Texas Rangers series was getting nowhere and Jim Newill was not too interested, so it replaced Newill with Ritter. *Gangster of the Frontier*, *Dead or Alive* and *The Whispering Skull* were still typical PRC productions but Ritter did give them some added pep and his singing was a gain. The Buster Crabbe–Fuzzy St. John westerns were still ground out. Some relief came with an entry like *Fuzzy Settles Down*, which focused on Crabbe's comic sidekick and was a bit of fun.

At Monogram the Johnny Mack Brown series galloped along with nine titles for the year from *Raiders of the Border* to *The Navajo Trail*, and Johnny found time to appear in the Monogram non-western *Forever Yours* with Gale Storm and C. Aubrey Smith. Brown was playing a continuing character in his westerns, Nevada Jack McKenzie, and sidekick Hatton was Sandy Hopkins. Directed mainly by Lambert Hillyer, the Brown films were stereotyped but lively and Brown was still in good shape.

The Monogram Trail Blazer series had run into Maynard trouble and Ken finally pulled out after *Arizona Whirlwind*. A surprise replacement was Chief Thundercloud to continue the trio, although the Chief was billed below Steele and Gibson. *Outlaw Trail*, *Sonora Stagecoach* and *Marked Trails* followed, then Thundercloud left and for the final films Steele was listed as "star" with Gibson just supporting him. *Trigger Law* in 1944 was the end of the Blazer trail. It was also the end of Hoot Gibson's cowboy star career. Steele had a few more films still to make. After all this, out of the ashes rose Ken Maynard. With producer Robert Tansey he made *Harmony Trail*, another effort at a trio western, with Max Terhune and longtime bit player (and fine singer) Eddie Dean. If Dean looked undernourished Maynard looked positively overnourished and Terhune was ineffective. *Harmony Trail* had a couple of nice Dean songs, including "On the Banks of the Sunny San Juan" but nothing else to recommend it.

A new cowboy at Republic, Sonny "Sunset" Carson (right), with Smiley Burnette.

It appears to have received little release, until in 1947 Astor picked it up, renamed it, for no apparent reason, *White Stallion* and unleashed it on the public. It was a starting point for Eddie Dean's singing cowboy career but the close of Ken Maynard's. Dean never amounted to much but Maynard had been one of the greats, and this was a sad end. Then, Ken had been living out a sad ending since about 1936.

Monogram was always looking for new cowboys and having decided it needed another singing cowboy, elevated Jimmy Wakely from longtime support singer to star in *Song of the Range*. Wakely had been receiving increasingly larger roles in Brown and Starrett pictures. He sang nicely as country and western singers go, and in his mannerisms and clothing imitated Gene Autry. Wakely denied this in later years but watching his early starring films it is inescapable. Monogram gave Dennis Moore to Jimmy as an action sidekick and Lee "Lasses" White as comic. *Song of the Range* was ho-hum. Jimmy sang well, Moore rode and fought well, White was not too bad. Possibilities were there for a nice trio.

RKO, with no regular cowboy since Tim Holt, tried the young and promising Bob Mitchum. Mitchum appeared in a western-comedy-musical, *Girl Rush*, with Brown and Carney and Frances Langford and then starred in the Zane Grey adaptation *Nevada*. The film was average but Mitchum caused excitement.

Meanwhile at Universal, Fuzzy Knight rode on as comic sidekick to another duo of heroes, separate and together. Tex Ritter finished his work there with *Marshal of Gunsmoke* and *Oklahoma Raiders*. Russ Hayden and Dennis Moore, respectively,

Top: *Tex Ritter circa 1944;* bottom: *Canadian born Rod Cameron, a late Universal cowboy star, in 1944.*

co-starred. They were good Ritter westerns and should have ensured Tex's retention at the studio but for some unknown reason that didn't happen. The Ritter option was dropped, he went to PRC and Universal brought in tall Canadian born stunt double Rod Cameron for four films, and also Eddie Dew from Republic for one, *Trail to Gunsight*, which had the advantage of Ray Whitley in support. Universal's next gambit, as the year ended, was to co-star Cameron and Dew. That was for 1945.

1 9 4 5

Eddie Dean—
In Living Color

Color had been used in minor westerns in the '30s but only in one-off features. In 1945 PRC "scooped" its rivals in the B western business by producing the first color series. Earlier in the year Screen Guild had two B westerns in color, both starring the endurable Bob Steele. *Northwest Trail* was an opportunity to highlight the red Mounties uniform. The other, *Wildfire*, was set in the USA, about a horse, and featured, as co-star to Steele, Eddie Dean. Dean had figured, as mentioned, in Ken Maynard's final abortive attempt at stardom in 1944. He had been in Hollywood for years, hardly ever rising above one of the heavies or singing group — for he had a fine baritone voice. In Tex Ritter's *Rolling Home to Texas* in 1940 he had been billed third and sung some songs, but nothing had come of it. Now further attempts had been made, not with any great success. Once again Dean sang well but looked and acted wooden beside Steele who, no great actor, dominated any scenes they were both in. Somebody at PRC didn't notice that because, with a color series in the works, the cowboy finally named as the bright new western star of the screen to appear in it was— yes, Eddie Dean. Released near the close of 1945, *Song of Old Wyoming* looked to be a bigger production than usual from PRC. Actually, the Cinecolor made it appear so; the basic script, direction and setting were much the same as usual, with the usual players. Color, however, made everything appear better. Except for Dean. Eddie Dean was not a handsome man and could hardly even be called good looking. His acting was dismal, his stature small and he had no dominating character. He could ride, just, but in fight scenes looked ineffective. Even worse, in *Song of Old Wyoming*, a supporting role, that of the Cheyenne Kid, shone out on screen more than the hero's. This was played by another "new discovery," Al LaRue, a most unique actor. Dressed in black, toting two guns and using a whip, LaRue appeared on screen as a combination Humphrey Bogart–Dead End Kid. He walked like Bogart, he snarled when he spoke out of the side of his mouth and he looked tough. Fact was he could barely ride a horse and at that stage knew nothing about staging fisticuffs. He could learn though, and as one writer (Don Miller) points out, "When a supporting player steals the attention from the debut of a new leading man, there's trouble ahead." Dean's singing was his only drawing point — that and the color process used, which, if not Technicolor, was certainly better than some of the later Republic Trucolor efforts.

Though not yet using color, Republic was certainly the top B western studio. In 1945 Roy Rogers cemented his "King of the Cowboys" tag by becoming the second, and only other, cowboy to list in the overall top ten film stars. Rogers "guested" at

Roy Rogers, now top cowboy at the box office in 1945, with the Sons of the Pioneers (Ken Carson, Bob Nolan and Tim Spencer on the ground, Karl Farr, Shug Fisher and Hugh Farr above) in Utah, *1945.*

Warner Bros. in its *Hollywood Canteen*, then appeared in hit after hit of his big scale western musicals: *Utah*, *Bells of Rosarita*, *The Man from Oklahoma*, *Sunset in Eldorado*, *Don't Fence Me In* and *Along the Navajo Trail*. Director Joseph Kane had left the series, Republic rewarding his years of service with Gene Autry and Rogers by giving him their bigger budget westerns to direct.

John English and Frank McDonald took over the Rogers films. Most interesting were *Don't Fence Me In*, which highlighted Gabby Hayes and had the big hit song, and *Bells of Rosarita*. The latter was a throwback to a trend in the '30s, used by Tom Keene, Gene Autry, Charles Starrett and Buck Jones, of westerns made about the making of westerns. In *Bells* Rogers plays himself, a cowboy movie star, between films getting mixed up with circus shenanigans and calling on fellow cowboy stars Bill Elliott, Sunset Carson, Allan Lane, Bob Livingston and Don Barry to help round up the bad guys and take part in a musical finale. Republic "cheated" to the extent that Barry and Livingston were no longer cowboy stars but that didn't matter — they were still fondly remembered. With his stock company of Hayes, Evans, the Pioneers and Trigger safely around him, Rogers, in movies, on radio, in books, soon comics and personal appearances, was building up a legend.

Joe Kane was at first delighted to be offered bigger pictures to direct and his first was to be *Dakota* starring John Wayne. But Wayne almost destroyed Kane's first assignment by refusing to appear opposite Herbert Yates' girlfriend, later wife, Vera Ralston. Wayne's reluctance was understandable; nobody wanted to appear with Miss Ralston, but Kane's resentment that the Duke had almost sabotaged his first picture remained with him all of his life. Kane never became a member of the John Wayne fan club. In the end Wayne reluctantly made the picture. It was one of Republic's two big westerns for the year, the other being *Flame of the Barbary Coast*. Both starred Wayne but neither was outstanding. Wayne did better elsewhere making *They Were Expendable* for John Ford. Biggest western of the year was Warner Bros.' *San Antonio*, a vehicle for Errol Flynn directed by David Butler, but that again was unillustrious. The most interesting bit was Tom Tyler as the baddie shot by Flynn, in one of Tyler's last major roles.

Gary Cooper made *Along Came Jones*, gently lampooning his own western characterization in a gentle film co-starring Loretta Young and Dan Duryea that never quite decided whether it was a comedy or western. Nothing could disguise the lack of a top class western film during the year though. Of more minor proportions were Universal's frontier comedy *Frontier Gal* with ex-series star Rod Cameron and Yvonne De Carlo, and Universal's cheap *The Daltons Ride Again*.

RKO's B efforts were isolated. Isolated because one star, Robert Mitchum, after *West of the Pecos*, was recognized as a rising star and elevated swiftly, and the other, James Warren in *Wanderer of the Wasteland*, was a totally inadequate cowboy hero. Warren actually made two more westerns, released slowly over the next two years, to further prove the point.

At Universal both B western and serial production were grinding to a halt as the studio assessed its future. The Rod Cameron–Eddie Dew–Ray Whitley group concluded with *Beyond the Pecos* and *Renegades of the Rio Grande*. Cameron moved up to bigger features, Dew disappeared and Whitley concentrated on his singing and personal appearances. Kirby Grant, of no western background and totally opposed to making what he called "filthy oaters," was pressed into service. Grant was a singer and although his three westerns for 1945 made little impact, the studio persevered with him, probably because they were just filling in time. Grant would later cut a more respectable figure as a Mountie at Monogram and on TV as Sky King and would actually learn to quite enjoy the job. The one stable factor in Universal B westerns over the last years was the sight of Fuzzy Knight, sidekicking to another cowboy hero, right to the end.

While its color Eddie Dean series captured the attention, at PRC Tex Ritter and Dave O'Brien completed the Texas Ranger group which, closing down with the fifth 1945 title, *Flaming Bullets*, was missed only for the departure of Tex Ritter from the western screen — although that was probably not obvious at the time. Buster Crabbe and Al St. John plowed on in *His Brother's Ghost*, *Shadows of Death*, *Gangster's Den* and five other similar adventures throughout the year. A certain degree of comfort must have come to the cinemagoers who knew they had seen it all before — yet still went along.

Columbia had narrowed its western production down to Charles Starrett in features as familiar as Buster Crabbe's but with a bit more style, and a group of hybrid musical-comedy-westerns, often featuring singer Ken Curtis who, even considering the crassness of the material, managed to display some potential. The first, *Sing Me a Song of Texas*, featured a grim Tom Tyler at the close of his starring career looking completely out of place. Starrett, with *Blazing the Western Trail*, his first 1945 entry, acquired the services of a singing saddle pal, Tex Harding. Harding was tall and nice enough looking, and seemed to have the necessary western attributes. Though Columbia gave him every chance by co-starring him in almost every 1945 Starrett western, he never caught on. During the year Columbia had been negotiating with Smiley Burnette, who was at a loose end. Burnette agreed to "come over and give some pep to Starrett's westerns," a statement that somewhat miffed Starrett when he found out about it. Starrett, having moved from eighth to seventh on the western players' top ten list by the end of the year, thought he was doing all right anyway. A noted happening during the year had been the making of *The Return of the Durango Kid* with Starrett's 1940 character, slightly modified, returning to the screen. In retrospect the Durango Kid is a highly ludicrous character but the masked man in black on the white horse proved to have immense pulling power and from that film on, Starrett was to play the character consistently.

Over at Republic Bill Elliott continued his very popular Red Ryder series in *Great Stagecoach Robbery*, *Phantom of the Plains*, *Wagon Wheels Westward* and others.

Left to right: *Wild Bill Elliott (as the second Red Ryder) with Bobby Blake and George Gabby Hayes in 1945.*

With Bobby Blake as Little Beaver, Alice Fleming as The Duchess and leading ladies like Peggy Stewart and Linda Stirling, the Ryder group looked a happy team. R. G. Springsteen became a regular director, and notable in the screenplays of Bob Williams, Randal Frey, Earle Snell and others were the cynically humorous villains, bad guys with a nice line in dialogue, often played by Roy Barcroft, Dick Curtis, William Haade or LeRoy Mason. It was a trend notable at Republic, especially in its later Allan Lane films.

Lane had finished his first short group at the studio, the best being *Corpus Christi Bandits* where he showed genuine acting ability as well as the usual virility. Sunset Carson was pulling in large audiences, in some parts of the country larger than those of Roy Rogers, so they said. Carson had nice leading ladies in Stewart and Stirling, who also helped him when he struggled with his lines. *Santa Fe Saddlemates* and *Sheriff of Cimarron* were typical Carson outings, all action, and just what his fans called for. He seemed to have a big future ahead of him.

Republic had also hired another singing cowboy, a Texan named Monte Hale, and had him around appearing in bits in the films of Elliott and Carson while they waited to hear whether Roy Rogers would go into the services. Hale was another very tall cowboy, like Sunset Carson, mild of manner and mild of voice and with a broad smile and Texan accent. At the close of 1945 the danger to the studio of Rogers departing was over and they promised young Hale a series of his own for the coming year. Having watched PRC's success with color, the studio also had ideas along that line.

Bill Boyd was off the screen for all of 1945 so that left only Monogram's cowboy stars, and they were the two—Johnny Mack Brown and Jimmy Wakely. Brown continued turning out Nevada Jack McKenzie tales, increasingly one much like the other. He and Raymond Hatton still made a good team but now the signs were starting to show of Brown's adherence to the good life. As with Ken Maynard, he was becoming a shade portly. Unlike Maynard, Brown always remained an easygoing, friendly man and retained his popularity. Monogram gave him a "special" for 1945 in *Flame of the West*, longer than normal and featuring Douglas Dumbrille, Joan Woodbury, Lynne Carver and Hatton relegated to a smaller role, in which Brown plays an idealistic doctor who finally has to buckle on his gun to provide justice. Although quite good, *Flame of the West* cannot disguise that it is another Lambert Hillyer directed B western, with the usual "suspects" in Harry Woods, John Merton, Steve Clark, Riley Hill, Bud Osborne and Jack Rockwell in the cast and the unfortunate addition of Pee Wee King and His Golden West Boys looking completely out of place.

Wakely's westerns, on the other hand, beginning with *Springtime in Texas*, were packed with musical numbers and produced and directed by veteran Oliver Drake. They were packed with musical groups (Foy Willing and his Riders of the Purple Sage got their first billing in *Saddle Serenade*) and were virtual country and western singing fests, rounded out by some riding and fighting. However, there was an audience for such "westerns" and Wakely himself, although mild in the action department, came

Jimmy Wakely, a '40s singing cowboy at Monogram.

across nicely when he sang. After *Springtime in Texas* Dennis Moore, who was under the impression that it was going to be his series with Wakely co-starring, was dropped, which caused some friction. Replacing him was John James. Unlike Moore he did not outshine Jimmy in the action department and he was retained for the rest of the year, which concluded with *Riders of the Dawn*, a remake in title of the 1937 Jack Randall starrer but not in content. The 1937 film had been full of action with three songs. Wakely's western was full of songs and the story was all about a baby Jimmy spends a lot of time crooning to. B westerns had been a bit more rugged in 1937, even singing cowboy ones.

One final Monogram initiative for 1945 was to begin a Cisco Kid series, the first time the Kid had been on screen since 1941 at Fox. Then he had been played by Cesar Romero, who had taken over the role from Warner Baxter. Monogram purchased the rights and starred Duncan Renaldo, with Martin Garralaga as Pancho in *The Cisco Kid Returns*. Two more 1945 films followed, both with this team.

1946

Home from the War

Nineteen forty-six was a pivotal year in the history of the western film. In response to public wants after the war more and more minor A westerns, those neither a B series nor a single epic drama, were produced. These films were usually about 90 minutes long, often in color and featuring players not normally associated with the western. They also, as a benefit of the war years, had a more cynical and tougher approach to them and often brutal violence was evident. Brutal, that is, for the time. It was also the year that the minor A cowboy came into his own, the likes of Randolph Scott and Joel McCrea who adopted the western as their form of film almost exclusively but were not classified in the cowboy listing. At least, in America. In Britain the likes of Scott and McCrea, and also players like Alan Ladd in later years, would be included in their top ten cowboy stars, a hybrid mixture of A and B players. In the United States, to be classified as a cowboy star related to the B series features only.

The year also saw the production of Universal's last western serial, the listless *The Scarlet Horseman*. Serials, after the heady days of the '30s, had declined rapidly in the '40s, at all studios producing them. Universal made its last notable one with *Riders of Death Valley*, although its 1944 *Raiders of Ghost City* starring the vagabond cowboy (he moved from studio to studio) Dennis Moore was a gallant effort. In 1946 the studio abandoned B features, both serials and series, in its ambition to be regarded as a major production company. Universal's last cowboy star was Kirby Grant, partnered by Fuzzy Knight, in a series that was hardly missed when it ceased.

Republic and Columbia continued to make serials, western and all, but the flame had gone even from the action studio. Serials became pedestrian and predictable with no innovation or inspiration. Although they lasted until 1956, after 1946 there was little of interest produced, especially in the western form.

One particular film of the year was regarded, upon release, as John Ford, back from the war, doing his finger exercises again on an "oater"—presumably before embarking on more serious fare. But *My Darling Clementine*, the best western of 1946, is a lovely film —"charming" may be the better word. Very loosely based on Wyatt Earp's battle with the Clantons, and highly romanticized, it was Ford's most optimistic picture of the Western frontier, a place where churches are rising and it will soon be "fit for a young man to grow up in." Beautifully lit and shot by Winston Miller, *My Darling Clementine* starred Henry Fonda at his most reassuring, mild, calm, in control and dandy enough to "smell of the desert flower." Rightly, scenes like the march of Fonda and leading lady Cathy Downs to the dance at the unfinished church, Fonda talking to the grave of his young brother and the first confrontation between Earp and the Clantons and Earp and Doc Holliday, have been singled out as masterpieces of construction in this tightly controlled but sweeping western. The famous battle at the O.K. Corral takes second place to the human structure, although it is well enough done. Walter Brennan turns in another of his splendid roles, this time as thoroughly nasty Ike Clanton, and among Ford's company is young Tim Holt, also returned from the war and set to resume his career at RKO.

Clementine was a great western, but at the time interest centered more on a much lesser production, David Selznick's epic *Duel in the Sun*, directed by King Vidor. An overlong, over-acted bore, *Duel in the Sun* gained its notoriety by its steamy performance by Jennifer Jones and its melodramatic and sexually charged ending as Jones and Gregory Peck die in the dust. In actual fact, though Vidor is the listed director, it is understood he did only about half the film. Selznick's demands became too much for him and other directors finished the filming. The cast was awesome, with Gregory Peck a promising actor, Joseph Cotten, Lionel Barrymore, Walter Huston, Lillian Gish, Charles Bickford, Harry Carey and many others. This cannot save *Duel in the Sun* from being a bad picture. It has some great scenes but is not in the same field as *My Darling Clementine*.

Also disappointing was the color remake of *The Virginian*, directed by Stuart Gilmore and starring Joel McCrea. The most notable thing about this film is that it signaled McCrea's determination to make such films on a regular basis, thus joining Randolph Scott as a major, or minor, A cowboy star. McCrea should have been ideal in the role, but the whole film is flat. Blame must lie at the feet of director Gilmore, who failed totally to capture the atmosphere that comes over in the 1929 early talkie.

More successful were Paramount's *California* with Ray Milland and Barbara Stanwyck plus stage Irishman Barry Fitzgerald, and Universal's *Canyon Passage*, another easygoing western with a nice cast: Dana Andrews, Brian Donlevy, Susan Hayward and Hoagy Carmichael singing his own songs.

Henry Fonda as Wyatt Earp in John Ford's first post-war western, My Darling Clementine, *20th Century–Fox.*

Selznick's 1946 production, Duel in the Sun, *with Jennifer Jones and Gregory Peck.*

Bad Bascomb was an MGM vehicle for Wallace Beery to play his rough, tough guy with the heart of gold. More credible was UA's *Abilene Town*, an old fashioned lawman versus cattlemen-homesteaders story starring Randolph Scott, Ann Dvorak and two young up-and-comers, Lloyd Bridges and Rhonda Fleming. A few other westerns were produced but none of note, apart from those at Republic where its A production had been taken over by director Joe Kane and in 1946 starred William Elliott, Wild Bill having been elevated to more gentlemanly status and bigger budget westerns.

Elliott's Red Ryder series concluded in early 1946 and Republic executives, especially boss Herbert Yates, had become impressed with the laconic cowboy. So they moved him out of B westerns and into their prestigious productions. Some say that Elliott did not want to go, others say the opposite. Whichever, as "William" he was starred in *In Old Sacramento*, a story by director Kane that had the ultimate in that Elliott is killed off at the end. Republic defects, including their now regular use of studio "exteriors" in their higher budgeted product, shone through this and later films, but Elliott proved a worthy A cowboy and follow-up for the year was *The Plainsman and the Lady*, big stuff (for Republic) of pony express riders and crooked politicians. Elliott was good even if he had to endure Vera Ralston as co-star. Interesting casting was provided by Donald Barry playing a snarling gunman who gets his comeuppance from Elliott. Wearing black and sneering becomingly, Barry proved an ideal bad guy. At the same time he made a guest appearance in Monte Hale's *Out California Way*, in the same outfit, as a hero.

Big news in the series world was the return of Gene Autry from service. Though he and Rogers got along fine off screen and there were no personal vendettas, it was a tricky situation for Republic. The studio stuck by its current cowboy king and continued to give Rogers more of everything. Gene's first pictures back were mildly entertaining affairs beginning with *Sioux City Sue* this year, while Rogers was in the big budget *Rainbow Over Texas* and *Under Nevada Skies*, the latter a particularly appealing film with a lighthearted climax as the Indians chase the baddies. Republic also gave Rogers a "special" for the year, the 79 minute *My Pal Trigger* with less music and much sentiment during which Rogers proved yet again that he really could act.

Bob Livingston drifted into secondary non-western roles at the studio, Don Barry also, and Republic was quite happy. They had Allan Lane, who had replaced Elliott, as Red Ryder. Lane was a more realistic Ryder and played the role with sincerity. Lane tried hard in everything he did, and his ambition to be the best put him off-side with many co-workers who took things more lightly. On screen, though, Lane delivered. Sunset Carson raced along the trail at breakneck speed in a series of action-all-the-way westerns like *Alias Billy the Kid*, *Rio Grande Raiders* and *Red River Renegades*, then, suddenly, was gone. Off screen young Carson had gone off the handle through drink and Herbert Yates first warned him — then fired him. Fans were astonished, not knowing the true story.

Republic's Roy Rogers "special" of 1946, My Pal Trigger, *with Roy taking on two bouncers in a night-club scene.*

Meanwhile Republic unveiled its Monte Hale series — in color. Magnacolor it was first called in *Home on the Range.* The untried Hale was given Adrian Booth, Bobby Blake, Bob Nolan and the Sons of the Pioneers to help him out first time up. *Home on the Range* was mild, as was *Man from Rainbow Valley,* in which only Booth was retained. For the final Hale entry of the year Republic changed its color process name to Trucolor and gave Monte an extra ten minutes in another story about film studios in action. *Out California Way* had a good story, an outstanding villain in John Dehner. Bobby Blake was back and Hale and Booth made a pleasant team. Add to that guest stars Roy Rogers and Trigger, Dale Evans, Allan Lane and Donald Barry, the music of Foy Willing and the Riders of the Purple Sage and the film was a sure-fire success. Hale himself, although nice enough, still failed to come across as a strong hero but the studio was pleased by *Out California Way* and continued Hale's series into 1947.

The only other color cowboy remained Eddie Dean at PRC. His second film, *Romance of the West,* looked pretty but was acted badly and Dean showed about as much emotion as a prairie cactus in scenes with a little boy shot by the baddies.

Emmett Lynn was Dean's sidekick at this stage. The follow up, *The Caravan Trail*, was better with Eddie singing "Wagon Wheels" in impressive fashion and, most of all, Al LaRue back in a secondary role, again as a black-clad gunman but allowed to remain upright at the close. Add Charlie King as LaRue's sidekick and Dean was outshone in about every department. *Colorado Serenade* was probably Dean's best, with nice songs and a fine performance from David Sharpe as a friendly gunman. In the fight scenes Sharpe absolutely dominated, leaving Dean looking foolish. Finally, *Wild West*, still in color and 73 minutes long, had LaRue back, with Lee Bennett forming a sort of trio as comic sidekick Roscoe Ates had replaced Lynn. Ates mugged his way through the rest of Dean's starring career.

A 1946 singing cowboy, Monte Hale, who, like Jack Randall, dropped the songs midway through his career.

Eddie then had a leading role in a country film, *Down Missouri Way*, playing a singing country bumpkin and, unfortunately, looking convincing. When he returned to westerns in *Driftin' River*, *Tumbleweed Trail* and *Stars Over Texas* the color had gone and Eddie rode in glorious black and white. A New York reviewer, trite though it may seem, was right in that "you could still see him." Don Miller in *Hollywood Corral* got it right when he pointed out the scene in a later Dean, *West to Glory*, in which Roscoe Ates and Dean change roles during a dream sequence, Ates being the hero and Dean the buffoon — "and the thing of it was, Ates looked better than Dean did."

During 1946 the unforeseeable happened. Buster Crabbe stopped making PRC westerns after 36 of them. Crabbe, as he told it later, got fed up with the penny pinching and walked out. As he also noted, PRC didn't miss a beat. They simply hired the man in black from Eddie Dean's pictures, Al LaRue, gave him a permanent whip, called him Lash LaRue and started off another series with Fuzzy St. John for 1947. LaRue had generated more fan mail than Dean, so it was a logical act.

Monogram seemed happy with its Johnny Mack Brown and Jimmy Wakely series and, having dropped Duncan Renaldo, continued the Cisco Kid series with Gilbert Roland in the role. *The Gay Cavalier*, *In Old Monterey* and *The Beauty and the Bandit* were made in 1946. Some Cisco Kid fans believe Roland to be the best of Kids, others differ. William Everson wrote that Roland was the best of the Kids while Jon Tuska said he was the worst. Biographer Francis M. Nevins (*The Films of the Cisco Kid*, 1998) sits on the fence.

There was trouble at the Monogram ranch, according to Jimmy Wakely, at that time between the champions of himself and Johnny Mack Brown. Wakely points the finger at Scott Dunlap for trying to downgrade his (Wakely's) image so that Dunlap's favorite (Brown) could prosper. Brown and Dunlap have never been available for comment so no more is known about that. Some of the songs did disappear from Jimmy's films after *Moon Over Montana*, *West of the Alamo*, *Song of the Sierras*, *Trail to Mexico* and *Rainbow Over the Rockies*. *Song of the Sierras* and *Rainbow Over the Rockies* were filmed at the same time, on location in the Rockies, one (*Song*) being released in 1946, the other in early 1947. After that Oliver Drake was replaced and the Wakely image made less fancy.

An even more radical change occurred in the Brown series. The first 1946 entry opened with Brown riding down the trail, singing. It was dubbed of course, and Monogram's (Dunlap's?) efforts to turn Johnny into a Jimmy came to nothing. The other departure was that Brown no longer played Nevada Jack, nor was Hatton in the role of Sandy Hopkins. Now their names changed from film to film. Possibly dubbing Brown in *Drifting Along* was Smith Ballew, briefly a singing cowboy at Fox in the '30s. Ballew also appeared as himself in *Under Arizona Skies* and sang a few numbers. Johnny's leading lady in *Drifting Along* (she was also in *Flame of the West* and *Crossed Trails*) was Lynne Carver, an interesting actress who had shown at Republic the capacity to play the sweet young heroine (in the Rogers *Sunset in the Desert*) and sharp-tongued, haughty villainess (in *Man from Cheyenne*). Johnny Mack Brown was increasingly showing his years, and Hatton plowed on. Brown still had six years of B westerns ahead of him.

Also in the longevity stakes was Charles Starrett at Columbia. As the Durango Kid he rode on through *The Fighting Frontiersman*, *Galloping Thunder*, *Frontier Gun Law*, *Land Rush*, *Two Fisted Stranger* and five other westerns, cheap but cheerful, for the year. With him rode Smiley Burnette, not everybody's favorite but a box office name on his own and, when he stuck to music and just a little foolery, not too bad. Columbia also continued its musical-comedy westerns with Ken Curtis, not really worthy of note. Columbia, in the coming year, had bigger fish to fry as it negotiated with a top cowboy about his future.

Finally for 1946 came the return of William Boyd to the screen in his own Hopalong Cassidy productions. *The Devil's Playground* and *Fool's Gold* compared favorably with the later United Artists titles and the new trio of Boyd, Andy Clyde and Rand Brooks as "Lucky" Jenkins appeared promising. Once again the Boyd-Cassidy laugh rang out from the screen and all seemed to be well in the world.

1 9 4 7

There's Room on the Prairie

"There's room on the prairie for both of us," Roy Rogers is alleged to have said about his rivalry with Gene Autry, but there wasn't room at Republic. After some lackluster films (the best being *Robin Hood of Texas*) Autry left the studio after much wrangling with Herbert Yates. Autry had made a good deal with Columbia. He would produce his own films for release through that studio. And they were to be in color, after the first 1947 title, *The Last Round-Up*. This first Columbia picture was well done, directed by John English, and showed a toned down Autry from this peak Republic days. It was Autry's own favorite.

Roy Rogers had a new director, William Witney. At first (*Roll on Texas Moon, Home in Oklahoma* and *Heldorado*, all 1946) the pictures remained much the same, but Witney wanted to change them and bring in more action. He gradually did. Color was introduced to the Rogers series in 1947 with *Apache Rose*, a pleasant but relatively mild feature. Next up, *Bells of San Angelo*, saw a new Rogers. Witney picked up the pace of the picture, songs were less and in one memorable scene Rogers is beaten up by David Sharpe and friends, emerging bloodied and bowed. Brutal action had come to the Rogers films courtesy of Witney. Along the way the Rogers "family" began to disintegrate. Gabby Hayes left to free-lance and, after *The Bells of San Angelo*, Dale Evans finally broke the yoke of B western "stardom" that had her billed lower than the horse and also left the series. Bob Nolan and The Sons of the Pioneers remained the link with the past endeavors. *Bells of San Angelo* was good but the next *Springtime in the Sierras* was even better, with rough and tumble action and a fascinating villainess in Stephanie Batchelor. Andy Devine was now comic sidekick, a

The first Gene Autry Columbia release, The Last Round-Up, *in 1947.*

passable substitute for Gabby. The last 1947 film, *On the Old Spanish Trail*, besides new leading lady Jane Frazee also featured Mexican singer Tito Guizar and Estelita Rodriguez and got a bit top heavy with songs again, but Charles McGraw and Fred Graham were great as heavies, Graham as a rather brain damaged ex-pug.

Republic also continued its Monte Hale color westerns, but Hale, though nice, failed to make a big impact. He had regular co-stars in Adrian Booth and Foy Willing and the Riders of the Purple Sage in *Last Frontier Uprising*, *Along the Oregon Trail* and *Under Colorado Skies*. The films were like Hale, pleasant. More action and drama was to be found in a new series starring Allan Lane, billed as "Rocky" Lane. Filmed in plain black and white and low budget, they benefited from literate scripts and the dedicated performances by Lane and his sidekick Eddy Walter, a less comic and more character-acting screen partner. *The Wild Frontier* (in which Jack Holt had a major role) and *Bandits of Dark Canyon* got the series off to an exciting start.

William Elliott's two larger scale westerns at Republic for the year were *Wyoming* and *The Fabulous Texan.* Co-starring John Carroll, who rather overshadowed Elliott, *The Fabulous Texan* is good but *Wyoming*, with Elliott aging over the years very effectively, was better. Carroll was again in *Wyoming*, but Elliott dominated the film. The killing off of George Hayes was a surprise but an essential plot motivation. Drawbacks to *Wyoming* included the casting of Vera Ralston as both mother and daughter but the film survives that calamity. Republic also filmed Nelson Eddy, of all people, riding along "singin' a song" in *Northwest Outpost*, directed by Alan Dwan, an interesting if unintentionally amusing picture. John Wayne, acting as producer, made *Angel and the Badman*, which turned out to be one of the best westerns of the year and probably the best non–John Ford one made by Wayne in the '40s. James Edward Grant, normally a writer, directed obviously with Ford in mind, but if one thing is lacking it is that extra touch that the likes of Ford would have given it. The story, of a gunfighter redeemed by a Quaker girl, sounds trite but is not allowed to sink toward pathos by the good work of Wayne, Gail Russell and Harry Carey in one of his last films.

Republic thus had a good year with westerns, as did Randolph Scott, who made *The Gunfighters* at Columbia and *Trail Street* at RKO, the latter directed by Ray Enright and the best of the two. Robert Ryan was in the cast as were former B heroine Anne Jeffreys and George Hayes, who had left Republic.

Joel McCrea was also heading west again after the failed *Virginian* the previous year. This time it was *Ramrod* at United Artists, directed by André De Toth and produced by Harry Sherman, the first of two outstanding westerns Sherman was involved with before his death. *Ramrod* is a stark, violent picture of the frontier, grim and unrelenting, about power games and twisted loyalties, and McCrea is perfect as the "ramrod" who strides stoically through it all, doing "what a man should do." A great performance by Veronica Lake as the dominant female lead is a perfect foil for the likable McCrea, and Preston Foster, Don DeFore, Charles Ruggles. Arleen Whelan and Donald Crisp are excellent, Crisp especially as the aging but dutiful sheriff, straight-backed and honest, who gets brutally murdered.

A similar dark hued western (a "film noir," it has been termed) was Raoul Walsh's *Pursued*, in which a bewildered but valiant Robert Mitchum struggles with his past and the dark secrets it holds. A compelling 100 minutes long, *Pursued* is a surprise from a director such as Walsh, who normally produced good but straightforward westerns. Other efforts at large scale westerns were not so successful, although, as usual, Cecil B. DeMille made money from his extravagant *Unconquered*, a dull affair starring Gary Cooper and Paulette Goddard. *Sea of Grass* at MGM was made as a vehicle for Spencer Tracy and Katharine Hepburn and was another dull epic. Michael Pitts calls it ponderous.

Westerns like *The Michigan Kid* and *The Vigilantes Return* at Universal, both with Jon Hall, were strictly routine affairs, as was the Raoul Walsh *Cheyenne* at Warners, the complete opposite to his excellent *Pursued* and featuring Dennis Morgan.

From United Artists in 1947 came Ramrod, *directed by André De Toth and featuring, in this scene, Don DeFore and Joel McCrea.*

Good points about *Cheyenne* were young Arthur Kennedy in an early role and Bob Steele and Tom Tyler, both former Mesquiteer partners, in bit parts.

The Prairie was an independent production released through Screen Guild of a James Fenimore Cooper frontier tale. A cast of mainly unknowns (the Indians were better known, being Chief Thundercloud, Chief Yowlachie and Jay Silverheels, than the leading players) with little budget was unable to come up with a quality production.

Of more interest was the return of Tim Holt to RKO. Besides appearing in Ford's *My Darling Clementine*, Holt also had a major role in *The Treasure of the Sierra Madre*. Release of the latter was held up till 1948 for some reason and Holt went back to sign a new contract at RKO to make westerns. Whether the critical acclaim he later received for *Sierra Madre* would have changed his thoughts is unknown. RKO set him off in 1947 with some Zane Grey stories, *Under the Tonto Rim* and *Wild Horse Mesa*. Notable was the pairing of Holt with a new sidekick, handsome Richard Martin, playing a slightly comic Mexican-Irish-American named Chito Rafferty. This pair remained together till the end of Holt's B western career.

Johnny Mack Brown at Monogram and Charles Starrett at Columbia remained two (now) old stagers who continued to be popular, even though the westerns they were making were cheap and sometimes shoddy with that cheapness. Brown's 1947 work began with a more literate than usual *Raiders of the South*, with the extra benefit of Evelyn Brent, still an attractive lady, playing a strong role. The rest of Brown's 1947 output was very routine but Johnny always did his best, looking committed in the fight scenes and still a fine rider. Starrett was playing the Durango Kid and enjoying the fact that a double could be used for most scenes behind the mask, leaving Starrett a minimal amount of work for himself. This is not meant to belittle Charles Starrett, who kept himself fit and athletic, right to the very end. More and more Columbia started using stock footage in these films. Famous is *Last Days of Boot Hill* in which about 20 minutes of new material was identified by Don Miller. Smiley Burnette filled up much of what was left with his musical and comic items. Columbia must have been making a suitable profit on the films because it kept churning them out. Monogram also, with both the Brown and Jimmy Wakely series. Wakely's 1947 films were directed by Thomas Carr, Ford Beebe and Howard Bretherton and contained more action, less music. Comic sidekick Lasses White was dropped for the last 1947 entry, replaced by Dub "Cannonball" Taylor, a sidekick liked by some, hated by many. Efforts to make Wakely an action cowboy were only mildly successful; Jimmy was just not a good horseman or screen fighter. He still remained best when being amiable and singing his songs.

Monogram brought its Cisco Kid series to a close in 1947. In his interpretation of the role, Gilbert Roland probably appealed more to adults than to children, but production otherwise was geared to the juvenile market. Neither one thing nor the other, the Cisco Kid films failed to make much of a mark. Roland's last film in the series was *King of the Bandits*, with Chris-Pin Martin as Pancho.

At PRC Eddie Dean in black and white made five 1947 westerns. *Shadow Valley* featured Jennifer Holt, daughter of Jack and a hard-working B heroine, as well as singing group Andy Parker and the Plainsmen. Ray Taylor was directing in his straightforward manner and the best part of any Dean feature remained Eddie's singing. Although PRC was struggling with financial problems, it also began a new series with Al LaRue, who had proved so popular in the Dean films. Billed as "Lash" LaRue and playing U.S. Marshal Cheyenne Davis, he gained a following in his eight 1947 westerns. Director Taylor worked overtime, doing these as well as Dean's, but the interest in the films was in LaRue, a unique personality who improved his western skills as he went along and, as Don Miller notes, "operated a mean, cracking whip." The whip, the two guns, the black outfit (including his horse)—all these gimmicks as well as LaRue's, well, slightly different personality brought out an interest in the cowboy that shimmered for years and would show many years later in his popularity at western conventions. *Law of the Lash* began the series nicely and *Cheyenne Takes Over* concluded it.

PRC's singing cowboy Eddie Dean with sidekick Roscoe Ates.

And Hopalong Cassidy? Boyd was distributing through United Artists but he had to find the money for the pictures. It soon became obvious in 1947 that most of that had been spent on the first two films. *Unexpected Guests*, *The Marauders*, *Dangerous Venture* and *Hoppy's Holiday* became increasingly pedestrian, sets were minimal and casts limited. Boyd, Clyde and Brooks remained an entertaining trio but it was only the loyalty of fans that kept things going. Boyd retained his position of number three cowboy on the box office listing but only through nostalgia rather than superior current work.

The 1947 top ten cowboy listing read: (1) Roy Rogers, (2) Gene Autry, (3) William Boyd, (4) Bill Elliott, (5) Gabby Hayes, (6) Charles Starrett, (7) Smiley Burnette, (8) Johnny Mack Brown, (9) Dale Evans, and (10) Eddie Dean.

1948

They Passed This Way

The year 1948 was a good one for western films. The much acclaimed *Red River* seemed the star of the show, hailed upon release as one of the great epics and overshadowing John Ford's film about the U.S. Cavalry, *Fort Apache*. As the years passed by, however, *Fort Apache* came to be seen as the classic it is, and *Red River* became one of those movies rarely recalled, apart from in reference to John Wayne's career. This is unfair to Howard Hawks' film which, while not in retrospect one of the very greatest westerns, is still the definitive cattle drive story and would have perhaps attained the top level of western classics had it not been for the controversial ending that Hawks provided. This ending spoiled the whole atmosphere of the film up to then, which was hard, gritty and mean. In other words, realistic. The sudden happy ending seemed false and still does. Nevertheless, the film provided a major boost for John Wayne in his acting as an older man that surprised everybody by its depth. Even Wayne's mentor, John Ford, was surprised. He said to Hawks, "I didn't know that big sonofabitch could act!" and spoke for many. The unlikely casting of Montgomery Clift proved a success and Walter Brennan played another garrulous old timer. Joanne Dru also shone in her pivotal role. *Red River* is worth catching up with if you have not seen it. Ignore the later TV inspired remake, as all remakes should be — ignored.

Fort Apache convinced the acidic critics that John Ford was a spent force and most of them found the film uninspiring. To a man (and woman) they missed the marvelous nuances that Ford conveyed in a complex story which they, the critics, took to be simple. As well as being complex, *Fort Apache* was also lyrical in its depiction of a dusty but noble cavalry and the mixture of men within. Sentiment,

John Wayne in his role as Dunson in Red River, 1948, directed by Howard Hawks and released by United Artists.

rough humor and good old-fashioned action were also present in what is now rightly seen as an outstanding western film. Henry Fonda, playing an egotistical glory hunting colonel dominates the film, with John Wayne stolid as his honest captain. Shirley Temple seems a little out of place as the colonel's daughter, the only glaring fault, but director Ford had a sentimental fondness for her. John Agar, then Temple's husband, made a forthright screen debut and the rough and ready army men portrayed by Victor McLaglen, Dick Foran, Pedro Armendariz and Jack Pennick are little more than "comic" characters, but memorably so. Western star George O'Brien returns to the screen after his war service, working for his old boss, Ford, Archie Stout provides the cinematography that highlights Monument Valley and Richard Hageman again, as in *Stagecoach*, provides a score rich with American folk tunes. And as if *Red River* and *Fort Apache* were not enough, the year also produced other westerns of near-classic stature.

To further exasperate the "serious" critics, director Ford also made *Three Godfathers*, a remake of the oft-filmed Peter B. Kyne story. Now I know I just criticized "remakes," but I meant modern (post 1962) remakes. Ford's *Three Godfathers* would be the last interpretation of the classic sentimental tale that would be out of place in any modern scenario. The film is not a "classic," it is too much of a personal production for that. The moralistic and sentimental strains are pushed a bit far in a story about a baby, three outlaws and religion. The religious aspect was especially close to director Ford's heart — he had recently made the supremely artistic but box-office flop *The Fugitive* based on Graham Greene's Catholic tale. For most audiences it was a little bit too cloying, but *Three Godfathers* did have lovely photography, many typically evocative Fordian scenes and good performances from John Wayne, Pedro Armendariz, Harry Carey, Jr., and Ward Bond. Ford dedicated the film to the late Harry Carey, "Bright Star of the Early Western Sky."

Released by RKO in 1948, John Ford's Fort Apache *featured* (left to right): *Grant Withers, Victor McLaglen, John Wayne, Henry Fonda, George O'Brien, Miquek Unchan and Pedro Armendariz.*

Blood on the Moon, directed by Robert Wise, was an intelligent, broody western starring the broody (and terrifically effective) Robert Mitchum. Marvelous atmosphere was created as Mitchum rides into the film and also the early town scenes, but the film is uneven, perhaps due to too many studio "exteriors," and does not quite keep its early promise. It is still a very good western and Mitchum is marvelous in his sleepy-eyed way.

The other outstanding western of the year was not as great as *Fort Apache*, or *Red River*, but in an odd way to this writer it is the most memorable film of the year. *Four Faces West* was produced by Harry Sherman and starred Joel McCrea. It was based on the Eugene Manlove Rhodes story *Paso Por Aqui* (*They Passed This Way*). Just for once the British distributors got it right; they changed the name to *They Passed This Way*, more suitable than *Four Faces West*. McCrea is perfect for the role of the honest man who makes a mistake and redeems himself for the love of (his off screen wife) Frances Dee, and Charles Bickford is the understanding lawman who chases him. It is a slow moving, gentle, picturesque western that did not appeal to the action fans but Sherman could be proud of it. It was far softer than the original story, in which the man is an out-and-out killer who surprisingly does "what a man should do" when the situation arises, but for his pains, still gets hunted down and shot dead by the lawman. As the law officer says, standing over the outlaw's body, "He was a murdering, thieving son-of-a-bitch — but he was a man!" The film's hero is far more gentle and righteous, but in McCrea's hands the role never becomes sanctimonious. Alfred Green directed.

Much tougher and more stark was William Wellman's best western, *Yellow Sky*, starring Gregory Peck and a sneering Richard Widmark. The tale of a gang of bank robbers who escape across the desert and end up in a ghost town with an old man and a girl is beautifully photographed and well acted. Anne Baxter plays the girl, whose influence turns Peck, the leader of the gang, to change his ways as the group squabbles over the old man's gold mine. As with most of these 1948 westerns, it was shot in black and white and suited to that, with its brooding desert settings and dusty towns. Of these five westerns only *Three Godfathers* was in color.

Other westerns for the year starred some unlikely western figures. For example, the gangster anti-hero of *This Gun for Hire*, Alan Ladd, was in *Whispering Smith* and at MGM Frank Sinatra made what would be one of a few excursions into the territory with *The Kissing Bandit*. Then, as later, Sinatra was totally out of place in the western. At RKO Dick Powell made a tough hero in *Stations West* and at Paramount top comedian Bob Hope rode west in *Paleface* with Jane Russell, a funny picture that would have an even funnier sequel. Good fun was had with Dan Duryea, a fine talent, in Universal's *Black Bart* directed by old Republic master George Sherman, and director Phil Karlson made two cheap but enjoyable westerns in *Adventures in Silverado* (starring William Bishop) and *Thunderhoof* (starring Preston Foster), both Columbia releases. At Fox, Victor Mature, after his venture as Doc Holliday in Ford's *My Darling Clementine* two years previous, made a passable star in *Fury at Furnace Creek*. More ambitious, but lacking substance, was Henry Levin's Columbia *Man from Colorado*. Glenn Ford, William Holden and Ellen Drew headed a talented cast with Ford impressive as the pyschopath cavalryman-judge.

Randolph Scott had a good year. *Albuquerque* and *Return of the Badman* were just average, if always enjoyable, and both were directed by Ray Enright who also directed *Coroner Creek*, a superior western notable for its revenge plot with Scott's role, as the avenger, very similar to his characterization some years later for Budd Boetticher. It was certainly Scott's best work since *Western Union* and a standout movie in a year of standout westerns.

Another interesting aspect of the year was the breakthrough into solid western stardom by former B player Rod Cameron, who made *The Plunderers* for Republic during the year and *Panhandle*, a sepia work directed by Lesley Selander for Allied Artists and a fine effort from the basically B director. *Panhandle* received good notices for its realism, unusual for a minor western. Cameron looked fair to become another Scott or McCrea — but never quite made it.

One other big western was made, directed by veteran Raoul Walsh, but it was not one of his best. *Silver River* had action and sprawl but seemed routine in the end, notwithstanding a good performance by Errol Flynn in a not too sympathetic part. His leading lady, Ann Sheridan, had been around in A and B features for years before slowly working her way to stardom.

In a year of so many good westerns the series version appears to have been pushed to the background. It was not so, but it was a fact that series westerns were now a little bit less important than they had been. They faced competition from the minor A version, which many of the above mentioned were. Notably from B ranks there was Bill Elliott, now the sober "William," appearing in A features at Republic. He made two during 1948, *The Gallant Legion* and *In Old Los Angeles*, both entertaining with fine casts and Elliott coming very much to grips with his more adult oriented cowboy style. And of the pure B western cowboys, only Rogers and Autry (and perhaps a fading Boyd as Cassidy) retained a big adult following, unlike the days of Mix, Jones, Gibson and Maynard.

Rogers, as King of the Cowboys at Republic, made fewer features, mainly because they were shot in color and took longer to produce. His 1948 output included his last appearances with the Sons of the Pioneers, whom Republic replaced with the cheaper Riders of the Purple Sage, no longer required for Monte Hale features because Hale had dropped almost all the music from his westerns, doing only the odd song, or part of a song, during the action. The musical content of the Rogers films, after the song-laden *On the Old Spanish Trail* and *Gay Ranchero*, also were cut back, as were running times from around 75 minutes to 70, then 68. But the Rogers westerns, directed by William Witney, were good — standouts for the year being *Under California Stars*, *Night Time in Nevada*, *Grand Canyon Trail* and especially *Eyes of Texas*, with the athletic Rogers showing his action credentials. Leading ladies Jane Frazee and Lynne Roberts (in *Eyes of Texas*) stood in for Dale Evans very well and in Rogers' last 1948 entry, *The Far Frontier*, a young Gail Davis was featured. A highlight of the year for Rogers and Pioneer fans was their appearance for Walt Disney in the full-length *Melody Time*, both on screen and telling the tale of "Pecos Bill." The lovely song "Blue Shadows on the Trail" proved a popular recording for the team, both Rogers and the group recording for RCA at that time.

Rival Gene Autry released just the one film in 1948, the color *Strawberry Roan*. This ambitious B western was meant as an answer to Republic's *My Pal Trigger* and captured some of the charm of that "special" horse story. Although the color and fine backgrounds gave it advantage, however, it never quite emulated the Rogers feature with Gene not as comfortable as Roy in the sentimental dramatic moments. It is a popular choice, though, of Gene Autry fans as one of his best pictures. After 1948 Autry expanded his program and features became more frequent.

Hopalong Cassidy made his last eight features in 1948, features sadly lacking the style and content of yesteryear. From *Sinister Conflict* to *Strange Gamble* the films were drab and slow and obviously suffering from budget restrictions. Hoppy remained

Johnny Mack Brown on horse Rebel, at Monogram, 1948.

popular and William Boyd retired from the screen with further aspirations, looking in the direction of television. He had bought up the rights to all his early pictures and now prepared to release them for small screen showing.

This year saw the "*finis*" for PRC studio. The last Eddie Dean features, cheap black and white affairs highlighted only by Dean's fine singing voice, were released through Eagle-Lion. *Check Your Guns* and *Shadow Valley* were diverting but *Prairie Outlaws* turned out to be just a trimmed down version of *Wild West!* with *The Tioga Kid.*

At Monogram nothing much had changed apart from Johnny Mack Brown's steadily expanding waistline. Brown still countered this by being tough in action and friendly of smile in pictures like *Crossed Trails* and *Triggerman*, the ever trusty Ray Hatton by his side. In *Sheriff of Medicine Bow* Max Terhune joined the cast but contributed little. During the year the star began to play himself and Ray Hatton played a variety of roles rather than Sandy Hopkins. After *Hidden Danger*, their last 1948 release, Brown and Hatton parted company after a long ride together, as Hatton went free-lancing.

Monogram's other cowboy, Jimmy Wakely, rode along being as nice as ever, and as mild. His features now had fewer songs and more action, and Jimmy wore plain Levi's and shirt. *Silver Trails* was pleasant and introduced a young cowboy who handled a whip and was billed as "Whip Wilson." Wilson was a personal "discovery" of producer Scotty Dunlap and was to be given his own series. He also sang, rarely, in a slightly unsteady baritone, but Jimmy remained the singing cowboy for Monogram — at least for a while yet.

Al "Lash" LaRue, the other whip waver, had signed for independent Western Adventure Productions, released by Screen Guild under producer Ron Ormond. First releases *Dead Man's Gold* and *Frontier Revenge* in 1948 were surprisingly good, with LaRue in his black, with two guns and a whip bringing a unique personality to the screen. Some people liked him, some didn't.

Well liked was veteran Charles Starrett at Columbia, now belting out Durango Kid westerns with partner Smiley Burnette. The pair were popular, notwithstanding that the Durango Kid westerns by then had become very cheap and trite. Ray Nazarro directed most of them, at breakneck speed. *Blazing Across the Pecos, West of Sonora, Quick on the Trigger* ... they were all much the same but that did not worry the mainly youthful audience who loved the masked man, Durango, and respected the smiling "Steve," the character Starrett normally played.

At RKO Tim Holt was dependable and productions were superior, especially *The Arizona Ranger* and *Indian Agent*. Richard Martin was his regular sidekick as "Chico," a departure from the usual bewhiskered or tubby sidekick, and casts included Noah Beery, Jr., Nan Leslie, Richard Powers (Tom Keene) and father Jack. Tim, honest and tougher than in pre-war films, never quite made the top as a cowboy star, perhaps lacking a little in charisma, but his westerns, right to the end, were classy B

Charles Starrett, a veteran by 1948.

features. In the same year Holt played an important role in director John Huston's *The Treasure of the Sierra Madre* starring Humphrey Bogart, once more exhibiting his acting talent. Critics were amazed that he chose to stay in B grade westerns. As to whether *Treasure* is a western, well, some say yes and some say no. I would classify it more as an action drama, and so do not add more about it here — but it is an outstanding film.

Republic remained the major producer of B westerns during the year with not only their Roy Rogers series but also the action-packed Allan "Rocky" Lane series and the quieter but likable Monte Hale group. Hale, after *Timber Trail*, had lost his color and his singing group, and before that his leading lady, Adrian Booth, but the simpler, starker black and white westerns he made would prove more suitable for his talents. Rocky Lane's westerns were fast, cheap and literate, their scripts and players rising above the low budgets, none more so than Lane himself. Among his 1948 releases *The Bold Frontiersman*, *Marshal of Amarillo*, *Desperadoes of Dodge City* and *Sundown in Santa Fe* stood out.

Finally for 1948, erstwhile Republic cowboy Sunset Carson, still trying to lick his drinking habits, started an independent series released through Astor just as another ex–Republic man, Don Barry, did the same at Lippert. Barry's westerns were cheap but rugged with the star still an attraction but the Carson ones were awful. Both of these series were mainly released in 1949–50, along with another cheap attempt at a revival for ex–Cassidy pals Russell Hayden and Jimmy Ellison. More on all those in the next chapter.

1949

"It Was All Over—but They Forgot to Tell Me"

Rex Allen, a cowboy singer from Arizona with a great voice, was signed up by Republic in 1949 to appear in musical B westerns. In later years Allen liked to wryly comment, "It was all over — but they forgot to tell me," meaning that as he came in B westerns were on the way out. Well, not exactly, but the writing was on the wall. There were three main reasons. One was that cheap westerns were no longer that cheap to make, rising production costs meant less and less profit, and B westerns were all about a dependable profit margin. Second, whereas the B cowboys of the '30s made westerns with adults also in mind, the current group was more and more child oriented, with their wholesome approach and "ten commandment" lessons for youngsters. The top cowboys were hugely popular but the adult following that Jones, Gibson, and even Boyd in his early days, had catered to was gone. Finally, and most damaging, was the onslaught of television. *The Lone Ranger* began on TV in 1949 to be followed by Hopalong Cassidy, the Cisco Kid and later Autry and Rogers themselves. The early TV westerns were cheap and shoddy, especially the *Lone Ranger* production values, but kids could stay home and watch them in their own living rooms, and in those days people watched most anything on television, to the horror of the studios that feared the worst.

With PRC gone Monogram and Republic were the only B film studios left and of the major film makers only RKO, with its Tim Holt group, and Columbia continued to make series westerns. With the Durango Kid still popular Columbia saw no reason to cease production and Gene Autry had a releasing arrangement with that studio. Monogram, as with Republic, even began a new series with Whip Wilson, as if to certify its confidence in the genre. However, at the close of the year the studio pulled the plug on the Jimmy Wakely series. Jimmy's last films were standard Monogram oaters, with sometimes only two songs, a come-down for a player whose main aptitude was his singing. Johnny Mack Brown carried on, making five westerns all with Max Terhune playing his character "Alibi." Brown's best effort of the year was a supporting role in the good Rod Cameron vehicle *Stampede*, directed by Selander and distributed by Blake Edwards and Allied Artists. New cowboy Whip Wilson debuted in *Crashing Thru*, a neat enough little B western with Andy Clyde, ex–Hopalong Cassidy co-star, joining him. Wilson was not handsome, more the rugged type. Producer Dunlap believed he had a likeness to Buck Jones, Dunlap's former friend and business associate. But he couldn't act like Jones and was relatively colorless. As one reviewer said, his whip had more personality than he did, which is a bit harsh, although later recollections from co-stars indicated Wilson wasn't very good with the whip at all.

Along with independent producers who made Sunset Carson (awful) and Don Barry (passable) westerns, United Artists got into the action in 1949 with four Cisco Kid adventures, all starring Duncan Renaldo with Leo Carrillo as Pancho. These were fair, with *Satin's Cradle* the best title, but Renaldo had thoughts in another direction and would soon begin filming for television release.

Ken Curtis, who had made some pseudo–singing westerns at Columbia, made two films for Astor release, *Stallion Canyon* and *Riders of the Pony Express*. He looked capable as an action star and had a fine singing voice, but Curtis had joined the Sons of the Pioneers group and his future lay there, and with his father-in-law, director John Ford.

Columbia's Durango Kid westerns picked up in 1949 after a bad spell of shoddiness. New director Fred Sears helped and films such as *Desert Vigilante*, *Lightning Guns* and *Across the Badlands*, though feeling the budget pinch, used less stock footage as well as utilizing a new player in one Jock, Jack, Jocko (he used all three) Mahoney, who not only doubled Starrett but played ever increasingly important roles in the films. Charles Starrett, still slim and athletic, seemed to be enjoying himself and Smiley Burnette had a following, and was not as bad as may seem when kept under tight rein.

Gene Autry's schedule expanded with release of the color *The Big Sombrero*, one of his best films mixing action, drama and song. But Autry had decided color was too expensive and would not use it again. His other 1949 releases were in black and white but still superior series westerns—*Loaded Pistols*, *Riders of the Whistling Pines*, *Rim of the Canyon*, *The Cowboy and the Indians* and *Riders in the Sky*, the last name using the big hit tune written by Stan Jones. John English was Autry's director and running times were around 70 minutes. A new, dusty and action-packed Autry was

New Monogram cowboy in 1949, Whip Wilson.

being revealed with songs gradually cut back. Not everybody thought it was a good thing, some believing that Gene was out of place in the "real" West, the only discordant feature in the group of intelligent films.

At Republic Roy Rogers kept the "fantasy" factor going in that his westerns were modern in period, with cars and trucks and missiles. They did provide blazing action thanks to director Witney, they were still in color and songs were, on average, three. This left a lot of the 67 minutes for action and plot, and the plots were good too with Roy battling some really nasty baddies. *Susanna Pass*, *Down Dakota Way* and *The Golden Stallion* (the last having some fine horse action and showing Trigger off magnificently in color) also heralded the return to the screen of wife Dale Evans. This was in answer to huge demand, but, as with the Autry question, some raised the query as to a wife appearing as "romantic" lead to her husband. Although, it is true, romance in B westerns was very limited by then, they had a point. Evans was also a different personality from the one who had captivated audiences in 1944–47, more maternal and less sexy, in keeping with her new found religious attitude.

With Rocky Lane and Monte Hale in full production, and newcomer Rex Allen making his first film, *The Arizona Cowboy*, Republic was well in command of the B western field. Allen's debut was not particularly good. The film was rather drab and Allen's fine voice and genuine action ability not fully utilized. But much better would come from the Arizona cowboy in the future. Monte Hale made a group of quietly enjoyable westerns, with *Outcasts of the Trail*, which featured the sparkling Jeff Donnell as leading lady, as the best. Hale failed to make a big "splash" at the time but in retrospect his films look good and Hale himself was a pleasant personality. Perhaps he was just not imposing enough. Rocky Lane, on the other hand, was imposing both on and off the screen. His co-workers found him hard to get along with but his westerns, standard in style, all were exciting and interesting with good scripts and Lane an impressive star. *Sheriff of Wichita*, *Death Valley Gunfighter* and *Powder River Rustlers* were very good, but they all were. The strange thing was that Lane never made it into the top ten at that stage, which is hard to understand now.

Tim Holt did make it, at number four, not surprising considering the quality of his RKO westerns. There was a certain sameness about them, but locations and stories were superior and Holt was one of the few current cowboy players who appealed to adults. Best of the bunch for '49 were *The Stagecoach Kid* (done in tongue-in-cheek fashion with Jeff Donnell outstanding), *Brothers in the Saddle*, *Rustlers* and *Riders of the Range*.

The last of the 1949 cowboys, but by no means the least, was Lash LaRue. Ron Ormond's Western Adventure releases did not have the distribution power of the studios, which may account for LaRue being outside the top ten cowboy stars too, but those who did like him found him fascinating. *Outlaw Country* was the best of his 1949 films and that ran 71 minutes and never got dull. Unfortunately others in the series contained more and more stock footage from previous LaRues. Still, to his growing number of fans, even 30 minutes of "new" LaRue was satisfying.

For the record, the top ten money making cowboy stars of 1949, in order, were: Roy Rogers, Gene Autry, Gabby Hayes, Tim Holt, Bill Elliott, Charles Starrett, William Boyd, Johnny Mack Brown, Smiley Burnette and Andy Devine. Considering that Hayes, Boyd and Devine were no longer involved with B westerns, the list is

Action ace Allan "Rocky" Lane at his peak in 1949.

a bit odd and hard on cowboys like Lane and LaRue. The only sure thing about the list over the years was that Rogers and Autry were way ahead of the others—their leadership was never disputed.

Bill Elliott is on the above list, though at Republic his films were A productions, note B. Elliott made two in 1949, *The Last Bandit* and *Hellfire*. *The Last Bandit*, directed by Joe Kane, was good and Elliott was backed by a cast of Andy Devine, Adrian Booth, Jack Holt, Forrest Tucker and Grant Withers, but *Hellfire* was special. Mainly studio bound and directed by R. G. Springsteen, *Hellfire* was a direct throwback to the days of William S. Hart with its story of sin and redemption. Elliott was outstanding as the gunman turned preacher and he was well supported by Marie Windsor, Forrest Tucker and Jim Davis. Both of Elliott's 1949 films were shot in Trucolor and *Hellfire* was a personal project of Elliott's, with the McGowan brothers. It must rank as one of Elliott's best efforts. At the time there were murmurings that Bill might play Bill Hart in his life story. It never came to pass but of all the cowboy players, or non-cowboy players who might have been considered, Bill Elliott was probably the pick.

The major western effort of the year came from John Ford, now making westerns on a regular basis. His *She Wore a Yellow Ribbon* is a work of art, beautifully filmed (Winston C. Hoch won an academy award for it) in color and a leisurely sentimental tale of the U.S. Cavalry and, most of all, renowned for one retiring captain played brilliantly by John Wayne. Playing a man much older than himself, Wayne proved once and for all his acting ability, although that acting ability never seemed to flourish quite as well under directors other than Ford or Howard Hawks. Young wrangler Ben Johnson was an up-and-comer after this film and old-time George O'Brien had a sympathetic role as the fort commander. Joanne Dru sparkled and John Agar and Harry Carey, Jr., bristled as the young officers. Ford regulars Victor McLaglen, Mildred Natwick, Arthur Shields, brother Francis Ford and numerous familiar faces gave the film that comfortable Fordian look. Over the years time cannot dim the charm of Nathan Brittles talking to the graves of his wife and family or the genuine sentiment contained in the scene where the troop present their retiring captain with a gold watch. It is a great western.

After that, 1949 contained surprisingly few good major westerns. Raoul Walsh made *Colorado Territory* with Joel McCrea and Virginia Mayo. It was a western remake of *High Sierra*, a '30s Humphrey Bogart thriller. The plot translated well enough into a western that was stark and brutal, with a violent, sad ending. It was not universally popular. For McCrea, a more traditional role was *South of St. Louis* from Warner Bros. and directed by Ray Enright, which was fun but fairly ordinary. Randolph Scott was busy with *Canadian Pacific*, *The Walking Hills*, *The Doolins of Oklahoma* and *Fighting Man of the Plains*—all average. *The Walking Hills* was contemporary and directed by John Sturges, probably the best of Scott's 1949 work.

The 1936 *Texas Rangers* was remade but it was a lackluster production called *Streets of Laredo*. William Holden once again proved inadequate as a western lead.

John Wayne in Monument Valley for Ford's 1949 She Wore a Yellow Ribbon, *a RKO release. Frank McGrath on left.*

Paramount's 1949 Streets of Laredo, *with stars William Bendix and William Holden.*

Only the ending was impressive in this Lesley Fenton directed film. *The Younger Brothers* from Warners continued a trend of highlighting bad men, Wayne Morris being the lead in a low key production. *Bad Men of Tombstone* furthered the trend, with Barry Sullivan an interesting star. He would make several more westerns and, though never reaching the heights of stardom, was a good actor. More bad men flourished in Universal's *Calamity Jane* and *Sam Bass*, historically inept but colorful with the beautiful Yvonne De Carlo and the rather less beautiful Howard Duff. John Wayne made a routine frontier tale for Republic, *The Fighting Kentuckian*, interesting in that Oliver Hardy played Wayne's comic sidekick in a rare moment without Stan Laurel. *Massacre River* starred two young hopefuls, Guy Madison and Rory Calhoun, and Samuel Fuller, a controversial director who made his debut with *I Shot Jesse James*, a minor affair starring John Ireland. *Roughshod* was a one-off minor western from RKO with an interesting cast including John Ireland, Robert Sterling, Claude Jarman, Jr., Jeff Donnell and Gloria Grahame. Mark Robson directed. All of these westerns were either mildly or generally entertaining but none reached any great heights. One must also include *Lust for Gold*, which was about the famous Lost Dutchman Gold-mine and starred Glenn Ford and Ida Lupino, a semi-western that covered familiar ground.

One other B group of westerns produced in 1949 went very much unnoticed. Eagle-Lion filmed a color group of Red Ryder films starring Jim Bannon as Red. Bannon actually looked more like the comic character than any of the other cowboys who had played him — but the films were not good and made no impact. Perhaps they symbolized the fate of B westerns in 1949 — it was over, but nobody had been told yet.

1950

Classic Westerns

After the slim pickings of 1949, 1950 burst forth with four truly classic western films plus other very interesting ones. The beginning of the new decade signaled a new outburst of creativity from both old and new film creators. At the same time, the B or series western began its swift 1950s ride to oblivion. Monte Hale, after a solid and entertaining stay at Republic, was first to go, to be followed over the next few years by a veritable stampede. At the close of 1950 Roy Rogers, Gene Autry, Rex Allen, Johnny Mack Brown, Charles Starrett, Tim Holt, Rocky Lane, Whip Wilson and Lash LaRue were still making westerns. Kirby Grant, ex–singing cowboy at Universal, began a new Monogram series as a Mountie with dog (Chinook). Don Barry concluded his Lippert work and finished his starring days, apart from one energetic but uninspiring effort in 1954. Two former Cassidy saddle pals, Russell Hayden and Jimmy Ellison, made a series of eight films for release by Lippert. The films contained the same cast, basically the same story and were all filmed in a month in one of the cheapest efforts yet in poverty row production. Television was beaming into most American homes and circling the globe. With it rode the Lone Ranger, Hopalong Cassidy, the Cisco Kid, Wild Bill Hickok (Guy Madison), Kit Carson (Bill Williams) and, in 1950, Gene Autry. Autry's rival, Roy Rogers, wished to get into the act too but his studio, Republic, forbade it. Newcomer Rex Allen had to sign a contract that specifically forbade him to appear on television. However, at the same time, Republic sold its own old movies to the small screen, causing Autry and Rogers to fight the company in court over this. Rightly, the two cowboys saw that whatever they could produce for a half hour TV series could not compare with the Republic production

169

values of former years. It was a battle that would drag on for years and finally be won by the studio, opening the way for hundreds of B westerns to flood the TV screens. Many retired cowboy stars, who received nothing from this, felt bitter, especially since they, in most cases, could not make it to the small screen. Even a popular cowboy like Bill Elliott who tried a sample 30 minute effort on sponsors was turned down. Non-singing cowboys especially found it hard going after their series came to a halt. The singers could front rodeos and shows as well as concentrate on their records and radio. The non-singers, or "action" cowboys, found employment hard to come by. Many ended up playing small roles in TV series. Many of course were near the end of their careers anyway and quietly retired. This was all coming in the next few years. In 1950 the writing may have been on the wall, but many tried to avoid reading it.

The four classic westerns of the year were *Broken Arrow*, *Winchester .73*, *The Gunfighter* and *Wagonmaster*. It is interesting that two of them (*Broken Arrow* and *Winchester .73*) starred James Stewart, an actor not associated with westerns, apart from his comic Destry in 1939's *Destry Rides Again*. Stewart had returned from war much more mature and finding it difficult to maintain the perennially youthful, mild, innocent character he had made his own in pre-war times. Looking for new pastures, he accepted two western roles for the year. Both turned out to be classics and the Stewart character, still mild on the surface, inclined to stammer and with that perpetual drawl, now added a sharp, violent edge, none more so than in *Winchester .73* in which he is out to kill his own half-brother in a grim revenge story. It was directed by Anthony Mann who had made his name by making mainly gangster-crime movies and now turned his attention in the '50s to westerns, becoming one of the great western directors in the process. With a standout cast of Stewart, Millard Mitchell as his patient partner, Stephen McNally, Dan Duryea (as a crazed gunman), Shelley Winters and Charles Drake, *Winchester .73* had all the ingredients that make a great western—fine story, action, scenery, sentiment and style.

Broken Arrow was directed by Delmer Daves, another relative newcomer to westerns. Daves, a quiet director, prided himself on the authenticity of his productions. *Broken Arrow* suitably captures the atmosphere of frontier life in its story of Tom Jeffords, Indian scout, who makes peace with Apache chief Cochise and marries an Indian girl. Stewart is suitably sensitive in the role and Jeff Chandler made a noble Cochise. Greeted at the time as a breakthrough in Hollywood's treatment of Indians, *Broken Arrow* was not the first western to raise the issue and did not have the courage to either cast Indian players or let the inter-marriage of white man and Indian girl prosper. The wife, Debra Paget, is killed off, thus preventing any problem with racial issues, and white actors played all the major Indians. However, *Broken Arrow* was a well meant tribute to the Indian way of life and a sensitive and entertaining film. Daves, although making many solid westerns, would never better it.

John Ford's *Wagonmaster* was an intimate "epic" wagon train story. Filmed in black and white without a major star, *Wagonmaster* was basically ignored by critics

A publicity still of James Stewart and Shelley Winters for Anthony Mann's 1950 Winchester .73.

as minor Ford and the general public also failed to respond. In actuality *Wagonmaster* contains some of Ford's most potent work, and was a personal project that turned out as he wanted and remained a favorite of his. Time and perception drew both western and film fans to it and it is now recognized by most people as the classic it is. Against a background of music sung by the Sons of the Pioneers, Ford's characters both decent and indecent make their way across the plains to "the promised land" in all their basic humanity. It is perhaps that, the humanity of his characters, that Ford most emphasizes in this film, from the tough, determined wagonmaster Ward Bond, his guides Ben Johnson (Ford's most likable hero) and Harry Carey, Jr., to showgirl Joanne Dru giving the second of two fine performances for the director and the host of Ford players, including Alan Mowbray's Shakespearean actor from *My Darling Clementine*. Just as distinctive are the outlaws, a rehash of the Clantons from that earlier film and even more vicious. *Wagonmaster* is a lyrical masterpiece.

The fourth outstanding western of the year also failed to generate much public appeal although critics did perceive its worth. *The Gunfighter*, directed by Henry King, was too somber, too realistic, for the average film fan. Dusty and unglamorous,

Henry King's classic The Gunfighter *with star Gregory Peck. The 1950 film was released by Fox.*

it stripped the life of a gunfighter of all its legendary romance. Sincere Gregory Peck gave his best acting performance as Ringo, the doomed gunfighter trying just to stay alive for one more year and escape the life of violence and fear he had undertaken. Millard Mitchell both looked and acted the part of an old-time lawman, once a gunman himself, trying to keep his town clean from such affairs and Skip Homeier was the quintessence of a young punk. Ladies Helen Westcott and Jean Parker played second fiddle to the men in what was, essentially, a man's world. No amount of modern "revisionism" could change that, although I know that if *The Gunfighter* was remade today it would conform to political correctness and show the ladies as main driving forces in the drama. *The Gunfighter* is a sad story and as William K. Everson pointed out in his history of the genre, one still keeps hoping when seeing it again that Ringo will escape his fate — to no avail.

Just missing out on classic western status was John Ford's second for the year, *Rio Grande*. Ford made this at Republic as part of the deal that Republic would produce his Irish film *The Quiet Man*. To many it is third in Ford's cavalry trilogy, in both sequence and quality. The links are there — John Wayne is Kirby York; Victor McLaglen, Ben Johnson, Harry Carey, Jr., and others are all there. Actually it is an underrated Ford, simply filmed in black and white but amidst scenic surrounds in which Wayne gives a sensitive performance as the lonely army man. The pairing with him of Maureen O'Hara was a lead up to *The Quiet Man* and they made a great team. The Sons of the Pioneers not only sang on the soundtrack but were also in the cast, and their singing of "I'll Take You Home Again, Kathleen" is a typical Fordian anachronism that all Ford fans can accept but critics sometimes blanch at.

Anthony Mann also directed *Devil's Doorway*, another film exploring the Indian question and though not remembered as *Broken Arrow* is, a very fine one. Robert Taylor, who had looked out of place in westerns when younger, gave a fine performance as the Indian trying to come to terms with the white man's world. Taylor also appeared in *Ambush* during the year, but that was ordinary. *Devil's Doorway* came from MGM, also never quite at home with westerns, but it did make two good Joel McCrea films during the year, *The Outriders* and especially *Stars in My Crown*, the story of a quiet preacher who tames the rowdy with the Word and a gun, directed by Jacques Tourneur.

McCrea's other westerns for the year were *Frenchie*, which was unremarkable, and *Saddle Tramp*, which had a nice little story about a cowhand and some youngsters. Randolph Scott was in three titles, none outstanding but he had a steady following now and his films made money. *The Nevadan*, *Colt .45* and *The Cariboo Trail* were routine but popular. A newcomer was war hero Audie Murphy, baby-faced and small of stature, but big of heart. *Sierra* showed only how green Murphy was on screen but *The Kid from Texas* and *Kansas Raiders* showed him more confident. In the latter Murphy played a young Jesse James and in the former, Billy the Kid. As Billy, Murphy's expressionless, low key performance was curiously disturbing — those cold eyes looked like those of a killer, which Murphy, in the war, was. Nobody realized at the time just how tortured an individual he was as he set out on a screen ride that would make him the last of the big screen cowboy players and would involve a series of good, if never outstanding, westerns over almost two decades.

Errol Flynn, no longer the heartthrob he had been, made two westerns in 1950, *Montana* and *Rocky Mountain*, the latter with its downbeat ending the slightly better of the two. Gary Cooper made *Dallas*, a far cry from his heyday as a western star and romantic idol. Cooper had been looking for a good western vehicle for some time without success. He would find it very soon. Republic made its usual few "prestige westerns," none of which stand out, although Joseph Kane added plenty of western know-how to *California Passage*, starring Forrest Tucker and Jim Davis. Republic's best efforts were Bill Elliott's last two films for them, the larger scale *Savage Horde*, directed by Kane in which B western star Bob Steele faces Elliott in a street gunfight, and the more personal project *The Showdown*, made by the McGowan brothers, shot almost entirely on sound stages and yet absorbing throughout, with Elliott playing to perfection the tough, grim man of few words he would characterize in forthcoming Monogram westerns. Support from Walter Brennan, Marie Windsor, Henry Morgan, Rhys Williams, William Ching, Jim Davis and others was excellent and *The Showdown* stands out in Elliott's career, full of classic confrontations and lines. "It's wet outside?" "It usually is when it rains."

Other westerns, apart from series ones, were produced during the year, the most ambitious being Anthony Mann's third, but least successful *The Furies*, starring a dominant Barbara Stanwyck. *Two Flags West* directed by Robert Wise looks like a Ford cavalry film without Ford, and *The Sundowners*, *Rock Island Trail* (from Republic), *Return of the Frontiersman* (with Gordon MacRae an unlikely western lead supported by the more suitable Jack Holt and Rory Calhoun), *High Lonesome*, *The Eagle and the Hawk* and *Dakota Lil* were routine. The last starred George Montgomery and Rod Cameron and, like *The Iroquois Trail* and *The Return of Jesse James*, were just one-off B westerns disguised as more prestigious items. MGM made *Annie Get Your Gun* with Betty Hutton, a boisterous musical comedy western, and Bob Hope sashayed forth out West again in *Fancy Pants*. Maureen O'Hara top billed in *Comanche Territory* and *Curtain Call at Cactus Creek* was fun with Donald O'Connor and Gale Storm. Lippert, besides completing its Don Barry group of B westerns, also made some mildly interesting cheapies, like *Bandit Queen* with Barbara Britton and *The Baron of Arizona*, directed by Sam Fuller and starring Vincent Price, who is more associated with horror films.

A departure from the norm was *The Kangaroo Kid*, a B western set in Australia and starring Durango Kid double Jock Mahoney. It was nice if very routine. Independent producer Jack Schwarz made two films starring the self-styled King of Western Swing, Spade Cooley. Cooley had nothing to offer but his music. Better at making westerns was singer Tex Williams, who had sung with Cooley's band at one stage.

Bill Elliott in The Showdown, *at Republic in 1950.*

With a fine deep voice and handsome persona Williams may have done well, given time and proper productions, but he only made a series of two-reel westerns for Universal, one reel of which would consist of stock footage from the studio's B library and the rest Williams and his pals singing. They didn't have the charm of RKO's previous Ray Whitley shorts but it was good to see Bob Baker and the like riding again, even if in long shot — Williams would dress for close-ups in similar gear to that of the long gone cowboys.

In the real B western world Monte Hale, as mentioned, concluded his Republic series with some particularly enjoyable films, *Pioneer Marshal*, *The Vanishing Westerner*, *The Old Frontier* and *The Missourians*. In the last one resident Republic heavy Roy Barcroft essayed a most unlikely Yugoslavian accent — it was good fun. Newcomer Rex Allen improved with *Hills of Oklahoma*, *Redwood Forest Trail* (helped by the perky Jeff Donnell) and *Under Mexicali Stars*, his singing a highlight, and Allan "Rocky' Lane continued his excellent series with films such as *Code of the Silver Sage* and *Vigilante Hideout*. He and his co-star, Eddy Waller, one of the most refreshing of "sidekicks," made a formidable team. But the star in Republic's B western crown was still Roy Rogers, his films in color, which gave him an advantage, and full of William Witney action. *Bells of Coronado* was top-notch, with the kindly old family doctor turning out to be the heavy. *Sunset in the West* introduced a new leading lady in Penny Edwards, who made quite a mark with B western fans in her short career, but best of all was *Trail of Robin Hood*, a Christmas-out-West fantasy of stolen Christmas trees in which all of Republic's current cowboys (Allen, Hale and Lane) come to help out at the end along with old-timers William Farnum, Tom Keene, Kermit Maynard, Ray Corrigan and Tom Tyler, and even heavy George Chesebro. Also not to forget was *North of the Great Divide* with Roy battling it out with bullwhips and heavy Jack Lambert.

Gene Autry released five westerns through Columbia and he got into the whip act too in *Mule Train*, singing the current hit song along the trail. *Cow Town* and *Indian Territory* continued the new Autry "realistic West" treatment and critics were most impressed. The sudden use of bullwhips by both Roy and Gene may have been inspired by the release of Lash LaRue's best known western — *King of the Bull Whip*. It was rather well done, with the whip-cracking LaRue and the heavy (actually Dennis Moore) going to it behind the credits and in the climax.

The other whip wielder, Wilson, produced standard Monogram westerns without creating much of a ripple, although the studio did get behind him with a publicity campaign. *Fence Riders*, *Arizona Territory* and *Cherokee Uprising* were typical and in story and production values very similar to Johnny Mack Brown westerns of the year, such as *Over the Border*, *West of Wyoming* and *Law of the Panhandle*. Brown had more personality than Wilson, but was fast putting on weight. Brown also featured in one of the better minor A westerns of the year, Allied Artists' (which was just upper-bracket Monogram) *Short Grass*, starring Rod Cameron and directed by Lesley Selander. Brown's own westerns were being directed by Lewis Collins and Wallace Fox, who also did the Wilsons.

Charles Starrett and Tim Holt retained their popularity during 1950, Starrett with the improbable adventures of the Durango Kid and Holt with his more serious RKO efforts, of which *Rider from Tucson* and *Storm Over the Badlands* were good examples.

In the top ten cowboy listing of 1950 Roy Rogers was number one and wife Dale

Allied Artists release Short Grass *from 1950, starring Rod Cameron, far left, with Johnny Mack Brown, center, supporting him. Frank Ellis to right.*

Evans number ten. In between, Gabby Hayes at two and William Boyd at five surprise, since neither had made a B western for some years. Bill Elliott, Tim Holt, Charles Starrett, Johnny Mack Brown and Smiley Burnette filled the other spots along with Gene Autry, seemingly permanently stuck at number two since he had returned from the war. However, there is no doubt that Autry and Rogers far surpassed the others in popularity.

1 9 5 1

On Big and Small Screen

On December 30 of 1951 the first *Roy Rogers Show* premiered on NBC network television. Rogers thus joined Gene Autry and the other TV range riders in what seemed to be the demise of the big screen small western, so to speak. Gene Autry of course had been smiling for some time; he was both on TV and making his own feature films, which he continued to do through 1953. Rogers, to get on television, had to end his association with Republic during 1951, the studio still being opposed to its cowboy stars featuring in TV series. With other older cowboy stars nearing the end of the trail, B westerns began their final slide into history. Yet there is some doubt as to whether television was the prime villain. There were, as noted in a previous chapter, a few factors like growing production costs, lessening profit margins, audience tastes.... It is worth considering this: Roy Rogers ceased making feature films for Republic in 1951 and went to television, apart from a 1952 appearance at Paramount. During the years 1952–54, however, Rogers continued to be voted by cinema owners as the top box office cowboy star, so presumably reruns of his old films were still bringing audiences in even while they could see him at home on TV. One distributor commented as to "why a patron should come to his theater to see Roy Rogers when he could see him at home on TV?" The answer to that was surely, as Rogers, Autry and others knew, they could not produce in a half hour TV program the same quality that a good Republic feature film could. Republic, fighting to the end, even produced two new short series of western films in 1951-52. It was to no avail. As older cowboys retired, they were not replaced. The series western was no longer a staple Hollywood product. B westerns were now the preserve of actors like Audie Murphy,

Cowboy ~ing Roy Rogers riding hard on Trigger in 1951's Republic film Heart of the Rockies. *Riding beside hi n is Rand Brooks, better known as a Hopalong Cassidy sidekick.*

making color westerns on budgets that would have amazed Republic or Monogram. Perhaps they should more accurately be called minor A westerns, the type, starring George Montgomery, Rod Cameron or even Randolph Scott, that had been in production since the late '40s. With their added ten to 20 minutes of running time, color and prestigious players, they brought in the audience and revenue that television could not yet compete with. Even they, though, would have their day by the mid–'60s.

Nineteen fifty-one was an unusual year in that no really outstanding major westerns were released. After 1950 that was a come down, and 1952 would offer superior productions. But 1951 was in many ways a case of near misses. The biggest near miss was probably MGM's *Across the Wide Missouri*, directed by William A. Wellman and starring Clark Gable. It should have been the definitive "frontier" western, the story of the mountain men, for hunters and the Indians, but it fell down, partly because MGM mucked about with the final production, and partly because though technically beautiful and widespread, it failed to quite capture the sentiments of the audience.

Kirk Douglas in his first starring western, Along the Great Divide, *a Warners film directed by Raoul Walsh.*

On a different scale and minus the romanticism was the tough, gritty *Along the Great Divide* from Raoul Walsh and starring Kirk Douglas in his first, and arguably, best western role. As the tortured lawman who had seen his father hung doing his duty, Douglas is convincing, especially in his relationship with accused killer Walter Brennan who reminds him of that dead father. Virginia Mayo adds spice as Brennan's daughter in a film that just falls short of greatness, perhaps due to too many studio exteriors. "Nicely done, full of suspense and well acted," states Michael Pitts, and I go along with that.

Randolph Scott, Joel McCrea, Audie Murphy, George Montgomery, Rod Cameron ... all players appearing regularly in the minor A productions during the year made numerous films between them, but few stand out. *Cattle Drive* with McCrea was nice and decidedly un-violent, but the story of a boy (Dean Stockwell) being gently matured by cowboy McCrea on the drive was actually just a remake of Spencer Tracy's *Captains Courageous* from years back. Scott's four westerns for the year were

Stephen McNally
Coleen Gray
ARTHUR SHIELDS
WILLARD PARKER

Apache Drums

Produced by: Val Lewton
Directed by: Hugo Fregonese
Screenplay by: David Chandler
Released: 1951
Running Time: 75 min.
Available in Color
★★★½ DAILY NEWS

These few held the Apache hordes at historic Spanish Boot.

Apache Drums *is an excellent minor western from Universal in 1951. Pictured are, from left, Willard Parker (standing), star Stephen McNally, James Griffith, Armando Silvestre and Arthur Shields (standing, right).*

all standard affairs, but Murphy did better, maturing with each outing, with Budd Boetticher's *The Cimarron Kid,* a serious and honest look at the unglamorous life of outlaws.

Alan Ladd made a couple of westerns, *Branded* and *Red Mountain*, which were passable, and Gregory Peck appeared, against his will, in the studio bound cavalry film *Only the Valiant*, which did him little good. Gary Cooper continued his below average work with *Distant Drums,* a good idea but lackluster from the variable Raoul Walsh, and Jeff Chandler revived his Cochise role in *Battle at Apache Pass.* More unusual was *Al Jennings of Oklahoma*, about a real-life bandit still alive at the time of filming. Dan Duryea was good as always, but the real Al Jennings was a little man of no great account, definitely a minor outlaw. The trend of filming real-life outlaw stories continued with *Best of the Badmen* with the James, Youngers, Quantrill and the lot getting together and wasting the talents of Robert Ryan and Claire Trevor. *Fort Defiance*, a minor affair, was better, with Ben Johnson given a leading role along with Dane Clark. Best of all the minor A westerns for the year was *Apache Drums*, directed by Hugo Fregonese, starring Stephen McNally and bringing a really frightening climax as the townspeople are besieged in the adobe church by the Apache, the Indians throughout having been a barely seen but always present menace.

Players as diverse as Burt Lancaster, Edmond O'Brien, Ronald Reagan, Wendell Corey, Ricardo Montalban, Dennis Morgan, Tyrone Power, Glenn Ford and even Mickey Rooney starred in westerns during the year, whereas once very few such would have. Most of the films they appeared in were average, not bad, tolerably good but certainly not outstanding. Even the return of Henry Hathaway to directing westerns after many years away from them brought only an average vehicle, *Rawhide*, with Power.

It was thus a good year, production-wise, for medium budget westerns, but lacking really top material. Possibly the best western of the year was not really a western at all: *The Red Badge of Courage*, based on the famous Stephen Crane story, is a straight Civil War tale, but some people still classify it as a "western." Brilliantly directed by John Huston, the film suffered from studio-director problems and was badly cut. Enough is left to reveal a small classic and outstanding performance from Audie Murphy as the sensitive, bewildered soldier. Perhaps he was just reflecting his own life.

Republic, as mentioned, tried two new ventures. Vaughan Monroe, a big-voiced singer and band leader who had made some high selling western recordings, was used in a few films like *Toughest Man in Arizona*, which tried to mix a realistic western background with Monroe's singing — uncomfortably. No more successful were Michael Chapin and Eilene Janssen in *Buckaroo Sheriff of Texas* and others similar that put these two youngsters in an adult western world. Don Miller got it right when he wrote (in *Hollywood Corral*) that young people didn't want to see their own kind riding, roping and catching baddies, they wanted to see adults doing it and thus identify with them. Republic had tried, but there were no new avenues left in the B western field.

Still hugely successful were Republic's Roy Rogers films. When Rogers' contract ran out in 1951 Republic wanted to sign him again, but the bogey of television came between. Thus after *Pals of the Golden West* the Rogers theatrical career virtually ended. The year had produced two excellent films, *Spoilers of the Plains* and *Heart of the Rockies*, both directed by Witney and featuring Penny Edwards, as good as ever, though Republic had dropped color after *Trail of Robin Hood* the previous year. Then followed *In Old Amarillo*, not quite as good, and unfortunately introducing Pinky Lee as a comic sidekick in place of Gordon Jones. Jones had only been so-so, but Lee was awful. The last two entries, *South of Caliente* and *Pals of the Golden West*, also brought back Dale Evans, which was not now a great advantage either.

Rex Allen had a lesser budget but his 1951 films were nice entertainment, with *Silver City Bonanza*, *Thunder in God's Country*, *Rodeo King and the Senorita* and *Utah Wagon Train*, directed by George Blair and Philip Ford. Allen had acquired a good sidekick in Buddy Ebsen and a semi-regular leading lady in Mary Ellen Kay. And when Evans displaced her in the Rogers series, Penny Edwards moved over to the Allens with *Utah Wagon Train*.

Alan "Rocky" Lane also worked hard all year with his usual dedication, partnered by Chubby Johnson for most of the year, with Eddy Waller absent for some reason *Rough Riders of Durango*, *Wells Fargo Gunmaster*, *Desert of Lost Men* and *Fort Dodge Stampede* were among these excellent little westerns. Lane was rewarded with a spot in the top ten cowboy star listing.

At Monogram Johnny Mack Brown and Whip Wilson turned out lackluster features, Wilson being joined by Fuzzy Knight (in place of Clyde) and, in five of Wilson's 1951 features, Jim Bannon, formerly Red Ryder. Bannon later claimed that his (Bannon's) job was to "pep up the series a bit" but most actors claim that sort of thing, notably Smiley Burnette when he had joined Starrett at Columbia in 1946. Starrett rather tartly said that he didn't think his films needed "pepping up." Whatever the case neither Bannon, nor Knight, could pep the Wilsons up. Brown, in what must have been a concerted Monogram casting effort, also found a new saddle pal into 1951, former Cassidy sidekick Jimmy Ellison, looking considerably younger than Johnny at that stage, who did add some new spice to the series. However nothing could hide Johnny's middle-age spread.

Lash LaRue "made" his last westerns in 1951—"made" part of them, anyway, since mostly they consisted of scenes from previous LaRues with some added footage. Only one of this films during the year, *The Daltons' Women* directed by Thomas Carr, showed individuality. And that was rather strange, with both the title and publicity for the film emphasizing big-bosomed women fighting each other. Lo and behold, after a few minutes of that, the film resolved into another LaRue–St. John adventure and not a bad one at that.

Charles Starrett, still straight of back and seemingly enjoying himself, made six Durango Kid adventures, partnered by Smiley Burnette and with less Jock Mahoney,

A late Johnny Mack Brown entry at Monogram in 1951, Oklahoma Justice. *Pictured are, left to right, Ed Cassidy, unknown, Brown, Jimmy Ellison and Lyle Talbot.*

who was busy on other productions during the year. Mahoney would return in full force for Starrett's final productions in 1952. Columbia's prime western releases remained the superior Gene Autry films, the emphasis in *Valley of Fire, Hills of Utah, Silver Canyon* and others being on somber realism. In many of these 1951 efforts Gene sings just two songs. In retrospect *Valley of Fire* and *Hills of Utah* are dull, the best for the year being *Texans Never Cry* and *Whirlwind*, a more typical Autry feature in which Smiley Burnette returned to partner Gene for a "oncer." However, after the demise of the Starrett series in 1952, Smiley would return to the Autry series for his final features, an appropriate casting. Strangest of the Autry films was *Gene Autry and the Mounties*, not because of the film itself, which is routine and pleasant, but because of the title, which seems to lower the level of his movies to that of the comics or children's novels then in vogue about Gene and Roy with titles like *Gene Autry and the ___* or *Roy Rogers and the ___.*

Al "Lash" LaRue, one of the more unique cowboy stars.

One other happy event for the year was Monogram's signing of Bill Elliott for a series. This group of westerns, filmed from 1951 to 1954, would straddle two worlds amidst changing times. Though B western in budget and presentation, the stories were adult and Elliott's performance decidedly so, a strong, silent characterization of a man neither completely good nor bad, who drank whisky and smoked and did unheroic things like beating up a suspected crook without giving him the chance of a fair fight. The first film in this group was *The Longhorn*, which managed, on its small budget, to capture the feeling of a cattle drive and the toughness of character and environment that Elliott was seeking. The writer was Dan Ullman and the director Lewis Collins, stock performers in their field, so it is fair to say that Elliott must have been the innovator for the "new look" cowboy who was, actually, just a throwback to the good old days of William S. Hart.

1 9 5 2

"Do Not Forsake Me"

High Noon, with its distinctive theme song of "Do Not Forsake Me Oh My Darlin'," was the western event of the year. Laurels went to director Fred Zinnemann, star Gary Cooper and music maker Dimitri Tiomkin, and former B western star Tex Ritter sang the hit song (as did many others including Frankie Lane, who made a bigger seller out of it than Ritter did). Cooper's honors were well deserved, with Hollywood rewarding an aging star, although his gaunt performance was made even more so by his being unwell at the time, and *High Noon* was taken up by the politically-minded as a parable for modern American politics. It is a good film but, as proven at the initial preview, slow without the background song. That, and Ritter's performance of it, really made the picture, one to be much imitated in following years.

A better western was Anthony Mann's *Bend of the River*. It had strong scenic values, a real wagon train atmosphere, an average budget and a riveting performance from James Stewart as the former Missouri raider set on redemption, battling his erstwhile friend, that fine actor Arthur Kennedy. It is, for this writer, Mann's best western, pictorially stunning, actionful, tense, violent and warm. Stewart was at his peak as a westerner, his earlier awkward screen persona now toughened, his friendly personality able to turn to menace when his character is under threat. *Bend of the River* is a very satisfying western, with an old-fashioned optimistic ending.

Another "best" western of the year failed to arouse much interest, maybe because it was dominated by women. William A. Wellman's *Westward the Women* was even more of an "epic" than *Bend of the River*, with outstanding wagon trek scenes, the

Best of the Anthony Mann–James Stewart collaborations, 1952's Bend of the River. *Stewart (left) and Arthur Kennedy pose for this publicity shot from the Universal picture.*

One of the very best, and last, of the wagon train westerns was 1952's Westward the Women, *directed by William Wellman and released by MGM. Star Robert Taylor and John McIntire comfort Renata Vanni while Henry Nakamuru looks on.*

hardships and frailties of the pioneering spirit as well as the grit and determination being captured. The story, about a wagon train of women headed for a new life westward, probably did not appeal to many men, but it was certainly not a "woman's" picture. Robert Taylor, in his best western role, was a forceful but likable lead and Denise Darcel, Hope Emerson, Julie Bishop and others headed a fine female supporting cast. Most of all Wellman captured, probably for the last time in western films, the "feel" of a wagon train moving west. It was the last of the great wagon train westerns, going back to the silent *Covered Wagon*.

Other interesting westerns included *The Big Sky*, meant to be Howard Hawks' follow up epic to *Red River* but falling short. Kirk Douglas was fine as the early frontiersman and the river boat scenes were well done but Dewey Martin was inexperienced and the love interest seemed to be added on as an afterthought. Basically *The Big Sky* is nice to look at but not satisfactory as a drama. *Viva Zapata!* was a Fox "historical drama" about the Mexican revolution with a mumbling Marlon Brando and virile Anthony Quinn. A nice looking picture thanks to painstaking direction from Elia Kazan, it is western enough to be included here, but not a notable success for anyone. *Rancho Notorious*, a Fritz Lang–directed vehicle for Marlene Dietrich, was a strange one. Lang's budget was restricted and resulted in numerous studio sets, *à la* Republic, and the revenge-hunted motif gave a haunted atmosphere to the story. Arthur Kennedy gives an earnest performance as the hunter, Mel Ferrer a dry one as Dietrich's gunman friend and Marlene herself comes across as an aging enchantress— certainly an interesting film.

Rock Hudson was an unlikely John Wesley Hardin in Raoul Walsh's *The Lawless Breed* and Clark Gable, another aging idol, a tough Texan in *Lone Star* with Ava Gardner. Westerns were made about horses (*The Lion and the Horse*), rodeos (*Rodeo* and *The Lusty Men*), outlaws (*Montana Belle* with Jane Russell) and railroads (*The Denver and Rio Grande*). Most were competent but not memorable. *Apache War Smoke* starred Gilbert Roland in one of his rare lead roles and *The Big Trees* gave Kirk Douglas a chance to flash his dimple and snarl, which, as always, he did effectively. *Bugles in the Afternoon* (Edmond O'Brien) was the cavalry versus Indians and *Kangaroo* an Australian western featuring Maureen O'Hara, Peter Lawford and Richard Boone. Robert Ryan was given the starring role in *Horizons West*, a Universal Budd Boetticher drama, Stewart Granger traversed *The Wild North* for MGM, and Rory Calhoun played an Argentinian cowboy in *Way of a Gaucho*. Charlton Heston showed his bare chest as *The Savage* and there was the comic side of the West, with the gentle *Sky Full of Moon* and, more notably, *Son of Paleface* with Bob Hope venturing west again, this time with not only Jane Russell but also Roy Rogers and Trigger. *Son of Paleface* is actually one of Hope's funniest films and Rogers (and Trigger) notably added to that fun.

During 1952 the minor A cowboy stars were busy: Sterling Hayden, Forrest Tucker, Rod Cameron and Gary Cooper made another western besides *High Noon*— *Springfield Rifle*, which was, however, mundane. Randolph Scott was popular in *Carson City* and *Man in the Saddle* but his best western of the year was *Hangman's Knot*, directed by Roy Huggins, an underrated western director, and featuring Donna Reed and a young Lee Marvin. Joel McCrea was relatively inactive and Audie Murphy appeared in *The Duel at Silver Creek*, a lighthearted but violent western directed by Don Siegel.

In short, 1952 produced many westerns but few outstanding ones. But *High Noon* so dominated proceedings that no one noticed. Also not noticed, except by devotees, was the further decline of the series western. The *Motion Picture Herald* seems not to have noticed it in its annual listing of the ten top western stars. It named ten even though there were not ten cowboys stars left making westerns in 1952. Re-releases were obviously the order of the day as Roy Rogers, Gabby Hayes, Dale Evans and William Boyd all made the list, along with Gene Autry, Tim Holt, Rex Allen, Bill

The last releases of Columbia's Durango Kid series came in 1952 and star Charles Starrett, seen here with Smiley Burnette (left), retired after 17 years with that studio.

Tim Hol- also made his last RKO westerns in 1952.

Elliott, Smiley Burnette and Charles Starrett. With *The Kid from Broken Gun* Charles Starrett and Durango rode into the sunset, as did Tim Holt, Johnny Mack Brown, Lash LaRue and Whip Wilson during the year. By the close of the year Autry, Allen, Lane and Elliott were still working in pictures, joined by the unlikely Wayne Morris at Monogram–Allied Artists, which had begun the last group of films universally recognized as B westerns.

At Republic during 1952 Rocky Lane's westerns had remained cheap but good, *Captive of Billy the Kid*, *Leadville Gunslinger*, *Desperadoes Outpost* and others still retaining Lane's enthusiastic approach and Eddy Waller being back as co-star, while Rex Allen had William Witney as director and *Colorado Sundown* was perhaps the best Allen ever made. Gene Autry's releases grew obviously tighter of budget and a little drab in *The Old West*, *Apache Country*, *Night Stage to Galveston* and *Barbed Wire*. But *Wagon Team* and *Blue Canadian Rockies* were brighter and had more songs, still Gene s forte, whatever his efforts to be a rugged, action cowboy.

The best of the minor westerns were those Bill Elliott made at Monogram, especially *Waco* and *Kansas Territory*, two of the most interesting B westerns ever made with Elliott, aging and grim, the man bent on revenge or accepting an outlaw's life. In many respects he was much like the character Randolph Scott molded together for Budd Boetticher. Elliott's other 1952 titles (*Fargo* and *The Maverick*) were not as good but *Waco* and *Kansas Territory*, along with *Bitter Creek* (1954) and Republic's 1950 *The Showdown* contained the best film work Elliott ever did.

One other Monogram series was still running in 1952. That was the Chinook the dog group with human star Kirby Grant as Mountie Rod. It should perhaps be classified as a B western series and Grant as a B western star. Although titles like *Yukon Gold* were cheap and predictable, they received quite wide distribution through not only the States but in Britain, Australia and New Zealand, though Kirby Grant never seemed to attain much popularity.

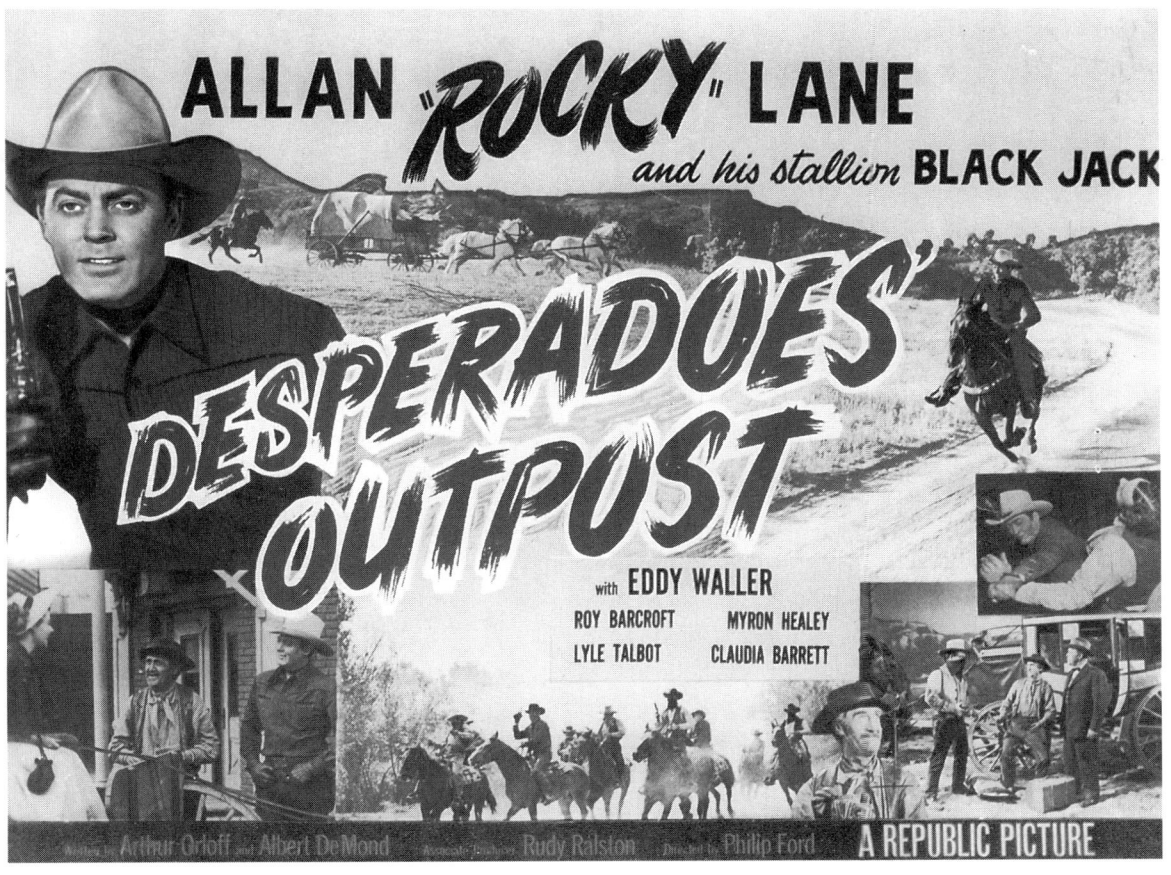

Still going strong in 1952 was Allan "Rocky" Lane.

As the B western died, 1952 was an example of the '50s decade that produced some of the greatest major westerns and a stream of very entertaining lesser ones. For some, though, the loss of the B western spelled the end of the trail — for those people the golden age would be over in 1954, just two years hence.

1 9 5 3

Shane

Director George Stevens set out deliberately to make "a great western film" and in 1953 released, through Paramount, *Shane*. Based on a fine story from Jack Schaefer, it deservedly was hailed as a classic, and remains to this day certainly one of the great westerns and for many people, *the* great western. *Shane* is a lovely, nostalgic, romantic and mythical story of the West as we would have liked it to have been. It is a parable and a morality play. The golden-hued but doomed figure of Alan Ladd as the gunfighter who wants to forget his past is classically molded through Ladd's finest performance, backed up by outstanding work from Van Heflin, Jean Arthur, Jack Palance (as a beautifully stylized villain), Emile Meyer and Ben Johnson. *Shane* is like a symphony, not a fanciful comparison since the music (composed and conducted by Victor Young) adds greatly to the shape of the film. Criticism of *Shane* is that it is too beautiful and simplistic, but that is the essence of the "myth" it upholds. A more valid criticism would be, strangely enough, of director Stevens' ultra-perfection in getting every scene just right. Stevens took a long time to film *Shane*. It is meticulous in its finished precision. As William Everson wrote, "In the time John Ford would complete three cavalry films Stevens molded his masterpiece into shape." But Everson goes on to admit his disappointment, on seeing the film again and again, in the "cold perfection" and lack of spontaneity. This is fair criticism. I have seen the film many, many times and still go back to it and I can see the clinical nature of many scenes. The flaws (there are flaws in everything — nothing is really perfect) get magnified with each viewing. But the beauty remains the same and I cannot listen to the first wave of music as Shane, behind the credits, rides over the hill and into

The year's great western was Shane, *arguably the best ever made. Alan Ladd, in the title role, and young Brandon De Wilde are pictured from George Stevens' Paramount release.*

the valley, without feeling the same gripping sensation as ever. And I cannot watch the ending without, after so many screenings, tears still coming to my eyes. *Shane* is 90 percent cinematic beauty and emotion and 10 percent banality that obviously did not seem so at first release but does now. That 90 percent is sufficient. It is a great western, a great movie.

While *Shane* was astonishing, B or series westerns were disappearing from the screen. Tim Holt's last one had been filmed in 1952, but was released in 1953. *Desert Passage* was still good quality B material. Gene Autry made his last theatrical features to concentrate on his television show. Smiley Burnette returned to partner him in what were quite enjoyable little westerns after *Winning of the West,* which was mainly stock shots. But *On Top of Old Smoky, Gold Town Ghost Riders, Pack Train, Saginaw Trail* and *Last of the Pony Riders* were good, even if budgets, obvious from the limited cast members, were kept low. Republic ceased its Rocky Lane series, the essential quality remaining to the end in *Bandits of the West* and *El Paso Stampede.* That left Rex Allen, Bill Elliott and Wayne Morris still operating. Allen made five Republic westerns that, despite Bill Witney's directorial efforts, looked cheaper and cheaper and by *Shadows of Tombstone* had running times of 53 minutes and no songs. Morris at Monogram, in *The Marksman, Fighting Lawman* and *Star of Texas,* was interesting as a laid back western lead and Elliott, after a couple of slow entries, *The Homesteaders* and *Rebel City,* was back to his best in the excellent *Topeka,* directed by Thomas Carr, and *Vigilante Terror* from Lewis Collins.

Taking over as the "bread and butter" westerns from the B's were the films, often now in color, starring the likes of Rod Cameron, Rory Calhoun and George Montgomery, with a further step up to Audie Murphy, Joel McCrea and Randolph Scott. In 1953 Murphy made three westerns, all good, solid and traditional in style: *Gunsmoke, Column South* and *Tumbleweed.* Murphy looked and acted more mature and had put on a bit of weight (he'd always looked a little undernourished beforehand). McCrea's one 1953 western was excellent, *Lone Hand,* which featured Barbara Hale. The part of the dedicated lawman who has to hide his true self even from his new wife and son fitted the dedicated McCrea mold of acting. He looked totally sincere. George Sherman directed *Lone Hand,* which is an unsung little gem. Randolph Scott's films for the year were unremarkable — some critics thought he was looking old — with *Man Behind the Gun, The Stranger Wore a Gun* and *Thunder Over the Plains.*

Other sound but unambitious westerns for the year were *Ambush at Tomahawk Gap, Gun Fury, Conquest of Cochise, Cow Country, Vanquished, The Tall Texan, The Stand at Apache River, Ride Vaquero, San Antone, Seminole, The Redhead from Wyoming, The Last Posse, Law and Order* and *Kansas Pacific.* These minor if often enjoyable films starred all sorts of actors who once would never have considered westerns— Sterling Hayden, Rock Hudson, Broderick Crawford, John Hodiak, Ronald Reagan, Edmond O'Brien, Robert Taylor, Montgomery, Cameron and others. *Law and Order* was interesting in that it was a remake of the 1932 classic, but was worlds

Gene Aut⁻y, seen here with sidekick Pat Buttram (left) and leading lady Gail Davis, released his last theatrical westerns in 1953.

Popular '50s star of medium budget westerns, George Montgomery.

apart, lacking all the creativity and realistic feeling of the earlier film. (It was also filmed under the same title in the early '40s by Johnny Mack Brown, but that was strictly a series western.)

There were better westerns released through the year. *Arrowhead* starred Charlton Heston in a bravo, chest-thumping role and the film is notable for its savagery toward the Indian. *Calamity Jane* was a light-hearted musical with Doris Day and Howard Keel that was fun, and *Escape from Fort Bravo*, directed by John Sturges, a thoughtful cavalry film starring William Holden, older and grimmer and looking more suited to the western than he had been in earlier years. *Powder River*, a small but likable Rory Calhoun starrer, used virtually the same script as that of *My Darling Clementine*, but carried it off well, thanks to steady direction from Louis King and the playing of Calhoun, an underrated western player, Cameron Mitchell, Corrine Calvert and ex–B western heroine Penny Edwards.

The biggest success of the year, initially beating *Shane* at the box office, was *The Charger at Feather River*, partly because it was in 3-D and partly because it was a rousing cavalry versus Indians affair with Guy Madison. *Pony Express* from Paramount was a large scale production, but with a B western plot and much loud action. Charlton Heston and Forrest Tucker as Wild Bill Hickok and Buffalo Bill Cody played their roles as if in a series or serial, as a couple of joking, sparring buddies. It was all good clean fun but unremarkable.

Another 3-D western, this time of some quality, was *Wings of the Hawk*. It was directed by Budd Boetticher and starred *Shane* player Van Heflin. Heflin, always an earnest actor, was just right in the role of a stubborn American miner working in revolutionary Mexico and getting unwillingly ensnared in local politics—and violence. Mostly forgotten now, *Wings of the Hawk* is entertaining. And there were a couple of unusual westerns that were not great hits at the box office but are worthy of consideration: Alan Dwan's Republic film *The Woman They Almost Lynched*, supposedly a parody of the western by the director, and Universal's *Take Me to Town*, a charming rural frolic with Ann Sheridan and Sterling Hayden.

A loose remake of the Wyatt Earp–Tombstone story, Powder River *in 1953 was minor but enjoyable. Cameron Mitchell is in the stagecoach (on the left) and star Rory Calhoun outside.*

Next to *Shane* the two best westerns of the year were *Hondo* and *The Naked Spur*. The latter was another James Stewart–Anthony Mann collaboration, and a stark, relentless account of one man's search for another and his struggle with his conscience over money or peace of mind, all beautifully filmed in magnificent surroundings with a small cast who give outstanding performances. Stewart is the dominating figure, though, and his western character is compelling. Robert Ryan, Janet Leigh, Ralph Meeker and Millard Mitchell make up the excellent supporting cast.

The other film was *Hondo*, directed by John Farrow (with, it is said, some help from John Ford) and dominated by John Wayne as Hondo Lane, scout with the army, strong, soft-spoken and deadly in action. It is definitely Wayne's finest performance outside his work with Ford and Howard Hawks. The depth and fierceness of the Hondo character is a look forward to Wayne's Ethan Edwards of *The Searchers* in 1956, without the pathological hatreds. Stage actress Geraldine Page, it seems, did not enjoy working with Wayne, but she gives a good performance as the lonely Plains woman.

So 1953 gave us some of the last B westerns, many enjoyable minor ones and a few outstanding examples, topped by what some (many) see as the greatest of them all—*Shane*. It had been a good year for westerns, sad though it may have been to part with the lowly series variety.

1 9 5 4

Sundown on the Prairie

It was just that for the old B or series western. Republic released *Phantom Stallion*, then closed the doors on its B unit. *Stallion* starred Rex Allen, "The Last of the Silver Screen Cowboys," and was a taut 53 minute story about a boy, a horse, two crooked ranchers and Rex and his pal Slim Pickens saving the day for good against evil. Straightforward and cheap, it was still directed with verve by William Witney, an innovator and outstanding B western and serial director, who was left to carry on with a few low budget features (including some Audie Murphy westerns) and television shows into the '60s. This was the fate of most B directors. Most of them who wanted it found work of some sort, although many were happy enough to accept retirement, after all, they had been around, these many years, since the silent days or early talkies. For the cowboy stars who had become redundant over the last few years it was not so simple. Big time players like Autry and Rogers had television, personal appearances and merchandising. Lesser lights struggled; parts in films and TV shows were not easy to come by for ex–B western cowboys. If they sang they had an advantage, as Rogers, Autry, Ritter, Wakely and Dean found out. For a younger player like Lash LaRue, or an elder statesman like Johnny Mack Brown, who had high tastes in living, it was harder going.

Even though Rex Allen was often called, in later years, "The Last of the Silver Screen Cowboys" (his son would perform a song about it) that honor really went to a player at Monogram–Allied Artists, Wayne Morris, who outlasted his fellow studio cowboy Bill Elliott by a few months. Elliott was of course one of the great cowboy stars, whereas Morris was minor in comparison. Elliott's last western was the taut

The last of the silver screen singing cowboys, Rex Allen, in 1954.

Generally recognized as the last B or series western made was Allied Artists' 1954 Two Guns and a Badge. *Pictured, left to right, are Damian O'Flynn, Roy Barcroft, I. Stanford Jolley, William Phipps, star Wayne Morris and Beverly Garland.*

detective-style *The Forty-Niners*, but his previous 1954 film, *Bitter Creek*, was outstanding, a tough, gritty B western with Elliott, vengeance-seeking, as grim as ever and refreshingly non–Boy Scoutish in his actions as he beats the hell out of a baddie while holding a gun on him, most unsportsmanlike, but very sensible.

Wayne Morris was also very good in the offbeat *The Desperado* and his *Two Guns and a Badge*, which was historically the last B western ever made, a tongue-in-cheek and enjoyable romp. Notable in both Elliott's *Bitter Creek* and Morris' *Two Guns and a Badge* was Beverly Garland, a refreshingly attractive and sensible minor production heroine.

At the time the demise of the series western was hardly noticed, but just taken for granted. Now, looking back over the years, it is a distinctive break in the history of western motion pictures and nostalgia has given it a mellow memory for many old fans who keep that memory alive. Television, after the first rush of child-oriented westerns like Cassidy, the Lone Ranger, Autry, the Cisco Kid, Rogers, Kit Carson and Range Rider, was now moving into the so-called "adult" era with *Gunsmoke* and others. Eventually these serious talk-laden half hour and hour long shows led to boredom on the prairie and many a viewer sighed and longed again for the thrill of galloping hooves, blazing six-guns and frenetic fist fights that had been the hallmark of the series western on the theater screen. Television westerns, into the '70s, would still capture large audiences but for different reasons and, as with the westerns produced for cinema release, would become the politically correct bores perpetrated upon the genre to this day.

The year 1954 did not produce a "great" western. It did produce quite a few interesting ones with some memorable moments, from the oddly bizarre *Johnny Guitar*, which became a "cult" classic, to the even more oddly bizarre *Jesse James' Women*, produced, directed and featuring ex–B western cowboy Donald Barry and reaching fresh depths of awfulness. *Johnny Guitar* came from Republic, which should have known better, and was directed by Nicholas Ray who, allowing star Joan Crawford her head as the hysterical woman empire builder, also should have known better. The whole thing involves "over-the-top" performances, from leading man Sterling Hayden to Mercedes McCambridge as Crawford's rival and has forever captured the applause of a slim group of cinema intellectuals who see something in the flames that is beyond the rest of us.

With no pretensions except to entertain, *Vera Cruz* and *The Command* are far better westerns, the former a romp for Gary Cooper and a smiling Burt Lancaster, the second another cavalry film with Guy Madison, filmed in the new CinemaScope, and directed by a no-nonsense David Butler. To show his versatility, Burt Lancaster, all teeth in *Vera Cruz*, made a serious story of an Indian brave, *Apache*, which, for its time, was hard hitting if once again timid by not casting any Indian players in leading roles. Other westerns dealing with Indians during the year — it was a popular subject — included *Taza, Son of Cochise*, which was routine, and *Sitting Bull*, starring Dale Robertson and further lowering the status of George Custer to a ranting megalomaniac. The lead in *Taza* was the physically impressive Rock Hudson, in retrospect one of the more unusual "Indians" given us by Hollywood, with Jeff Chandler playing a minute role as the dying Cochise, as one writer said, "a role he had made his own."

A good little film, not receiving much recognition then and virtually forgotten today, was *The Raid*, which may or may not be a western according to your criteria. This Van Heflin starrer was a thoughtful story, based on fact, of an incident during the Civil War, nicely directed by Hugo Fregonese. Another part-western, set in modern times, was *Track of the Cat* with Robert Mitchum, from a Walter Van Tilburg Clark story, and just getting in as a western-style musical was *Seven Brides for Seven Brothers*. More traditional were *The Siege at Red River* with yet another unlikely westerner, Van Johnson, and *Drum Beat*, a Delmer Daves–directed film starring Alan Ladd that had some picturesque moments but was not memorable.

The Command *was released in CinemaScope by Warner Bros. in 1954. Star Guy Madison is hatless, bending over the map, while James Whitmore (wearing scarf) is at his right shoulder.*

A Monogram looked like a Monogram, major westerns bore the stamp not so much of the studio making them, but the artist doing so. Thus a John Ford or Howard Hawks film looked like just that, whether it was released through Columbia, Universal, MGM or Paramount; the fact that Paramount, for example, released the classic *Shane* in reality made not one whit of difference to that film. It would have been the same George Stevens creation if released by RKO or Republic. With the demise of the B western came the demise of the studio-stamped formula. Historian William K. Everson once wrote an essay in which he claimed, even as a child, to have been able to identify the different products from Monogram, Republic or Universal just by the look and sound of each film. He was right, with regard to series westerns.

In a year of plenty, production-wise, there were other serviceable westerns made. Personal preference is a great thing. Some of these other films, which I lump together as much of a sameness, might well be a particular favorite of somebody. Take *River of No Return* for example. It has an interesting cast, with Marilyn Monroe and Robert Mitchum starring and Rory Calhoun featured, directed by Otto Preminger. And there was *Broken Lance*, an Edward Dmytryk film for Fox with Spencer Tracy, Robert

Wagner, Jean Peters and Richard Widmark. It is sure to be someone's favorite. For me, a pleasant outing was Warners' *Boy from Oklahoma* with Will Rogers, Jr., in the sort of easygoing role his father, Will, would have once played and Nancy Olson a nice heroine. *Arrow in the Dust*, starring the solid Sterling Hayden and directed by B favorite Lesley Selander, was notable for featuring ex–singing cowboy Jimmy Wakely playing a supporting role that gave him a chance to pluck his guitar and sing. The film itself was only average, as was *Garden of Eden*, a disappointing Gary Cooper–Richard Widmark pairing from director Henry Hathaway. Barbara Stanwyck, who increasingly appeared in westerns, roles in which her strong character was perfectly suitable, made *Cattle Queen of Montana*, a late RKO film directed by Allan Dwan and interesting now mainly because Ronald Reagan played opposite Stanwyck, not an easy task.

Nineteen fifty-four had a western for most everyone, if only a few last B features for the fans. Speaking of which, it is worthwhile considering here, with the closure of series features, the role that studios themselves had or did not have in the making of a western film. The whole Hollywood studio system was on the wan in 1954. Independent-minded stars, directors and producers were now getting their own way in production, whereas once the studio ruled the roost. Small studios like RKO and Republic were struggling to survive. Monogram had vanished into Allied Artists. With B westerns, each studio making them stamped its own trademark upon the films—a Republic B western looked like a Republic B western.

1955

A World Without B
or Series Westerns

To be honest, the series western had been on the slide for some years so nobody really noticed that in 1955 it had vanished. In its place, as B pictures, were the westerns of regular stars like Rory Calhoun, Rod Cameron, John Payne, George Montgomery, Sterling Hayden and the three "biggies" of the lower budget group, Randolph Scott, Joel McCrea and Audie Murphy. Of course these "lower-budget" westerns were majestic of budget to the makers of true B westerns. Filmed in color, they were B films only in comparison with the even bigger, high prestige films made with Hollywood players who, some years before, would hardly have considered making westerns. Now everybody made them. It might be said that the western had reached its highest state of respectability. James Cagney, Spencer Tracy (in the magnificent *Bad Day at Black Rock*, a fringe western), Claudette Colbert and Fred MacMurray are names brought to mind, and the likes of Robert Mitchum, Kirk Douglas, Burt Lancaster, Robert Taylor and Clark Gable added more titles to their growing lists of westerns.

Bad Day at Black Rock, directed by John Sturges, had to be the best western of the year — if it is a western. Very contemporary, it would have to be called, and not a horse in sight. My own inclination is to not count it as a western, against the judgment of historians like Michael Pitts and Phil Hardy, but there it is. I would just say that it is a great film and that Spencer Tracy is superb.

Kudos for best western of the year would thus fall to Anthony Mann's Columbia

Audie Murphy, war hero and mainstay of the 1950s minor A western.

release, *The Man from Laramie.* This was the last western Mann made with star James Stewart, the last of five excellent films, and *The Man from Laramie* must be ranked up there with the other two best, *Winchester .73* and *Bend of the River.* Aided by a fine supporting cast of Arthur Kennedy, Donald Crisp, Alex Nicol and the soft-spoken Cathy O'Donnell (and a nice cameo by Jack Elam), Stewart is at his most determined as he sets out to find the killer of his brother and unravels the sad story of cattle baron Crisp's two sons, one neurotic and weak, the other (the excellent Kennedy) friendly and reasonable on the surface but underneath, cold and murderous.

No other western matched *The Man from Laramie* in 1955 but there were several very good ones. Raoul Walsh, whose work had become very variable, gave us one of his better efforts in *The Tall Men,* a cattle drive story from MGM with Clark Gable and Robert Ryan battling over Jane Russell, and King Vidor returned to the western after a long spell away with *Man Without a Star.* Like his 1946 *Duel in the Sun,* it was a little bit too intense, with one of the most intense actors, Kirk Douglas, seemingly given full rein. Jeanne Crain is the leading lady but in a supporting role longtime favorite Claire Trevor gives a warm-hearted performance as the saloon girl. Better was *Wichita,* directed by Jacques Tourneur for Allied Artists. Joel McCrea played a placid, likable Wyatt Earp (probably a long, long way from the true character) and was partnered by the always reliable Vera Miles in a film that was, although basically about violence, surprisingly amiable and peaceful.

The Davy Crockett craze, unleashed by Walt Disney on television, came to the big screen as Fess Parker repeated his role in *Davy Crockett — King of the Wild Frontier,* which was actually a hitching together of the three television stories. And still back in early frontier days, Charlton Heston and Fred MacMurray played Lewis and Clark in Rudolph Maté's *The Far Horizons* for Paramount. Historically inaccurate, the film was let down by obvious budget constraints. When all is said and done, as good as anything else released in 1955 was another Mann-Stewart collaboration, *The Far Country.* Western historians are divided over this one; some see it as the least of

A scene from Columbia's 1955 The Man from Laramie, *directed by Anthony Mann. That's star James Stewart with his back to the camera and in the distance, closest to Stewart, is longtime character actor Wallace Ford.*

the five Mann-Stewart films, others praise it highly. Once again Stewart plays a man alone, but this time he is just trying to get by staying alone, rather on the trail of personal vengeance. That is until his friend Walter Brennan is killed and Stewart goes into action against the amiable but corrupt John McIntire and his gang.

Two stars took it upon themselves to direct their own films in 1955. Burt Lancaster made *The Kentuckian*, a mildly successful early frontier tale and at Republic Ray Milland, not normally a westerner, starred in and directed *A Man Alone*. Republic would not give Milland much of a budget so most of the film was made on the studio sound stages. Milland, as the gunman seeking to clear his name of bank robbery, gives an interesting performance. Republic was indeed very busy in 1955, probably trying to stave off the creditors at that stage. It also produced *Sante Fe Passage*, *Timberjack*, *The Road to Denver*, *The Vanishing American* and *The Last Command*. The first three were average vehicles for John Payne, Rod Cameron and Sterling

Hayden *The Vanishing American*, starring Scott Brady in the role originally played by Richard Dix, was a remake of the Zane Grey story, and not in the class of the silent screen version. More interesting was *The Last Command* because it was the John Wayne–planned script. Wayne had left Republic still wanting to make his story of the Alamo.

Herb Yates had put it off time and again and it took Wayne nine years after he left Republic before he could bring it to the screen himself. In the meantime, Republic held on to the original script and made it with Sterling Hayden in the role that would have been played by Wayne, that of Jim Bowie. Frank Lloyd was given the director's job but his work was routine. B director William Witney directed the action scenes and those stand out. An interesting failure would be a fair summing up.

Other releases for the year included another Anthony Mann film, *The Last Frontier*, inferior to his best and starring Victor Mature, whom some liked, and many didn't; Robert Taylor in good humor battling with Eleanor Parker in MGM's *Many Rivers to Cross*; Kirk Douglas all chin-jutting aggression as *The Indian Fighter* and Raymond Massey at Allied Artists essaying the role of John Brown in *Seven Angry Men*. George Marshall directed *Destry* for Universal, the same story he had made in 1939, except that this time it was played straight with hero Audie Murphy. And there were other westerns starring favorites Randolph Scott, Joel McCrea, George Montgomery and Rory Calhoun (outshone by that scene-stealer Gilbert Roland in *The Treasure of Pancho Villa*). That western musical to end all western musicals, *Oklahoma!*, was filmed and mention must be made of two more westerns.

One, *The Violent Men*, directed by Rudolph Maté for Columbia, is an oddly compelling film with strong performances from Edward G. Robinson, as the wheelchair bound cattle baron, Barbara Stanwyck as his unfaithful and ruthless wife, Brian Keith as her lover and Glenn Ford as the quiet man who wants to stay away from violence but finally takes up the role of sorting all things out — and gaining the hand of Robinson's daughter, Dianne Foster. This writer, who does not normally like Glenn Ford on the screen, finds this an absorbing film. Also during the year Universal continued its effort to turn ex–Tarzan Lex Barker into a cowboy star. The studio had featured him with Randolph Scott, then starred him in a minor 1954 western, *Yellow Mountain*. Now came *The Man from Bitter Ridge*. It was another failure and the studio gave up the attempt. The irony is that Barker did become a well-known western star, but in the unlikely screen studios of Germany, where he made many films based on the literary characters of James Fenimore Cooper. Perhaps another irony, looking at 1955's films, is that villain of *The Violent Men*, Brian Keith, who looked so good as an evil man, went on to become one of westerns (and Walt Disney's) nicest and most affable leading men. In the film business, you never knew....

1 9 5 6

"Name's Ethan"

John Wayne named a son after the character he played in John Ford's 1956 *The Searchers*. Wayne regarded the role of Ethan Edwards as the best he played, a verdict shared by many, who would also rank *The Searchers* as the best western ever made. It is indeed a beautiful and powerful work from a great director, an odyssey patched with humor and action and colorful characters. Some of the most memorable scenes Ford ever made are in *The Searchers*. Released through Warner Bros. and based on a novel by Alan LeMay, it is both an enchanting and brutal film. The long search for the white girl captured by Indians and the almost maniacal progress of Ethan Edwards through the wilderness of his own tortured thoughts was also the most unusual western Ford had made. All the great Fordian scenes were there — riders etched against the Monument Valley skyline, the broad humor, the brawling, the music ... plus the never-to-be-forgotten opening and closing scenes as the door opens, then closes on Ethan Edwards. There are flaws, which fans tend to overlook, and faults in construction of the film that the younger Ford, of 1939–41, would not have tolerated. But there have always been flaws in Ford's work, that great naturalness that helps bring us closer to the artist and his work. The greatest western ever...? Perhaps ... perhaps not. If not, it would probably be ousted by some other Ford film. Jeffrey Hunter, Ward Bond, Vera Miles (who worked well for Ford) and a host of Ford stock company players including Hank Worden as a Shakespearean "fool" play their part in this epic.

Released the same year, on a completely different scale, was the Budd Boetticher–directed *Seven Men from Now*, the first of what would become a famous series

From the first collaboration of Randolph Scott and director Budd Boetticher, Warners' Seven Men from Now, *Randolph Scott and Gail Russell are pictured.*

of films featuring Randolph Scott as star. This film was made on a small budget, with B running time and a small cast but is, in retrospect, one of the great westerns. Scott was aging and this was utilized to perfection by director Boetticher who, with the star, created a William S. Hart–style character of a lonely man, haunted by some past deed, forever searching for … something. In this case it is for the murderers of his wife, the seven men of the title. Riding along is bad man Lee Marvin, the first of the many "badmen" characters in this series who are really quite likable and whom, like the Scott character, you desperately want to keep alive. Inevitably, however, Scott has to face them down, gun to gun. The doomed actress Gail Russell, fighting personal problems, played the heroine in a nice performance, and among the supporting players is former cowboy star Don Barry playing a moronic gunman companion of Marvin. Marvin casually disposes of Barry at the film's conclusion before meeting Scott over a money box of gold that had been the driving force behind the gang, and Marvin's ride with Scott. In a touching ending Scott tried to dissuade Marvin from trying to take the gold by "going over him." Scott, as he does so often in these films, later rides away alone, but with the hint that he and Russell will meet up again. The script was from the talented Burt Kennedy, a writer who later went into directing but never made the same impact there as he did with his writing.

Two great westerns in any one year is more than satisfactory. There were plenty of other contenders, but no rivals. George Stevens made *Giant*, a sprawling contemporary western, but could not recapture the spirit of *Shane*. William Wyler directed the borderline western *Friendly Persuasion* about a Quaker family and the Civil War, and Gary Cooper gave his last outstanding performance as the sincere father. Making a rare western appearance at MGM was James Cagney in *Tribute to a Badman*, based on a short story by Jack Schaefer, author of *Shane*. This was a good study in power and abuse, Cagney as always being convincing in a genre that never quite suited him. Delmer Daves directed *Jubal* starring Glenn Ford, which was an interesting account of ranch life. Glenn Ford was also in *The Fastest Gun Alive*, not a particularly good western. Better was another Daves film, *The Last Wagon*, with Richard Widmark playing a somewhat savage hero who saves a wagon train by brutal methods. Widmark, who could be savagely powerful as well as likable on screen, was also in *Backlash*, an average outing. More interesting was Universal's *Walk the Proud Land*, based on the recollections of an Indian agent and starring Audie Murphy. Murphy gives a satisfactory performance but the film is too slow and the love interest involving both Anne Bancroft (an unlikely Indian maiden) and Pat Crowley gets in the way of an otherwise absorbing story. Playing Geronimo, in an interesting break away from his Tonto characterization, is Jay Silverheels.

Speaking of whom, in 1956 the Lone Ranger returned to the big screen for the first time since Republic serial days in a Jack Wrather–Warner Bros. production. Filmed with an A budget and directed by Stuart Heisler, *The Lone Ranger* follows traditional lines and is predictable, but is well done, Clayton Moore and Silverheels assured in their roles and the film looking good in color. Lyle Bettger, a reliable '50s heavy and Bonita Granville, former child star married to producer Wrather, led the rest of the cast.

There were other entertaining westerns released in 1956. *The Spoilers* was remade, this time with Jeff Chandler, Anne Baxter and Rory Calhoun; Greer Garson of all people starred in *Strange Lady in Town*, a peaceful, preachy piece from Mervyn LeRoy; Dean Martin and Jerry Lewis went west in *Pardners*; and Clark Gable ambled through MGM's *The King and Four Queens*. Writer-director Richard Brooks meant *The Last Hunt* to be an indictment of the slaughter of the buffalo but MGM, not for the first time, interfered with matters in fear that such a topic would flop at the box office. *The Last Hunt* thus was turned into a tale of rivalry between Robert Taylor and Stewart Granger, with Brooks' heavy social comment all but obliterated.

Frank Sinatra out West in *Johnny Concho* was, well ... Frank Sinatra out West, but more edifying was Republic's *The Maverick Queen*. Republic, like most smaller studios, was struggling to exist by 1956. Its major stars, John Wayne and Roy Rogers,

The Lone Ranger *on the big Warner Bros. screen in 1956 — star Clayton Moore.*

had left the studio in 1951 (and Autry before then) and now their regular A western director, Joseph Kane, was leaving. His last film for the studio was *The Maverick Queen*. Nicely filmed on location, it was notable for fine performances from stars Barbara Stanwyck and Barry Sullivan.

Finally for 1956, a year belonging to John Wayne and Randolph Scott, an event occurred that was scarcely noticed by industry or fans. Columbia released the last known American serial, and aptly it was a western, *Blazing the Overland Trail*. Small time B western hero-heavy-bit player Dennis Moore starred, he and Lee Roberts, his co-star, being dressed in outfits closely resembling those worn in the 1939 serial *Overland with Kit Carson* so that most of the action from that earlier film could be used. The history of the serial, or cliffhanger as it was affectionately known, went back a long way, to the early silents, and it had been important entertainment in its day for young and old alike. Over the years it had grown cheaper and cheaper in production as the studios that made them (almost exclusively Universal, Columbia and Republic — before that Mascot, in the sound era) tried to get the most out of the least. With *Blazing the Overland Trail* it all came to a far-from-blazing end.

1 9 5 7

There Are Some Things a Man Can't Ride Around...

These were immortal words in the voice of Randolph Scott, among the many succinct such phrases written for Scott by Burt Kennedy, scriptwriter for Budd Boetticher in those marvelous Scott-Brown productions of the '50s. Two of them came out in 1957, both classics—*The Tall T* and *Decision at Sundown*. Little westerns in scope and running times, these masterpieces were not seen as such, especially in America, upon release. Not for the first time it was the Europeans, often with more respect for the mythical western than their U.S. counterparts, who picked them up and gave them the status they deserve. *Decision at Sundown* was a taut town western and the bleakest of all the Boetticher-Scott combinations, with Scott riding away at the end a bitter, broken man, devoured by his own hatred and call of vengeance. *The Tall T*, after some grim moments with outlaw Richard Boone and his moronic companions, the ending is optimistic, Scott and Maureen O'Sullivan (in a rare western role) walking away arm in arm as Scott comments on what a nice day "it's gonna be!"

If these Randolph Scott classics stand now as the highlights of a good western year, it was not always so. Far bigger at the box office, and with serious critics, was the Paramount film *Gunfight at the O.K. Corral*. Directed by John Sturges and starring the sure-fire combination of Burt Lancaster and Kirk Douglas, *Gunfight* told, not for the first or last time, the Wyatt Earp story, a certain drawing card. Claiming to be the "truthful" account, it was really no more so than any other film about the

219

Rod Steiger, star of Samuel Fuller's Run of the Arrow, *released through RKO in 1957.*

famous gun battle, but was entertaining. Also arousing much interest, but not the same box office hit, was independent director Sam Fuller's *Run of the Arrow*. Fuller produced, directed and wrote the story that broke some new ground in the eternal white man versus Indian question. Rod Steiger's overacting (when I first saw it I thought he was playing a German, or some fellow mid–European, with his accent, before realizing it was meant to be Irish) is balanced by calmer work from Brian Keith, Ralph Meeker (adept at playing handsome but weak-willed officers) and Sarita Montiel. Even old-timer Colonel Tim McCoy gets a role in a film that must have met his approval. Fuller also directed the cheap but rambling-plotted *Forty Guns*, featuring a storming performance from Barbara Stanwyck, well-matched by Barry Sullivan in what is a curiosity of a western and well worth a watch.

More conventional were *3:10 to Yuma*, directed by Delmer Daves and starring Glenn Ford and Van Heflin, a tense affair released by Columbia and well received, and *The Tin Star*, from Anthony Mann and starring Henry Fonda as the world-weary lawman who educated young sheriff Anthony Perkins. Perkins looked out of place in the West but Fonda was good, as always.

Night Passage was to be another James Stewart–Anthony Mann collaboration but Mann backed out of it, not happy with the script. As directed by James Neilson for Universal-International, it came over as an enjoyable western lacking any depth that Mann might have brought to it. Stewart was partnered by Audie Murphy, playing against type as Stewart's outlaw brother. Both stars did well but for Stewart the main satisfaction in the film was that he got to play his accordion. Murphy also made the enjoyable *The Guns of Fort Petticoat*, nothing ambitious but solid western fare.

Fox renamed the Jesse James saga. Called *The True Story of Jesse James*, it was nowhere near as good a western as the 1939 Tyrone Power–Henry Fonda starrer, and certainly no truer. Young players Robert Wagner and Jeffrey Hunter looked what they were, nice young men from the '50s. Also unsuccessful were films like *Gun for a Coward* (Fred MacMurray) and *Three Violent People* (Charlton Heston) but *Gun Glory* directed by Roy Rowland for MGM and starring unlikely westerner Stewart Granger

Anthony Mann's The Tin Star, *1957. Anthony Perkins and Henry Fonda are in a scene from the Paramount release.*

with the flaming-haired Rhonda Fleming was an enjoyable outing, Chill Wills somewhat stealing the show as a larger-than-life parson.

Another western made that year centered about the Indian-white relationship and the effect of one woman, who has a baby, on her captor, an Apache chief. Barbara Stanwyck was unusually sensitive as the female lead but the amiable Joel McCrea was outstanding as the tough but gentle soldier, an ideal part for him as *Trooper Hook*. The story came from Dorothy Johnson, an award-winning western writer, and added viewer (listener?) appeal came through Tex Ritter singing the theme through the film. It was directed by Charles Marquis Warren, not notable as a director and more well-known as producer of TV shows such as *Rawhide*.

Apart from Murphy, Scott and McCrea, other actors more and more associated with westerns were busy in 1957 — Guy Madison, Sterling Hayden, George Montgomery, Jock Mahoney, Rory Calhoun.... Their western films could well be seen as replacing the old series version, being, in their own way, just as predictable and stylized. Rory Calhoun was particularly busy, making four westerns — *Utah Blaine, Ride*

Out for Revenge, The Hired Gun and *The Domino Kid*—which was about the same number Monte Hale and Roy Rogers had been making in the mid to late '40s at Republic when both cowboys were in color. And Randolph Scott, with three western releases, had one of his most prolific years at a time when he must have been contemplating retirement.

All in all, 1957 produced a well balanced blend of the traditional and new, both major and minor A westerns. It was interesting though that many of the Calhoun, Montgomery and even Randolph Scott westerns at this time were referred to by reviewers as "B" films; makers of real B westerns in the '30s and '40s would have been overwhelmed by such budgets to play with under the realm of such "B" westerns.

1958

Once Upon a Horse...

Dan Rowan and Dick Martin were a comedy duo from television who made a film comedy called *Once Upon a Horse*. This received limited release in 1958 and normally a history of western movies would not even mention this unmemorable film except for that popping up as "guest" stars in it were old-time cowboys Kermit Maynard, Bob Steele, Bob Livingston and Tom Keene, a poignant reminder of other days. In the more conventional scenes, 1958 was actually a very good year for westerns, the last one in which it could be said a large number of very good ones were released. There were disappointments, Anthony Mann's *Man of the West* with an aging Gary Cooper being the most notable. This fierce, almost neurotic western pleased many critics but I find it overdone and unbalanced in both its violence and sexual overtones exemplified by Julie London in a revealing blouse. The biggest western of the year, *The Big Country*, was more compelling but failed to quite convince despite veteran director William Wyler being at the helm and Gregory Peck, Charlton Heston, Burl Ives, Jean Simmons, Carroll Baker and Charles Bickford giving it an imposing cast. It reminded me, not particularly in content but in cast and intent, of the 1946 *Duel in the Sun*.

Better entertainment came from the little known now *From Hell to Texas*. This Henry Hathaway western starred the relatively unknown Don Murray and Diane Varsi, was good to look at and powerfully acted by the stars and a restrained Chill Wills. A simple old-fashioned story of a loner falsely accused and chased, *From Hell to Texas* just never caught on at the box office but was both artistically and emotionally a satisfying and well paced western. Also satisfying and both funny and harshly

223

A little known western but a very good one was Henry Hathaway's 1958 From Hell to Texas. *Stars Don Murray, Diane Varsi and Chill Wills are pictured from this Fox film.*

violent at moments was Budd Boetticher's Randolph Scott feature *Buchanan Rides Alone*. Another Scott-Brown production, the film was partly tongue-in-cheek with Scott allowed to display his dry humor before, at about the halfway point, the story turns more serious and ends with the streets of Agrytown littered with corpses before Scott rides away, his work done. I have seen it described as "witty but grim" and that would be apt.

The sincere form of Gregory Peck was back out West in *The Bravados*, directed by the man who made *The Gunfighter*, Henry King. A grim revenge story, *The Bravados* was not in the same class although Peck was his usual dedicated self. More interesting was MGM's *The Law and Jack Wade* directed by John Sturges. It is a fact that though MGM produced more and more westerns as the '40s passed and the '50s took over, they seldom managed to make the great ones that lesser studios, prestige-wise, did. *The Law and Jack Wade* is yet another stylish effort from a very good director that falls short of greatness. Richard Widmark, in one of his unsympathetic roles, and Robert Taylor as the good guy struggling to stay good, make a fine pairing in this film, Taylor having matured greatly since his earlier western efforts at the studio like *Billy the Kid* in 1941, where he looked awkwardly out of place. In fact, since the 1950 *Devil's Doorway* Taylor had become MGM's most dependable western player.

Fascinating to many viewers was the oddly casted *Left Handed Gun* from Warners with Paul Newman playing a neurotic, psychotic Billy the Kid. Director Arthur Penn had made the original television version of this also starring Newman and written by Gore Vidal, an unlikely western author. Leslie Stevens did the film script but it was based on Gore's work. The end result was a New York method acting–directing affair that appealed to the high minded and baffled the traditional western film fan. It is always worth a look.

In the minor league back on screen came the Lone Ranger with Clayton Moore and Jay Silverheels again playing the Ranger and Tonto in *The Lone Ranger and the Lost City of Gold*, old style B entertainment with the addition of wide screen and color. It was good fun, as were minor efforts like George Montgomery's *Badman's Country* directed by old Durango Kid–maker Fred F. Sears, and United Artists' *Fort Bowie*, which had the very likable and under-used Ben Johnson in the lead role. Less interesting was *Fort Dobbs*, a vehicle for Warner Bros.' television star Clint Walker, a very large and expressionless actor. One more minor production, from United Artists, but worthy of mention is *Terror in a Texas Town*. This was directed by Joseph H. Lewis, former B western director who made only a few cheap but always interesting westerns outside the B field. This one has both an unusual story (a Swedish immigrant takes on the baddies and kills the opposing gunman with a harpoon) and cast, of Sterling Hayden, Sebastian Cabot, Carol Kelly and Ned Young as the black-clad gunman with problems.

In what was, as mentioned, a good year for western movies, Audie Murphy, Alan Ladd, Guy Madison, Jock Mahoney and Glenn Ford, regular faces now in such movies, all were busy and if no single, great western stands out the overall quality was good. There were bad moments. Fred MacMurray went west again in *Day of the Badman*, another one of those talkative, conscience-stricken stories that did so well on hour long TV shows but was boring on the big screen. Fred MacMurray was a good and sincere actor, but not a westerner, proven, unfortunately, too many times. A good hard look at 1958 would provide a cautionary note to the sharp eye, namely that too many westerns featured players who were not entirely at home in the environment. This was balanced out by said westerns being directed by a whole group of artists who were at home out West — Sturges, Mann, Boetticher, King, Wyler, Hathaway ... but many were veterans now and not being replaced by younger directors with a real feel for their material.

I have left till last the film that was one of the biggest grossers of the year, surprisingly, and that is *The Sheepman* directed by George Marshall and starring Glenn Ford and Shirley MacLaine. *The Sheepman* was acclaimed as a rousing comedy, with some traditional western action and hugely liked at the time. Seeing it today one is

A minor, but unusual western, again from 1958, from former B director Joseph H. Lewis and distributed by United Artists, Terror in a Texas Town. *That's star Sterling Hayden with the harpoon, Victor Millan on right.*

perplexed as to just why. The comedy seems muted, the action dull and the stars uninteresting (one writer's verdict of course). Some films, though, just do not stand the test of time. Luckily, in the western genre, so many do and rewatching of most of the 1958 westerns mentioned is as rewarding as ever.

1959

The Year Creeps Slowly By...

"Lorena" is a lovely old Civil War song used by, among others, John Ford in *The Searchers* in 1956. Ford used it again as theme for the relationship between star John Wayne and Constance Towers, his leading lady, in the 1959 *The Horse Soldiers*. This Ford cavalry film based on an incident during the war was a pleasant, always pictorially satisfying but rather flat western that did not compare with the same director's earlier cavalry trilogy. John Wayne did indeed star in the leading western for the year, but it was for director Howard Hawks in *Rio Bravo*, next to *Red River* that director's most satisfying western. Wayne plays the stolid lawman who meets the baddies face to face in this town-based film in a display of professionalism that Hawks and Wayne meant to be the answer to *High Noon*'s politically motivated revelations of the weakness of democracy, a particular sore point with the super-patriot Wayne. Helped by Dean Martin, Ricky Nelson and Walter Brennan, Wayne is compelling in the role. Angie Dickinson provides a combative heroine to match the dominating Wayne and *Rio Bravo* deserved its success as both entertainment and a taut western. It would be Hawks' last outstanding western, two follow-ups with Wayne in the '60s and '70s showed a deterioration, whereas Ford still had some greatness to come.

Bud Boetticher directed Randolph Scott in *Westbound*, which was a disappointment, lacking all the strengths of their previous films together. The lack of Burt Kennedy's scripting showed but Boetticher and Scott were back in top form with *Ride Lonesome*, in which Scott, as intense as ever, grimly hunts down and brings in James Best, but for his own to-be-revealed purposes, involving Best's outlaw brother, Lee Van Cleef. Pernell Roberts and James Coburn are the two cowboys who yearn to go straight and can do so by bringing in Best themselves. The marvelous ending when Scott and Roberts front up for custody of Best is one of this series' most satisfying moments. And I won't reveal the result here just in case someone has not seen it.

Joel McCrea's *Gunfight at Dodge City* looked tired, as did its star. Audie Murphy made three westerns during the year, one of which, *No Name on the Bullet*, gave him the chance to play a cold-blooded killer in an offbeat role that showed again Murphy's latent acting talent. Edward Dmytryk directed the long *Warlock* with Henry Fonda, Anthony Quinn, Richard Widmark and Dorothy Malone, and Fonda in particular gave a powerful performance. But the film was too long and rather turgid in parts, though good in others. *The Hanging Tree* was another dark and brooding western although director Delmer Daves did successfully capture the atmosphere of a frontier mining community. Gary Cooper, however, seemed old and tired. He did not have long to live.

Entertaining without being outstanding were *The Jayhawkers* (Jeff Chandler and Fess Parker), *Last Train from Gun Hill* (Kirk Douglas, Anthony Quinn) and *These Thousand Hills* (Don Murray), and *Day of the Outlaw* had a chilling quality but was a little too static. Robert Ryan and Burl Ives starred.

Robert Parrish, an old Hollywood hand, directed *The Wonderful Country*, a sprawling south-of-the-border western that was wonderful for the slumbering but compelling Robert Mitchum, always a delight. In the comedy field Bob Hope went west again, in *Alias Jesse James*, not as good as his earlier Paleface films but interesting in that a whole range of mainly TV guest stars appeared, including Gary Cooper and Roy Rogers. Stranger was the British film directed by western veteran Raoul Walsh, *The Sheriff of Fractured Jaw*, filmed in England and starring the essentially British Kenneth Moore and, even unlikelier, Jayne Mansfield. It had some laughs and pop star Connie Francis did the singing for Miss Mansfield.

Still working away were westerners like George Montgomery in *King of the Wild Stallions*; the younger Jock Mahoney, whose B western career had been cut short, was making lackluster westerns like *Money, Women and Guns* and would soon branch off into the role of Tarzan.

By the time we come down to films like *Curse of the Undead*, which was a western, believe it or not, we enter the dregs of the year's production and there were a few of these tawdry and very minor westerns around, trying through some sort of shock effect to cover up slim budgets and still get away with challenging television's increasing stranglehold upon the genre.

It was now the end of a decade that had promised much and delivered many outstanding western films. Unfortunately it had also witnessed the demise of the series western. At the time it had not seemed such a big shame — most of the B cowboy stars were aging, television seemed to have picked up the mantle and there were so many good A and minor A westerns being produced. However, television was a leaden provider with its westerns proving over time to be more domestic dramas than honest to goodness action fare, and a large part of the cowboy film audience was lost there, replaced by responsible mothers and a general television audience that became as bland in its wants as the producers (advertisers) in meeting them. Add to this a gradual falling away in total western film production and you were left with two schools of thought. One was that the cutting away of the grist, or bad western movies, would leave the genre like a rose bush, set to bloom with bright new flowers. The other was that the future for the western film was, if not grim, certainly uncertain.

1 9 6 0

A New Decade—Old Players

As the new decade began western movies were in their 58th year and not many were being made. What were made were still popular, probably because the players and technicians were the same ones who had been making westerns for some years and people knew, and were confident in, the product they produced. The challenge of television was extreme and in that medium the old B style cowboys had now all gone from the small screen, the new breed of television cowboy being earnest, tall and invariably dull (this is, of course, the opinion of the writer — large audiences held other views). But at the movies old performers like director John Ford, with *Sergeant Rutledge* and major star John Wayne, who made his own large scale version of *The Alamo*, still held sway. Wayne's effort was actually an overlong bore that lost money for the star. Ford's film, starring black player Woody Strode with Jeffrey Hunter, was a well-meaning western on racial issues that failed to capture the best of that director's work. Wayne suffered from the problem later actors like Kevin Costner would, an inability to control themselves when handed a big project. Wayne knew his business, but he still needed the firm hand of Ford or Howard Hawks to guide him.

Anthony Mann made his last western, a remake of *Cimarron*, which proved a disaster. Star Glenn Ford lacked Stewart or Fonda's intensity and somehow Mann just never came to grips with the sprawling Ferber story. His style of film making suited more the intimate, small story practiced so successfully with star Stewart.

Well known directors Henry Hathaway, John Sturges and John Huston all made westerns in 1960. Huston's was a good effort that was not popular, again probably because of the racial theme in *The Unforgiven*, in which Audie Murphy, who always

A major success of 1960, The Magnificent Seven, *directed by John Sturges for United Artists, stars Yul Brynner and Steve McQueen on their famous ride to the cemetery.*

worked well for Huston, gave one of his best performances as the racist brother of star Burt Lancaster. Hathaway directed the hugely popular adventure-comedy *North to Alaska* with John Wayne in a rollicking mood while Sturges had the biggest western hit of the year, *The Magnificent Seven,* a beautifully composed western based on the Japanese *Seven Samurai* with a nigh on perfect cast, many of whom (James Coburn, Charles Bronson, Steve McQueen) went on to stardom after careers as bit players. Main star Yul Brynner was surprisingly effective as the leader of the Seven and the music also proved a hit.

In 1960 Elvis Presley made *Flaming Star,* strictly for fans, and real western star Audie Murphy had a couple of westerns, the best by far being *Seven Ways from Sundown,* a neat little western that included a good performance by Barry Sullivan as the unrepentant gunfighter Murphy has to bring in and then face at the showdown.

However, the very best western of the year, if not most popular, was director Budd Boetticher's *Comanche Station,* the last in his group covering five years with Randolph Scott. Packed with jewels from scriptwriter Burt Kennedy, this final homage of Scott and Boetticher to the lonely odysseys of the grim Scott character, this small, just 73 minute, western is a classic tragedy. The simple revenge story — which is not so simple in the end for the relentless Scott, nor for the flawed but likable bad guy, Claude Akins, he encounters along the way of his task of bringing Indian captive victim Nancy Gates home — packs more succinct dialogue and silent, compelling images into that short running time than most so-called epics.

Randolph Scott retired after this film and it seemed that, in a world that seemed to be increasingly at odds with the "Some things a man can't ride around" attitude of that player's character, only Wayne was left (and perhaps Murphy) to carry the tradition onward. Joel McCrea was also making his last, rather weak films as he headed for retirement. A maverick director and a film regarded as a failure by its studio makers would, in two years, leave both stars with the chance to retire with the dignity they deserved. In the meantime John Wayne continued to lift his increasing bulk into the saddle. He also was just two years away from what, for him, was not the climax to a great career but would be a worthy one for the partnership between him and his mentor, John Ford.

1961
Near the End of the Trail

In 1961 either everybody was watching television or it rained a lot. Very few western movies were made and of those there was little of top quality. John Ford gave us *Two Rode Together*, a film not liked by critics, historians or Ford himself, but one that this writer believes is underrated. Even its critics admit it contains some vintage Fordian moments and one of these is the conversation on the river bank between stars James Stewart and Richard Widmark, done in one incredible shot with the camera implanted in the river itself. The story, touching on racial and sexual conflicts, is grim but Stewart is encouraged to make his role semi-comic with some biting if throwaway lines. His "What the market will bear" is surely a cynical Ford comment on (then) modern society. *Two Rode Together* also has the distinction of being solidly non-violent in an age that was becoming increasingly so, both on and off screen. But non-violence in his westerns was a Ford trait and had proven many times that a good western does not need flaming guns with writhing bodies to entrance.

The Deadly Companions was a vehicle for Maureen O'Hara but new director Sam Peckinpah made it his own using his TV star Brian Keith and favorites of Peckinpah like Strother Martin. The film met with mixed reaction and certainly nobody would have expected the same director's 1962 *Ride the High Country* to emerge with the charm and beauty it has. More on that to come. Burt Kennedy had his first directorial job with *The Canadians*, an acceptable but not outstanding western starring Robert Ryan, and Marlon Brando both directed and starred in *One-Eyed Jacks*, an overwrought, jumbled western best forgotten. Clark Gable and Marilyn Monroe were the stars of *The Misfits*, a modern western best remembered for Miss

Not a favorite of the film's director, John Ford, but a better western than is generally acknowledged, is Columbia's 1961 Two Rode Together. *Richard Widmark and James Stewart are pictured and behind them, on horseback, are Shirley Jones and Andy Devine.*

Monroe's temperamental habits than anything else (apart from being Clark Gable's last film).

More traditional, with no pretensions and much more fun, was Michael Curtiz's *The Comancheros*, a sprawling affair of cheerful lack of logic featuring John Wayne at his most superhuman. Sadly this film would point the way for a style of mindless westerns, often starring Wayne, that mocked themselves and presented mindless, if also unrealistic, violence and storyline.

On the other few westerns made, *Gold of the Seven Saints* from Warner Bros. was simply an excuse to use television star Clint Walker on the big screen, *The Last Sunset*, directed by Robert Aldrich, was a stunning looking western starring an intense Kirk Douglas and laid-back Rock Hudson but featuring an unpleasant story of incest in the West, and *A Thunder of Drums* was an attempt by Joseph Newman to make a cavalry epic without John Ford — and a failure.

On the other hand, a very minor *Posse from Hell* starring the always reliable

Audie Murphy and produced by Republic veteran Gordon Kay (Herbert Colman directed) was quite entertaining, only lacking in ambition and budget. Of brief nostalgic mention was the appearance of former cowboy star Allan Lane, brief because he is violently shot dead by killer Vic Morrow in the first minutes of the film.

Those few western movies represented the year 1961, hardly a vintage one. Around the corner into the new year were some projects of true class that would surprise in 1962, but also, sadly, serve as a farewell, not a revival, of the old style western film.

1 9 6 2
Glorious Beginning—
Sad Farewell

Some hoped it would be the beginning of a bright new era, in fond hope that the western movie would rise from the ashes it was descending into, and, in a blaze of glory gallop off through green, new pastures. They failed to notice a few things. One was that very few westerns were actually being made and two, that one of the two great westerns of the year was made by an old man at the close of a distinguished career. Add to that the not-so-good quality of many others and the recipe for optimism was based purely on that — optimism.

Also it was fueled by the comments of two influential writers, George Fenin and William K. Everson who, in their classic and trail-breaking history *The Western — From Silents to Cinerama*, published in 1962, concluded, "Even at this writing, three new westerns have been released which restore much integrity to the genre." These three westerns turned out to be two and a half on the scale of greatness and, as will be revealed, constituted the sad fading of the western, rather than the new rise.

All three films were concerned with the demise of the old West, and all were sad and nostalgic. The "half" was David Miller's *Lonely Are the Brave* starring Kirk Douglas as a lone cowboy fighting the "new" West of automobiles and trucks and losing out after a gallant resistance. The film and Douglas were good, but it fell short of greatness. Of the two great westerns released that year, the veteran director John Ford was responsible for one, *The Man Who Shot Liberty Valance*. Based on a Dorothy Johnson story, this was a black and white homage by Ford to the ashes of the old West

239

One of two great westerns of 1962 is John Ford's The Man Who Shot Liberty Valance. *James Stewart with his back to us addresses the meeting while John Wayne sits to his right. At the table is Edmond O'Brien.*

and his final great artistic achievement. It was not Ford's farewell to the genre, his later *Cheyenne Autumn* in 1964 would be big, pleasing to the eye but essentially a tired work by a tired man. *Valance*, filmed on cramped sets and under gloomy lighting, was full of Fordian magic moments and obviously a personal statement of "print the legend." Even the unexpected, but apt, insertion of the Abe Lincoln theme music from Ford's 1939 Henry Fonda feature seemed to intensify the bitter, melancholy mood of the John Wayne character, the symbol of the old, dying West, making way for the new, flower bedecked one of lawyer James Stewart. The ending when the train conductor says, "Nothing's too good for the man who shot Liberty Valance," and Stewart is left, numbed, by the consequences of the lie that has made him rich and famous, is beautifully filmed. The train disappears around the bend to consecrate the last rites on John Ford's West. Stars Wayne and Stewart are admirable as is Vera Miles, an actress who reserved her best for Ford, plus the cast of Ford regulars from Andy Devine to John Carradine.

The other great western of 1962 is Sam Peckinpah's Ride the High Country, *an MGM release. In the foreground are Joel McCrea and Randolph Scott and behind them Ron Starr and Mariette Hartley.*

From the last vintage year, 1962, is an enjoyable minor A western, Six Black Horses. *Audie Murphy is attending to Joan O'Brien while Dan Duryea lurks in the background.*

The other classic was *Ride the High Country*. This gentle requiem to the passing of gritty, honest lawmen, filmed in magnificent country, was not looked upon highly by the production studio, MGM. For some reason they thought it a "bomb" and hid it away on release as second on a double bill. It was the British (where it was named *Guns in the Afternoon*) and other Europeans who first claimed it as a "classic." Soon independent-minded Americans came to the same conclusion and today it stands as just that, a great western movie. Just how much is attributable to director Sam Peckinpah is unknown. Peckinpah came from television where among his success was the writing, and directing, of the great little series *The Westerner* starring Brian Keith. Inevitably this series failed in the ratings game and was dropped after a few episodes, which tells us a whole lot about television. In 1961 Peckinpah was given *The Deadly Companions*, starring Keith again, plus Maureen O'Hara, to direct, with mixed results. MGM then entrusted him with *Ride the High Country* and gave him old-timers Randolph Scott and Joel McCrea as stars. Peckinpah went over budget and time and argued with the studio, but the end result was a lovely western film of two aging lawmen on one last mission that ends in McCrea dying gallantly at the end to enter his house "justified," as he longed to do. Both the old cowboys, Scott and McCrea, were wonderful in fitting farewells to the screen. (McCrea would return in later years in a couple of minor roles.)

With the late-coming praise behind him Peckinpah looked to be the man who would take over from Ford as the great western director, but this brilliant but erratic man never reached those heights. Bedeviled by drink and drugs and an increasing penchant for violence on screen, he provided one other western regarded by critics (but not by me) as a classic, *The Wild Bunch*, but his other work was uneven and basically a failure.

So in a sense these two westerns, the classics of the year 1962, also were swan songs and the last of a dying breed. Neither were actually the big money maker of the year, that was the over-inflated, star-studded but ultimately boring cinerama effort *How the West Was Won* from which only the short Civil War episode directed by John Ford came out with honor.

There wasn't much else to "write home about" in 1962. Sinatra and his pack remade *Gunga Din* calling it *Sergeants Three* and Chuck Connors was a wooden, muscle-bound *Geronimo*. More interesting was a minor western, Audie Murphy's *Six Black Horses*, co-starring the ever-entertaining Dan Duryea. This was written by Burt Kennedy and used many lines from his work for Budd Boetticher, but director Harry Keller was no Boetticher so, although good fun, the film never rose above that.

Conclusion

So ended the golden years of the western film. It had been a wonderful ride down the trail of B westerns, A westerns, great cowboy stars, action westerns, singing cowboys, epics and all. Fans had their favorite movies and their favorite cowboys. Now it was over as Hollywood, under the threat of the television-dominated home western, made less and less of the genre, with fading stars who never seemed to be adequately replaced by younger talent, no more than the talented directors or writers were interested in the genre any longer. It got so bad that the western scene became dominated by films from countries like Italy, Spain and even Germany, often using Hollywood players who could not find work in their home town. These pseudo westerns remained but pale shadows of the real thing. Westerners like John Wayne, old and successful, made films that almost parodied their former selves. Now and then Wayne, an American icon, would turn out something better, none more so than in his last role in 1976, Don Siegel's *The Shootist*, playing, poignantly, an old gunman dying of cancer, from which Wayne himself would succumb just three years later.

Films like that were few and far between. America entered that strange period of political correctness, which led not only to television westerns that were devoid of all but actionless moralizing but also to films that preached all the "isms" of current society carried back in time to the 1880s. In an era that saw Snow White "corrected" to Snow Person, might we assume we would get *The Person Who Shot Liberty Valance* or *Seven Persons from Now? Height-Impaired Grass?* The mind boggles.

During the '80s even television lost interest in westerns and the complete demise of the genre was somberly announced by many. Then, in the '90s, came two academy winning westerns, Kevin Costner's *Dances with Wolves* and Clint Eastwood's *Unfor-given*. Amidst the acclaim it was little noted that neither were really good westerns, Costner's being an overblown bore whose subject had been covered in earlier films and was not the sudden revelation the yuppies of the '90s claimed it to be; Eastwood's was a turgid attempt to make the "authentic" film of the West and, in effect, the last word. As a gloomy bit of muck, it succeeds.

On through the '90s and into the new century they came, limpid, politically correct interpretations of westerns, with freshly swept and polished saloon floors that William S. Hart would have winced at. Remakes of classics served only to underline the paucity of ideas that current writers and directors have. Revisionist history turned scenes from 1890 into 1990 visions. The only bright sign as the century closed (and opened) was that some westerns continued to be made, usually for television, each year. Unfortunately, they cannot compare with those of old.

Until the miracle happens and some new John Ford and John Wayne emerge, we who love the western film can only live on with it by way of video tape, on which most films from the past are now available. And mainly they are from that golden era, in so many ways— the golden years of 1929 to 1962.

Bibliography

This is a selection of the best books on western films I have read over the years, some for their entertainment value, some for their reference value, but not always for both.

Adams, Les, and Buck Rainey. *The Shoot 'Em Ups*. Metuchen, NJ: Scarecrow Press, 1987.
Anderson, Lindsay. *About John Ford*. London: Plexus Publishing, 1981.
Barbour, Alan. *A Thousand and One Delights*. NY: Collier, 1971.
_____. *The Thrill of It All*. NY: Collier, 1971.
Bogdanovich, Peter. *John Ford*. London: Studio Vista, 1967.
Bond, Johnny. *The Tex Ritter Story*. Chappell Music, 1976.
Calder, Jenni. *There Must Be a Lone Ranger, The Myth and Reality of the American Wild West*. London: Hamish Hamilton, 1974.
Cline, William C. *In the Nick of Time*. Jefferson, NC: McFarland, 1984.
Drew, Bernard A. *Hopalong Cassidy: The Clarence Mulford Story*. Metuchen, NJ: Scarecrow Press, 1991.
Everson, William K. *The Hollywood Western*. NY: Citadel, 1992.
_____. *A Pictorial History of the Western Film*. NY: Citadel Press, 1969.
Fenin, George N., and William K. Everson. *The Western — From Silents to Cinerama*. NY: Bonanza Books, 1962.
Gallagher, Tad. *John Ford, the Man and His Films*. Berkeley, CA: University of California Press, 1986.
Griffis, Ken. *Hear My Song*. CA: JEFM Foundation, 1974.
Hardy, Phil. *The Aurum Film Encyclopedia: The Western*. London: Aurum Press, 1983.
Hoffman, Henryk. *"A" Western Filmakers*. Jefferson, NC: McFarland, 2000.
Leonard, John W. *Wild Bill Elliot*. Self-published, 1976.
McClure, Arthur F., and Ken D. Jones. *Heroes, Heavies and Sagebrush*. NJ: A.S. Barnes, 1972.
Magers, Boyd, and Fitzgerald, Michael G. *Westerns Women*. Jefferson, NC: McFarland, 1999.
Miller, Don. *Hollywood Corral*. NY: Popular Library, 1976.
Nevins, Francis M. *The Films of Hopalong Cassidy*. NC: The World of Yesterday, 1998.
_____. *The Films of the Cisco Kid*. NC: The World of Yesterday, 1998.
Nott, Robert. *Last of the Cowboy Heroes*. Jefferson, NC: McFarland, 2000.
Parkinson, Michael, and Clyde Jeavons. *A Pictorial History of Westerns*. London: Hamlyn, 1972.
Parrish, James Robert. *Great Western Stars*. NY: Ace Books, 1976.
Pitts, Michael. *Western Movies*. Jefferson, NC: McFarland, 1986.
Rainey, Buck. *The Fabulous Holts*. Nashville, TN: Nashville Western Press, 1976.

_____. *Serials and Series*. Jefferson, NC: McFarland, 1999.

Rothel, David. *The Gene Autry Book*. NC: Empire Publishing, 1988.

_____. *The Roy Rogers Book*. NC: Empire Publishing, 1987.

_____. *The Singing Cowboys*. NJ: A.S. Barnes, 1978.

_____. *Those Great Cowboy Sidekicks*. Metuchen, NJ: Scarecrow Press, 1984.

Rutherford, John A. *From Pigskin to Saddle Leather*. NC: The World of Yesterday, 1996.

Smith, Packy, and Ed Hulse (editors). *Don Miller's Hollywood Corral*. Revised edition with additional material. CA: Riverwood Press, 1993.

Thornton, Chuck, and David Rothel. *Allan "Rocky" Lane*. NC: Empire Publishing, 1990.

Tuska, Jon. *The Filming of the West*. NY: Doubleday, 1976.

_____. *The Vanishing Legion*. Jefferson, NC: McFarland, 1982.

Witney, William. *Trigger Remembered*. AL: Earl Blair Enterprises, 1989.

Wood, Robin. *Howard Hawks*. London: Secker and Warburg, 1967.

Of further interest are some of the magazines I have enjoyed and used for reference over the years.

The Big Reel
Classic Images
Cliffhanger
Favorite Westerns and Serials
Nostalgia Westerns (Westerns N–Z Chapter)
Screen Facts
Screen Thrills Illustrated
Serial Report
Under Western Skies
Western Clippings
Western Film Collector
Wild West Stars
Wildest Westerns
Wrangler's Roost

Index